DRAFTING

&
PATTERN DESIGNING
(1924)

by
Woman's Institute
of Domestic Arts and Sciences

*Principles, methods, and proportions
for drafting to measurements and
designing individual, modish patterns*

LACIS
PUBLICATIONS
Berkeley, California USA

PUBLISHERS NOTE :

Pattern drafting, the key to garment design permits the creation of the *FLAT PATTERN* for any design for any figure. The pattern drafting method as fully taught in this volume focuses on the contemporary styles of the early '20s and should be an important resource for costumers involved with this period of dramatic costume innovation.

Designed as a text for students seeking a career in the apparel industry, this book is a republication of the original 1924 edition by the same title published by the Woman's Institute of Domestic Arts & Sciences. Each section is followed by examination questions to insure comprehension of the preceding information. Reflecting the styles of the period, contemporary fashion illustrations have been added by this publisher.

While the combination drafting square and curve as illustrated in this book is no longer a readily available tool, the readily available standard pattern maker's square and separate curves will satisfy all requirements of this volume and can be found in any tailoring supply center .

SUPPLIES:

LACIS, 2982 Adeline Street, Berkeley, CA 94703
Books, tools and materials relating to costume, millinery, embroidery and lace making

LACIS PUBLICATIONS
3163 Adeline Street
Berkeley, California 94706

© 1994 Lacis
ISBN 0-916896-56-0

PREFACE

It is said about cooking that any woman can become a successful cook if she will take up the subject scientifically and first learn to measure accurately and to follow recipes carefully. In drafting, the same is true. Any woman can master the art of drafting if she will treat it as a science, learning to measure accurately, to study proportions, and to follow the rules and laws set down as the basis of dress designing and pattern drafting.

In this Volume all drafting tools and materials are described or pictured, and their uses explained or illustrated. The Picken square takes the place of the measuring cup in cooking, a sharp-pointed pencil, the place of the mixing spoon, and instead of food stuffs, straight lines and curves are added to one another and blended to produce the finished product.

After the tools and their uses are treated, the foundation drafts are developed. These comprise the plain waist, the plain and circular skirts, and the plain sleeve, as well as the collar and cuff drafts, from which all variations are derived. Explicit directions for the making of these drafts, together with explanations and reasons for the steps, are given so that, at the outset, students of drafting can understand the logic and natural sequence in the processes that, step by step, make up the finished draft.

Many are the waists that are drafted with the plain waist as a foundation, among them a mannish shirt waist and several kimono waists and tight-fitting waists. The result is that no matter what the size of the person, whether undersize or oversize, and no matter how ill-proportioned the shape, perhaps because of some physical deformity, a proper-fitting draft can be made. Also, no matter what the prevailing style tendency may be, whether toward very snug-fitting garments or toward those of extreme looseness, the correct drafts, which will follow and emphasize the characteristic lines, can be made.

One chapter deals with the subject of underwear and lingerie. It shows how the waist drafts may be changed to form patterns for brassiéres, corset covers, and pajama tops, and how extensions may be added to certain waist drafts to form patterns for nightgowns and slips. Also, it covers the drafting of patterns for several types of drawers, knickerbockers, pajama trousers, and various combination suits, thus completing a chapter that can be of unlimited value to the woman who designs.

The chapter on aprons and caps should make an especial appeal to the home woman, for it makes possible the developing of any type of apron from the daintiest of serving aprons to the most enveloping of house aprons, with caps to match. Some of these aprons show the alteration of a foundation pattern, while others are evolved on entirely new lines, making a better assortment of aprons possible.

For the woman who sews for others, either professionally or as a part of her home keeping, the chapters on patterns for girls of all ages, for boys, and for men will prove their worth. The instruction for the drafting of outer garments as well as underclothes for the wee baby, the little tot, and the growing girl or boy is supplemented by instruction concerning the making of various patterns for the grown-up men in the family. Such instruction wins for the home woman much appreciation from those whom she desires most to please with just the right garments.

A chapter on coats and capes is included especially for those women who have found pleasure and satisfaction in the drafting of simple garments and who are desirous of increasing their skill and utilizing their ingenuity still further. A good-fitting wrap is not always easy to find, especially in the case of persons whose measurements do not coincide with model measurements, but with the mastery of this chapter comes the realization that outer garments of a perfect fit can be had with no great difficulty.

When one considers the possibilities in drafting, the analogy between cooking and drafting can be carried still further. When a woman has mastered the fundamentals of cookery and has familiarized herself with the correct combinations and proportions, she no longer limits herself to the recipes prescribed by others; she figures and alters until she has something new, the creation of her own ingenuity. Likewise in drafting, the woman who has become familiar with the meaning of certain proportions and the relation of the various lines of a draft, finds herself able to alter or develop any pattern to suit her needs. Thus, the last chapter in this Volume guides her in the use of commercial patterns of all types, not the slavish use, but the kind of adaptation that chooses a feature here, another there, and so on, and combines them all into an artistic design, a veritable work of genius. With the acquiring of such knowledge, the dressmaker becomes a true designer.

Elite Styles, January 1922

Elite Styles, January 1922

Elite Styles, January 1922

Elite Styles, January 1922

iv

CONTENTS

Elite Styles, January 1922

Delineator, March 1924

Elite Styles, January 1922

Delineator, March 1924

vii

Delineator, March 1924

Elite Styles, January 1922

Elite Styles, January 1922

Elite Styles, January 1922

viii

Delineator, March 1924

Delineator, March 1924

Delineator, March 1924

Elite Styles, January 1922

ix

Elite Styles, January 1922

9706

Elite Styles, January 1922

Elite Styles, January 1922

Delineator, March 1924

x

CHAPTER I

PATTERN MAKING FROM MEASUREMENTS

ART AND INTEREST IN PATTERN DRAFTING

1. The artist, to make beautiful pictures, and the architect, to have perfect rooms, must, first of all, know proportion. Just so must the dressmaker or modiste who designs, cuts, and fits dresses, know the proportion of the human form and the way in which to combine measurements harmoniously if she is to obtain right results.

Some persons instinctively know proportion just as some portrait painters make beautiful pictures without ever having had instruction, but such cases are exceptional. An accurate guide is essential to the majority of workers. The carpenter's rule is as important as his hammer; the engineer must have his steel tape for measurement; the architect needs his scale of proportions. And so it is with the dressmaker. To cut into fabric and shape it to the human form, to meet the requirements of fashion, utility, and type, she must know how to divide the material into right proportions. And to do this, she must have a knowledge of **pattern drafting**, which is the laying out and drawing of lines so as to form a *draft*. A draft, when properly cut apart, forms a *pattern*, which is a model or guide used in cutting out materials to be made up into wearing apparel.

2. On first thought, you may feel that the drafting of patterns is too difficult a subject for the average person to master, but you will find it not only simple but fascinating as taught in this Volume. It does not require, as is sometimes thought, a laborious, preliminary training; rather, its mastery is dependent on a good understanding of the lines of the human form and interest in the subject as a whole. And to be able to draft a pattern does not necessarily mean that a person must know how to draw; for, with pencil and paper, a smooth, flat surface, and a special dressmaker and tailor's square, such work is quickly accomplished.

3. Importance of Measurements.—Closely allied with a knowledge of the lines of the human form are the measurements used in pattern drafting. The bust measurement, which of itself usually denotes the size of the individual, is the chief one. Some artists need to know only the bust measurement and the height to make beautiful patterns. While this may be accomplishable by all after they are thoroughly familiar with the rules of drafting, to the one who is learning, each measurement should have a special significance and its place on the draft should be perfectly understood.

So, first of all, learn the rules that apply to all measurements and their use in pattern drafting as they are given in this Volume. For instance, the first line drawn in making a waist pattern is the foundation center-back line. To the length-of-back measure, you add $\frac{1}{2}$ inch to allow for the shaping out of the neck in the back. The next line drawn is the foundation back neck line, which is one-sixth of the neck measure, this being the right proportion whether the neck measure is 11 or 14 inches. The third line drawn is the bust line, which is one-half the bust plus the fulness you desire in the waist, tight-fitting waists requiring little fulness and blouses requiring considerable. From the bust line, you build the waist up and down, putting in lines and curves that correspond with the measurements you are using and that will result in a correctly proportioned pattern.

4. Art in Pattern Drafting.—In pattern making, work for beauty of line and proportion rather than for the exact location of points. When you have learned the subtraction, multiplication, and division rules, for such they really are, your square, pencil, and paper will be all you will need to assemble measurements in a wholly artistic way. Then you can develop any pattern, from a tight-fitting waist to the most intricate shapings that fashion may indicate. And your patterns will save material as well as time in cutting and fitting and in making alterations.

All this requires study and practice, but in applying the rules, try to understand the "why" of each line and each location and the proportion used to obtain it rather than to follow the rules slavishly. Then, drafting will be an interesting, creative work that you yourself can develop to meet your every pattern requirement.

_____

LINES USED IN PATTERN DRAFTING

5. Since pattern drafting means the drawing of lines to form a draft, the various kinds of lines as well as the terms relating to them must be understood from the very beginning. When thought of according to the direction in which they run and the shape which they assume, lines are *straight, curved, parallel, horizontal, vertical,* and *diagonal;* and when thought of according to the manner in which they are made, they are the *light full line*, the *heavy full line*, the *dotted line*, the *broken line*, and the *broken-and-dotted line*.

6. A **straight line** is a line that extends uniformly in one direction, while a **curved line** is one that is continuously bent so that no part of it is straight.

Parallel lines, Fig. 1, are lines that lie in the same plane and never meet, no matter how far they are

FIG. 1   FIG. 2

produced. Any two parallel lines have the same direction and are everywhere equally distant from each other.

A **horizontal line,** Fig. 2, is a line parallel to the horizon or to the surface of still water.

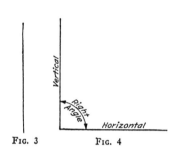

FIG. 3   FIG. 4

A **vertical line,** Fig. 3, is an upright line whose upper end is directly over its lower one. A vertical line is said to be *perpendicular* to a horizontal one.

A vertical line that meets a horizontal line at any point is said to form a **right angle.** Fig. 4 shows a horizontal line joined at right angles to a vertical line, the space between these lines, which is indicated by the arrow, being a right angle.

A **diagonal line** in pattern drafting is a straight line that is neither vertical nor horizontal; that is, a

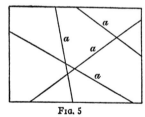
FIG. 5

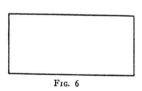
FIG. 6

slanting line. All lines marked *a* in Fig. 5 may be considered as diagonal lines.

A **rectangle,** Fig. 6, is any four-sided figure whose opposite sides are parallel and whose angles are right angles.

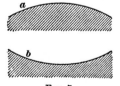
FIG. 7

A **convex curve,** as illustrated at *a*, Fig. 7, is a curve that rounds outwards; and a **concave curve,** as at *b*, is a curve that rounds inwards.

An **arc** is any part of a line that forms a *circle*, which, in turn, is a plane figure bounded by a curved line everywhere equally distant from the center. Thus, the concave and convex curves shown in Fig. 7 are arcs.

7. Describing an Arc.—A simple device to use in drawing, or describing, an arc, and one that is always available, consists of a pencil to which a string is attached. Cut a notch in an ordinary lead pencil about 1 inch from the point of the pencil. Tie a string around the pencil at the point where the notch is located so that the string will not slip out of place.

8. If you wish to draw, or describe, an arc that will pass through two points, as *a* and *b*, Fig. 8, and that does not form a semi-circle, you must first locate a center, as at *c*, from which to describe the arc.

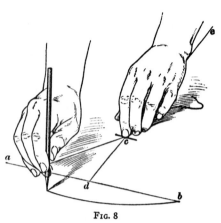
FIG. 8

To accomplish this, first join *a* and *b* with a straight line, then find a point *d* midway between *a* and *b*, and at the point *d* draw line *de* at right angles to the line joining *a* and *b*. Any point, such as *c*, on the line *de* may be used as a center for the arc passing through *a* and *b*.

Now, with the pencil held vertically, place the point of the pencil at *b*. Measure out from the pencil on the string the distance from *b* to *c* and place a pin at this point, crosswise of the cord. The pin will help to hold the string firm so that it will not slip and cause an irregularity in the arc.

With the pin directly over the center point *c* and held securely in position with the forefinger of the left hand and with the point of the pencil at *b*, swing the pencil from *b* to *a*, as shown. Be careful to keep the pencil in a vertical position while describing the arc, or the pencil point will swing to one side of *a* instead of meeting it exactly.

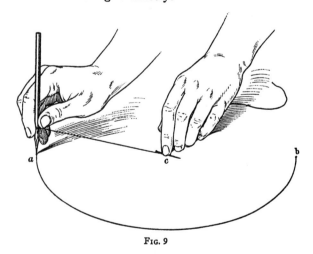
FIG. 9

9. To draw an arc in the form of a half circle, as shown in Fig. 9, proceed in exactly the same manner

2

as in drawing the arc just explained, but in this case let point *c*, or the center of the arc, fall midway between *a* and *b*.

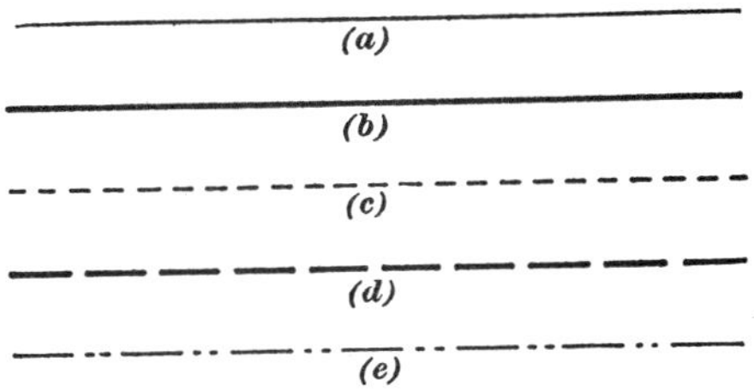

10. The lines used in pattern drafting, named according to the way in which they are made, are shown in Fig. 10.

The **light full line,** illustrated at (*a*), is used for construction and foundation lines.

FIG. 10

The **heavy full line,** shown at (*b*), is used to represent the pattern lines.

The **dotted line,** shown at (*c*), consists of a series of very short dashes. This style of line is used in designing to show new lines other than the foundation and pattern lines.

The **broken line,** shown at (*d*), consists of a series of long dashes; it is used in connecting points, as in the bottom of skirts.

The **broken-and-dotted line,** shown at (*e*), consists of a long dash and a couple of dots repeated regularly. Such a line is used to indicate the center of a pattern.

THE PICKEN SQUARE

MEANING AND DESCRIPTION

11. The dressmaker and tailor's square—the **Picken square**—used in connection with the drafting of patterns in these sections and shown in Figs. 11 and 12, is a convenient and ingenious device designed for the purpose of laying out drafts for patterns in the quickest and most efficient way. It is the very secret of simplicity in drafting. In appearance, the Picken square is similar to an ordinary **L** square, such as is used by mechanics, yet it contains different graduations that serve to lighten the labor of the user by avoiding the use of fractions in making measurements. And, in addition, it contains curves based on those of the human form, which will enable any one to obtain well-balanced lines for figures of any shape.

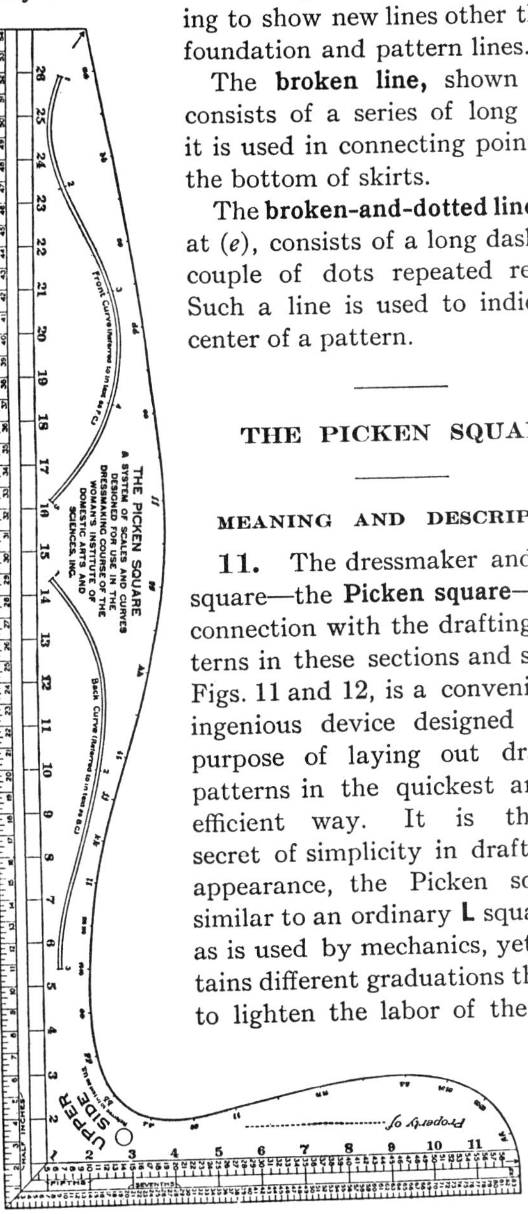

FIG. 11

12. To determine just what curves were to be placed on this square, more than five thousand drafts were made for figures of various shapes. These curves are so arranged that they will blend with any line drawn to correspond with the instructions given in the text of these sections; so by following instructions one may draft a pattern for any kind of garment, no matter how large or small the figure may be, nor how close or tight-fitting the garment is to be. It will readily be seen that a square constructed according to such ideas will give perfect lines and thus be the means of saving much time in the constructing and fitting of any garment.

13. A word of caution before you consider the Picken Square in detail. This instrument is your tool. Your aim in becoming acquainted with it should be to understand its uses and possibilities so that you may adapt it to your purpose. Never follow instructions for its use blindly or simply as rules. Try to see the reason for the various operations so that after you have had practice you will be able to make drafts without any thought of following a rule.

Also, since every curve and line of the square has a relation and meaning with reference to human beings, make a point of studying the human figure. Study the people you see as you walk along the street; notice people in the shops, on the street cars, everywhere. Compare their lines and curves. Compare stout women and thin ones, and try to see wherein they differ. You will discover that the thin ones have more lines and angles than curves, that the stouter ones tend to curves, and that, in general, the stouter people are, the more definite are their curves.

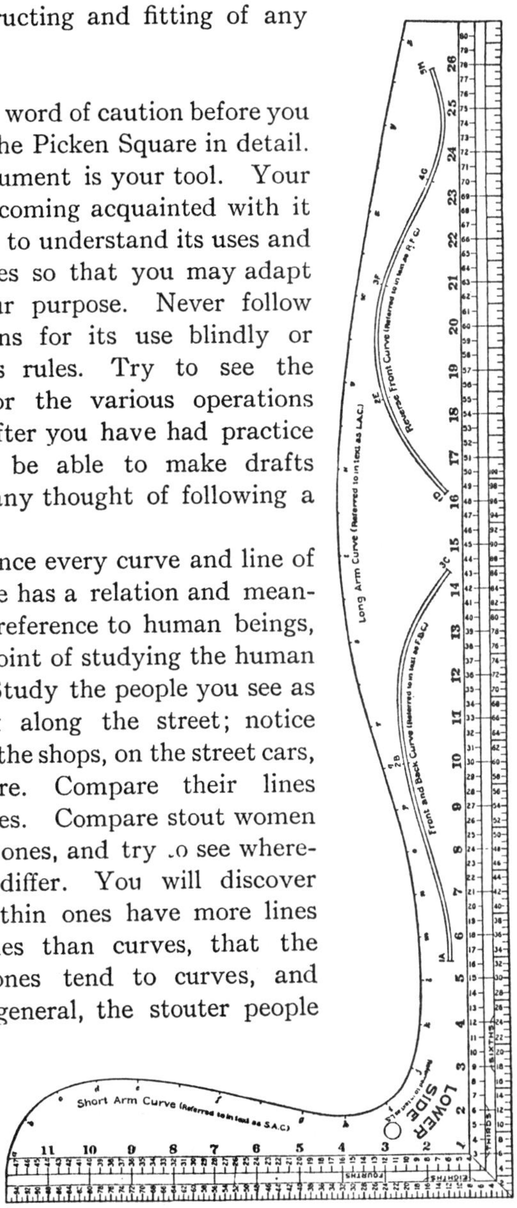

FIG. 12

14. The Picken square has two sides—the upper side, referred to as U. S. in this book, and illustrated in Fig. 11, and the lower side, referred to as

3

L. S. and illustrated in Fig. 12. It has, also, two arms —the *long arm*, which is 27 inches in length, and the *short arm*, which is 12 inches. The outer edge of each of these arms is straight and the inner edge of each has an irregular curve, one known as the *long-arm curve* and the other as the *short-arm curve*. Although the long- and the short-arm curves are designated on the lower side only, the same curves, lettered differently, appear on both sides.

15. Upper Side.—On referring to Fig. 11, you will see that the straight edge of the long arm of the upper side of the square has inch and half-inch graduations and that the short arm is graduated into inches, fifth inches, and seventh inches. Inches are marked on the inner scale, while the fractions of an inch occur on the outer edge.

The *long-arm curve*, referred to in the text as L. A. C. for the purpose of brevity, begins with the arrowhead near *aa* and extends to the point *qq*. Between these points are 1-inch graduations, these being lettered *aa*, *bb*, etc. at 2-inch intervals until *ii* is reached. From *ii* to *tt* of the short-arm curve, every 1-inch graduation is lettered, as *ii*, *jj*, etc.

The short-arm curve, referred to as S. A. C., extends from *qq* to the arrowhead at the end of the short arm and is divided and lettered in the same way as the long-arm curve, the letters continuing from *qq* to *zz*. From *qq* to *tt*, the intervals are 1 inch long; from *tt* to *vv*, 2 inches long; and from *vv* to *zz*, 1 inch long.

16. In the long arm, between the straight and the curved edge, are two additional, irregular curves. These curves are used for the upper and the under parts of the sleeve; one of them is called the *front curve*, referred to as F. C., and the other the *back curve*, referred to as B. C. The front curve is divided into four equal parts by the points *1* to *5*, and the back curve, into two equal parts, by the points *1*, *2*, and *3*.

17. Lower Side.—As shown in Fig. 12, the straight edge of the long arm of the lower side of the square is graduated into inches, third inches, and sixth inches, and the short arm into inches, fourth inches, and eighth inches. The short-arm and the long-arm curves on this side are marked off into 1-inch spaces and lettered with single letters to avoid any possibility of confusion with the double letters on the upper side. The short-arm curve extends from *a* to a point midway between *i* and *j*, and the long arm, from this point between *i* and *j*, to *z* and a short distance beyond, that is, to the end of the square.

On this side, too, between the straight and the curved edges, are the opposites of the curves on the upper side; they are called the *front and back curve*, referred to as F. B. C., and the *reverse front curve*, referred to as R. F. C. The former is divided into two equal spaces by the points *1A*, *2B*, and *3C*, and

the latter, into four spaces, by the points *1D*, *2E*, *3F*, *4G*, and *5H*.

18. Abbreviations Relating to the Square.—The abbreviations mentioned in the foregoing articles are tabulated so that you can easily refer to them. They should, of course, be memorized before you proceed very far with drafting, and they can be memorized very easily by a few references to the following table:

U. S.	Upper side of square
L. S.	Lower side of square
L. A. C.	Long-arm curve
S. A. C.	Short-arm curve
F. C.	Front curve
B. C.	Back curve
F. B. C.	Front and back curve
R. F. C.	Reverse front curve

USE OF CURVES

19. Purpose of U. S. Curves.—The next important matter to learn in drafting is the purpose of the curves of the square. The principal uses are tabulated here, for easy reference. In studying them, do not be content with simply reading them over; rather, become so thoroughly acquainted with them that you can, on looking at your square, identify each of its curves with the purpose for which it is used. Then, when you begin to draft patterns, you will not be handicapped by the necessity of becoming acquainted with the instrument on which all your drafting success depends.

20. The curve from *ff* to the arrowhead (long arm, U. S.) is used in obtaining:

(1) For waists, coats, and skirts, the correct curve from the waist line to the hip line.

(2) For waists and coats, the correct curve for the under-arm line from the waist line to the bust line.

(3) For sleeves, the correct line from the elbow up and down.

(4) For similar curves in drafts of underwear and children's garments.

The curve from *dd* to *ii* (long arm, U. S.) is used for the under-arm curves of waists, coats, and underwear when tight-fitting garments are worn.

The curve from *jj* to *tt* is adjusted to the different points on the draft to form the front armhole.

The curve from *ii* to *tt* is used for front armhole lines for large measures.

The curve from *mm* to *ss* is used for front armhole lines for small measures.

The curve from *mm* to *gg* is used for the back-shoulder curve.

The curve from the arrowhead on the short-arm curve around to *uu* or *tt* (depending on the size of the armhole), is used to lay off the back-armhole curve.

4

The curve from the arrowhead on the short-arm curve to *tt* forms the front-neck curve and is used in obtaining curves in yokes, collars, and cuffs, also lapel lines, and in outlining various points in flat designing, as is explained in some of the later chapters.

The front curve, F. C., is employed in drawing the front upper curve of sleeves, and can be used for any size of armhole and style of sleeve. The back curve, B. C., is used in drawing the back under curve of sleeves and, like the F. C., can be used for all sizes of armholes and all styles of sleeves.

21. Purpose of L. S. Curves.—The curves on the lower side of the square serve practically the same purpose as those on the upper side, and their arrangement is such that in many cases the lines may be drawn from either side of the square, and thus make turning the square unnecessary.

However, unless one is an expert in the use of the square, one should not attempt to substitute a L. S. curve for a U. S. curve, for one might become confused and make a wrong curve that would throw the entire draft out of proportion. It would be safer to turn the square over and use the designated curve. One very important L. S. curve, the one from *j* to *m*, is the back-neck curve.

USE OF SCALES

22. Nature of Scales.—The purpose of the graduated scales on the upper and the lower side of the square is to avoid calculations and the use of fractions in connection with the drafting of patterns. Besides the scale of inches, there are seven scales; eighths, fourths, halves, fifths, sevenths, thirds, and sixths.

23. Making the Scales.—To understand these scales thoroughly, as well as to appreciate their value, it will be advisable for you to lay out each one on a sheet of paper with a pencil and the aid of the square itself, using Fig. 13 as a guide.

24. Begin by drawing eight horizontal, parallel lines on the sheet of paper, making them about 4 inches long and marking spaces on them 1 inch apart, as shown by the vertical lines in the illustration. Then, using the straight edge of the long arm of the square and the inch marks on it as a guide, and remembering that the inch marks are the large figures on the inside of the scales, divide each of these eight lines, beginning at the left end of each, into inches, as shown. Draw a vertical line at right angles to the horizontal line at each inch division, and mark the first vertical line on each of the eight horizontal lines 1, the second 2, and the third 3, as is clearly shown in (*a*), Fig. 13.

With the scale of halves on the square, divide the first inch of the second line into two equal parts, or *halves*, and then treat the second and the third inch in the same way, as shown in (*b*) of the illustration, using short vertical lines to indicate these divisions. In this way, six half-inch spaces are secured in a 3-inch space when measured on the scale of halves on the square. Thus, to find one-half of any given distance by means of the square, use the half-inch scale.

For instance, if the bust measure is 40 inches and the drafting directions say to find one-half of 40, it is not necessary to determine what one-half of 40 is; all that has to be done is to locate the point opposite 40 on the scale of halves on the square.

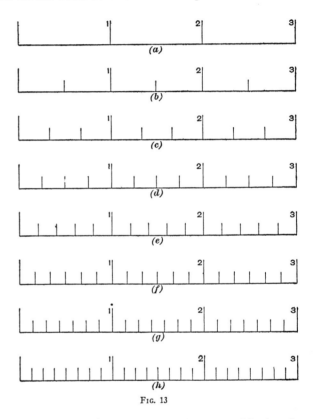

FIG. 13

Next, as in (*c*), divide the third line of inches into *thirds;* that is, divide each of the three inches into three equal parts, as shown by the short vertical lines. To locate these points exactly, place the scale of thirds on the square along the line to be divided and mark the short vertical lines opposite each $\frac{1}{3}$-inch mark. Thus, when directed in the instructions to locate a point one-third of the armhole measure, for example, when the armhole measure is 15 inches, simply measure out to 15 on the scale of thirds.

Proceed in the same manner with the remainder of the lines, dividing them in the order given into fourths, fifths, sixths, sevenths, and eighths.

25. Although the graduations on the square for the first inch are not clearly shown for all scales, as in the case of thirds, fourths, and fifths, this will

5

not inconvenience you in drafting, for it is very rare that a line of 1 inch has to be divided into fractions.

In using scales on the square, begin your measurements at the corner of the square. This means that sometimes the measuring edge will be on the upper side of the line and sometimes on the lower side.

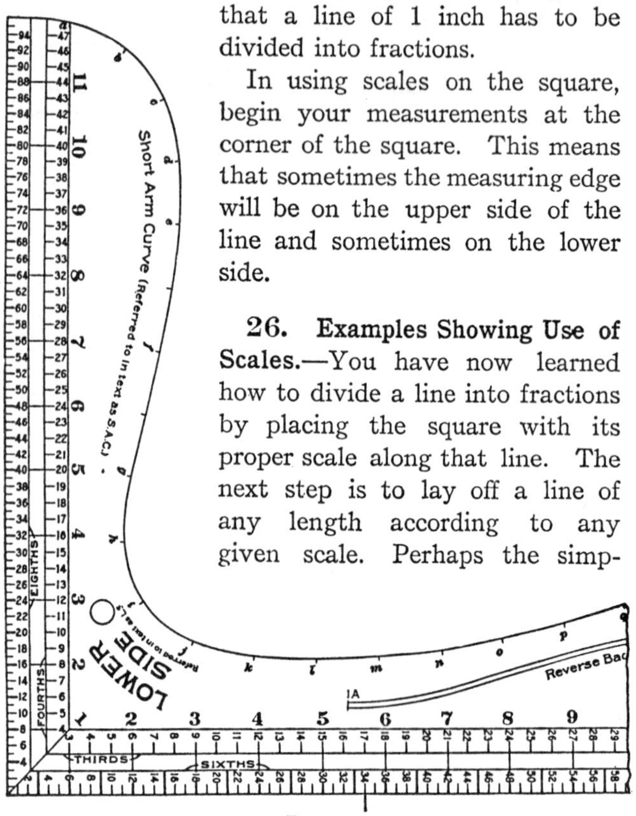

26. Examples Showing Use of Scales.—You have now learned how to divide a line into fractions by placing the square with its proper scale along that line. The next step is to lay off a line of any length according to any given scale. Perhaps the simp-

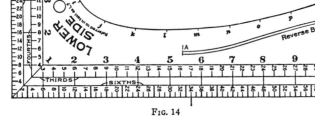

Fig. 14

lest way to learn this is by means of illustrated examples.

EXAMPLE 1. If you desire to lay off a line $\frac{1}{3}$ of 17 inches, use the scale of thirds, which is inside the scale of sixths on the Lower Side of the square on the long arm. Lay the square with the scale of thirds along the line and the corner of the square at the beginning of the line; then look down the scale of thirds until you come to 17, as indicated by the short line extending from the edge of the square in Fig. 14. This is the desired point.

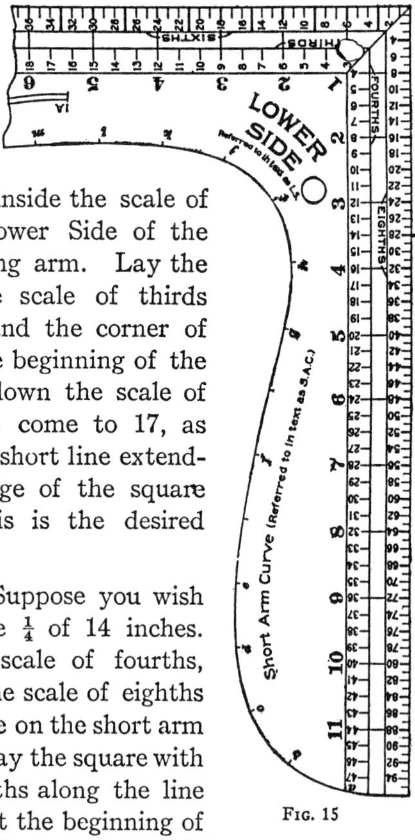

EXAMPLE 2. Suppose you wish to lay off a line $\frac{1}{4}$ of 14 inches. First, find the scale of fourths, which is inside the scale of eighths on the Lower Side on the short arm of the square. Lay the square with the scale of fourths along the line and the corner at the beginning of the line; then follow the scale of fourths until 14 is reached, as indicated in Fig. 15 by the short line on

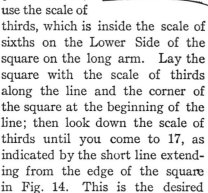

Fig. 15

the outer, or straight, edge of the short arm. This is the desired point.

EXAMPLE 3. Suppose you wish to lay off $\frac{1}{8}$ of $8\frac{3}{4}$ inches, which is perhaps a little more difficult. The scale of eighths is on the outer straight edge of the short arm of the L. S. Measure up to 8 on the scale of eighths, also $\frac{1}{8}$ of $\frac{3}{4}$ inch, or between 8 and 9 on the scale of eighths. To be exact, divide this small space into fourths and make your mark exactly opposite $8\frac{3}{4}$ on the scale of eighths, as shown in Fig. 16.

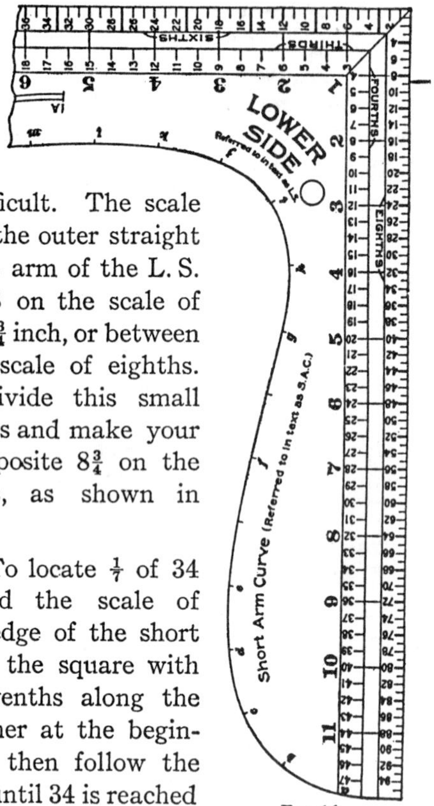

EXAMPLE 4. To locate $\frac{1}{7}$ of 34 inches, first find the scale of sevenths on the edge of the short arm, U. S. Lay the square with the scale of sevenths along the line and the corner at the beginning of the line; then follow the scale of sevenths until 34 is reached as shown in Fig. 17. The mark representing where you stop is the desired point.

Fig. 16

27. Another point that you should master at the beginning of your use of scales is that of adding a number of inches to a fraction of a line. The following illustrative example should make this clear:

EXAMPLE 5. Suppose that you must make a line $\frac{1}{6}$ of 40 inches plus 2 inches. This does not mean $\frac{1}{6}$ of 42, but $\frac{1}{6}$ of 40 inches, plus 2 inches.

Lay the square with the scale of sixths up, follow this scale from the corner of the square to 40, represented by point a, Fig. 18. Then add 2 inches to this measure, bringing the correct point opposite 52 on the scale of sixths, or at point b.

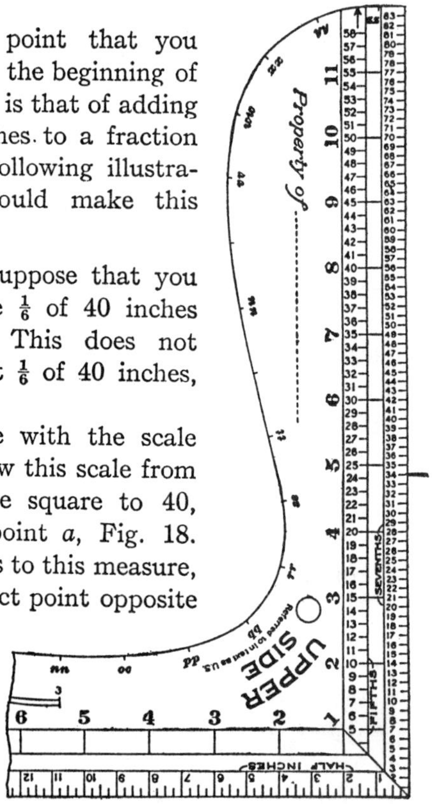

Such measuring is necessary in the drawing of horizontal lines,

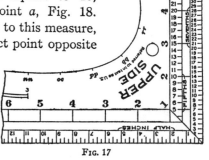

Fig. 17

such as the bust and hip line, where additions to actual measures are made to give ease or provide fulness.

28. The taking of measurements in dressmaking is a matter that should not be regarded lightly, for the accuracy of the measurements governs the accuracy of the drafts made from them.

Seventeen measurements are required for drafting the foundation waist, sleeve, and skirt. They are: (1) the neck, (2) the bust, (3) the front, (4) the chest, (5) the width-of-back, (6) the length-of-back, (7) the center-back depth, (8) the armhole, (9) the inside sleeve length, (10) the elbow, (11) the hand, (12) the waist, (13) the hip, (14) the dart, (15) the front length, (16) the side length, and (17) the back length.

29. A great aid in the work of taking the measurements just enumerated is the **Woman's Institute**

FIG. 18

measure slip, Fig. 19. This slip is so arranged that a complete record of measurements and notes relating to the work in hand may be kept. There is space at the top for a person's name, address, and telephone number, the date on which the measurement is taken, the name of the magazine from which the design is selected, and the design number. The measurements are arranged in the order in which they should be taken, with a space for recording details relating to the work, all of which should be evident from the slip. Such slips can be made on the typewriter or they can be obtained already printed in pads of fifty or one hundred.

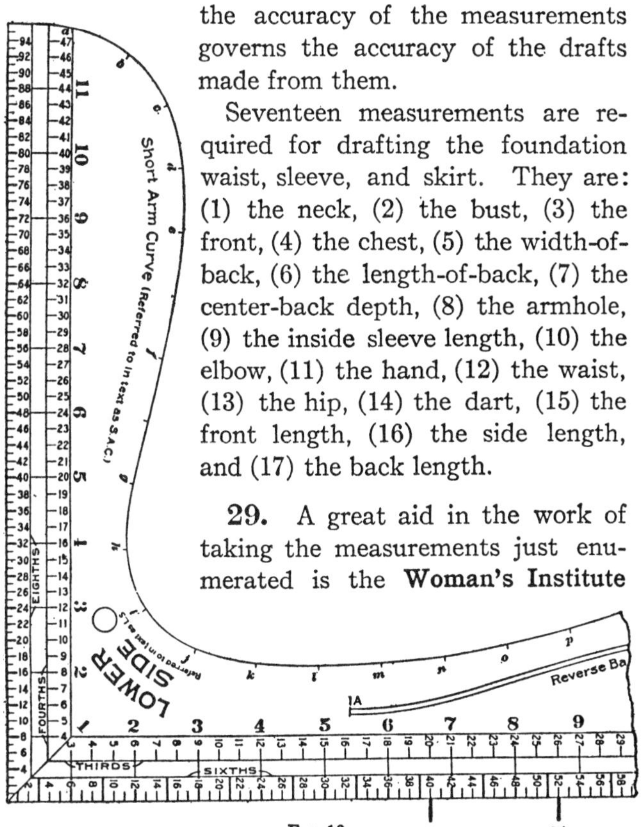

30. Importance of Taking Measurements Accurately.—As has already been emphasized, the form of a person for whom one is drafting a pattern must be studied carefully. Two figures may have the same neck, bust, and waist measure, and yet be so different in the chest measure and in the width and the length of the back or the front that their forms assume entirely different proportions. Individually drafted patterns take care of these differences if the measurements are correct; therefore, the importance of knowing just how to take measurements correctly

and of taking them with accuracy cannot be over-emphasized.

Practice in taking measurements will help to obtain accuracy. The measures of several different figures should be taken, as should also the measures of one figure two or three times, so as to come to an appreciation of the importance of placing the measuring tape correctly and thus getting the measurements the same each time.

31. Preparation for Taking Measurements.—The procedure in taking measurements is simple; yet it is essential for you to study the illustrations, noting just how the tape is placed for each measure, and to read carefully the instructions relating to them. It is a good plan, also, before taking measurements, to compare the tape with the square to see that the graduations agree. Frequently, an old tape measure

WOMAN'S INSTITUTE MEASURE SLIP

Name_____

Address _____

Telephone No. _____Date_____

Magazine_____ Design No. _____

Name of Measurement	Size
Neck_____	
Bust_____	
Front_____	
Chest_____	
Width of Back_____	
Length of Back_____	
Center Back Depth_____	
Armhole_____	
Inside Sleeve Length_____	
Elbow_____	
Hand_____	
Waist_____	
Hip_____	
Dart_____	
Front Length_____	
Side Length_____	
Back Length_____	

Designed by_____Cut by_____

Pattern_____Garment_____

Material_____Made by_____

FIG. 19

becomes so stretched that it is practically useless for taking measures. Then, too, a new one sometimes has a great deal of "give" or stretch. Try to procure a tape measure whose graduations correspond with those on the square.

The person whose measurements you are taking should stand erect, but not in an unnatural manner.

figure, regardless of where the armhole, neck, or waist line comes in the garment that she is wearing. Then, the measurements will be those of the human form.

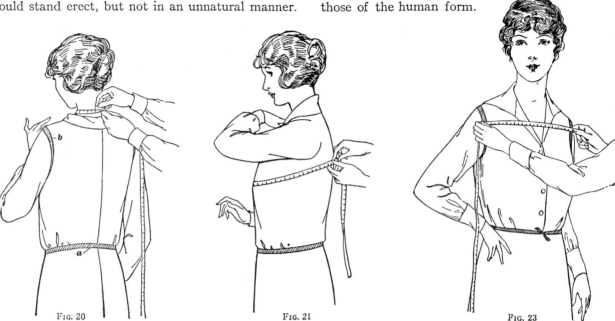

FIG. 20   FIG. 21   FIG. 23

You will frequently find persons who, when being measured, stand very straight with their shoulders thrown back, but not erect and natural. A good idea is to observe the person in repose; then you can judge more easily and accurately whether or not she is assuming an unnatural position when she is being measured. A pattern made from measures taken while a person is standing unnaturally is likely to produce a garment that is not good-fitting.

32. Before taking the various measurements, directions for which follow, it is necessary to form lines by means of tapes on the person about to be measured.

FIG. 22

Tie a tape snugly around the waist, as shown at *a*, Fig. 20, pushing it down well on the figure. Observe this tape during the measuring process to see that it does not creep up. Next, place a tape around each armhole, as shown at *b*, being careful to have it fit well up around the arm and up to the point of the shoulder, where it should be pinned to the garment in order to keep it in place. These lines are of great importance if an accurate draft is to be made.

In taking measurements, never be guided by the lines of the waist or the skirt that a woman is wearing, but place the tape exactly where it belongs on the

TAKING THE MEASUREMENTS

33. Take the **neck measure** in the manner shown in Fig. 20, usually around the base of the neck. The garment is generally cut to fit close at this place, even though the neck is to be cut lower later, for an accurate neck measure is essential if the waist or blouse is to fit properly at the neck line. It is sometimes a good idea to take an additional neck measure at the top of the neck. This is a great aid in fitting high collars on figures having a full neck.

Another method used is to take the measure at the top of the neck and add $\frac{3}{4}$ inch to this for the lower measure. The first method, however, is more accurate.

34. Take the **bust measure,** as illustrated in Fig. 21, around and over the fullest part of the bust and loosely over the fullest part of the shoulder blades to the center of the back. Because a blouse that is too snug through the bust is most uncomfortable as well as unbecoming, great care must be exercised in placing the tape in the exact position that the bust line of the garment will assume.

FIG. 24

In taking this measure, stand directly behind the person. Hold the tape together in the back; and step around in front to see that it is over the fullest part of the bust. Insert two fingers crosswise underneath the tape over the bust, sliding them around to the back to avoid drawing the tape too tight.

35. Take the **front-length measure,** as shown in Fig. 22, by placing the end of the tape at the prominent bone at the back of the neck and around the base, and then down over the fullest part of the bust to the center front of the waist line. The front measure is taken from the back of the neck because of the fact that there is no definite place on the shoulder from which to take it.

FIG. 25

36. Take the **chest measure,** as shown in Fig. 23, by placing the tape 2 inches below the top of the breast bone at the neck and then measuring across from the outside edge of one armhole tape to the outside edge of the other.

37. Take the **width-of-back measure,** as shown in Fig. 24, across the back from the outside edge of

38. Take the **length-of-back measure,** as shown in Fig. 25, by measuring from the prominent bone at the base of the neck to the bottom of the tape at the waist line.

FIG. 26

39. The **center-back-depth measure,** as illustrated in Fig. 26, requires first that a tape be placed across the back directly under the arms and up across the chest in front, where it is pinned securely, and that care be exercised so that the tape runs in a straight line across the back from armhole to armhole. Then, with a tape line, take the measurement from the prominent bone at the back of the neck down to the top of this tape.

40. Take the **armhole measure,** as shown in Fig. 27, by placing the tape around under the arm, bringing it close to the body, and then up around the arm to the shoulder point, as at *a*, taking care not to draw it tight.

It should be remembered, however, that while you should not take this measure too tight, neither should you go to the opposite extreme of taking it too loose. A good-fitting armhole in both the blouse and the sleeve depends on the accuracy of this measure.

FIG. 27   FIG. 28   FIG. 29

one armhole tape to the outside edge of the other and about 4 inches below the neck in the back, as shown at *a*. Be careful in taking the chest and the width-of-back measures that the tapes around the armholes do not slip out of position.

41. Take the **inside-sleeve-length measure,** as illustrated in Fig. 28, by having the arm held out straight, as shown, and then measuring from the tape around the armhole at the hollow of the arm down to where the wrist joins the hand, as at *a*.

42. Take the **elbow measure** by having the arm bent, as shown in Fig. 29, and then placing the tape around the arm at the elbow joint, as at *a*.

This measure is not used in the actual drafting, but it is often of help in measuring for short-sleeve finishes and in preventing a sleeve from being made too snug at this point.

43. Take the **hand measure,** as illustrated in Fig. 30, by measuring around the hand at the fullest part, including the thumb.

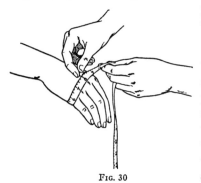

FIG. 30

44. Take the **waist measure,** as shown in Fig. 31, by placing the tape line snugly around the waist exactly where the waist band of the skirt should come.

45. Take the **hip measure,** as shown in Fig. 32, around the fullest part of the hips, which as a rule is from 6 to 10 inches below the waist line. The tape should not be drawn tight; it should be held around the figure, in an easy manner, but close enough to stay up all the way around. A pin should be placed in the skirt at the side over the hip, even with the top

47. Take the **front-length measure,** as illustrated in Fig. 34, by measuring from the tape around the waist, at the center front, down to the floor.

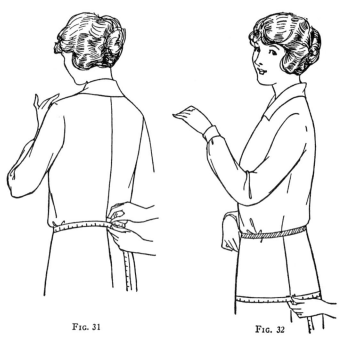

FIG. 31   FIG. 32

48. Take the **side-length measure,** as illustrated in Fig. 35, by placing the tape at the waist line, letting it fall over the fullest part of the hip, and then measuring to the floor.

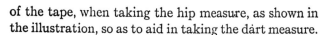

FIG. 33   FIG. 34

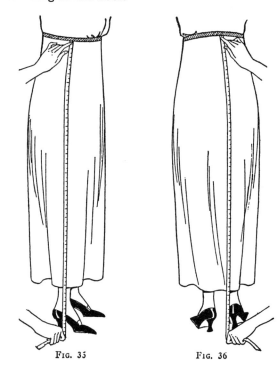

FIG. 35   FIG. 36

of the tape, when taking the hip measure, as shown in the illustration, so as to aid in taking the dart measure.

46. Take the **dart measure,** as shown in Fig. 33, from the waist line to the pin, over the fullest part of the hip, as shown at *a*.

49. Take the **back-length measure,** as illustrated in Fig. 36, from the tape at the waist, at the center back, down to the floor.

50. Average Measurements.—So that you may become familiar with the different measurements and their relative proportion to one another, the measurements of five hundred women were taken, averaged, and arranged in a table, designated here as Table I. This table you will find an excellent guide in taking measurements, because by referring to it you will be able to tell at a glance whether or not the measurements you take are in the correct proportion one to another.

TABLE I
AVERAGE PROPORTION OF MEASUREMENTS IN INCHES

		Waist							Sleeve				Skirt				
Bust	Neck	Front	Chest	Width of Back	Length of Back	Center-Back Depth	Arm-hole	Inside Sleeve Length	Elbow	Hand	Waist	Hip	Dart	Front Length	Side Length	Back Length
30	$12\frac{1}{2}$	19	$12\frac{1}{4}$	12	$14\frac{1}{2}$	$6\frac{1}{2}$	$13\frac{1}{2}$	16	9	$7\frac{1}{4}$	24	33	$6\frac{1}{2}$	37	37	$37\frac{1}{2}$
32	$12\frac{1}{2}$	$19\frac{1}{2}$	$12\frac{1}{2}$	12	$14\frac{3}{4}$	$6\frac{3}{4}$	14	16	$9\frac{1}{2}$	$7\frac{1}{2}$	24	35	$6\frac{1}{2}$	38	38	$38\frac{1}{2}$
34	13	20	$13\frac{1}{4}$	13	$14\frac{3}{4}$	$6\frac{3}{4}$	14	$16\frac{1}{2}$	10	$7\frac{3}{4}$	26	37	$6\frac{3}{4}$	$38\frac{1}{2}$	39	$39\frac{1}{2}$
36	$13\frac{1}{2}$	$20\frac{1}{2}$	14	$13\frac{1}{2}$	15	7	15	17	$10\frac{1}{2}$	8	28	39	7	39	40	$40\frac{1}{2}$
38	$13\frac{1}{2}$	21	$14\frac{1}{2}$	14	15	$7\frac{1}{4}$	$15\frac{1}{2}$	$17\frac{1}{2}$	11	8	30	41	$7\frac{1}{2}$	$39\frac{1}{2}$	$40\frac{1}{2}$	41
40	14	$21\frac{1}{2}$	15	$14\frac{1}{2}$	$15\frac{1}{4}$	$7\frac{1}{4}$	16	18	$11\frac{1}{2}$	$8\frac{1}{4}$	32	44	8	40	41	$41\frac{1}{2}$
42	$14\frac{1}{2}$	22	$15\frac{1}{2}$	15	$15\frac{1}{4}$	$7\frac{1}{4}$	$16\frac{1}{2}$	18	12	$8\frac{1}{4}$	34	46	$8\frac{1}{2}$	41	42	$42\frac{1}{2}$
44	$14\frac{1}{2}$	22	16	$15\frac{1}{2}$	$15\frac{1}{2}$	$7\frac{1}{2}$	17	$18\frac{1}{4}$	12	$8\frac{3}{4}$	$35\frac{1}{2}$	49	9	$41\frac{1}{2}$	$42\frac{1}{2}$	43
46	15	$22\frac{1}{2}$	$16\frac{1}{2}$	$15\frac{1}{2}$	$15\frac{3}{4}$	$7\frac{3}{4}$	17	$18\frac{1}{2}$	$12\frac{1}{2}$	9	$37\frac{1}{2}$	51	$9\frac{1}{2}$	42	43	$43\frac{1}{2}$
48	$15\frac{1}{2}$	23	$17\frac{1}{2}$	16	16	8	$17\frac{1}{2}$	19	13	9	$39\frac{1}{2}$	$53\frac{1}{2}$	10	$42\frac{1}{2}$	$43\frac{1}{2}$	$43\frac{1}{2}$
50	16	$23\frac{1}{2}$	18	$16\frac{1}{2}$	16	8	18	19	$13\frac{1}{2}$	9	41	56	10	43	44	44

REVIEW QUESTIONS

1. Define pattern drafting and tell how a pattern is formed.

2. Draw an arc.

3. What is the purpose in pattern drafting of: (a) A light full line? (b) A heavy full line?

4. What is the purpose of the Picken Square?

5. What are the advantages of the scales on the Picken Square?

6. Draw a line showing: (a) $\frac{1}{3}$ of 7 inches; (b) $\frac{1}{6}$ of 12 inches; (c) $\frac{1}{7}$ of 8 inches.

7. Why is it necessary to take accurate measurements?

8. How should a person whose measurements are being taken stand?

9. (a) Describe the taking of the bust measure. (b) How is the center-back-depth measure taken?

10. Why should the human form be studied in connection with pattern drafting?

CHAPTER II

PATTERNS FOR FOUNDATION WAISTS

PRINCIPLES GOVERNING FOUNDATION DRAFTS

1. With drafting lines and the use of the Picken Square, with its curves and scales, well in mind, drafting should prove to be an interesting and delightful occupation. But before taking up the real study of the drafts, it will be well for you to know that there are certain drafts, known as *foundation drafts*, from which all others are developed. They are the plain waist, the plain sleeve, and the plain and the circular skirt drafts. In this chapter, the foundation waist drafts with their sleeves, collars, and cuffs are taken up.

2. In the making of drafts, remember that lengthwise measurements, that is, measurements that are taken up and down the figure, such as length of back, length of front, skirt lengths, and sleeve lengths, are used in drafting just as they are taken; and that crosswise measurements, such as bust, waist, hip, and hand, are usually located on the pattern in halves. The reason for this is that a pattern is drafted for only one side of the body. It will therefore be a good idea for you to make a note of one-half of all the crosswise measures before beginning to draft.

Drafts are constructed on a scale of proportions from these actual measurements and may therefore be used at all times. The proportions given for these drafts hold good for nearly all figures; so it is necessary simply to study them and to practice making them in order to master them thoroughly and thus come to an understanding of garment construction.

3. As you make a draft, try to comprehend what every line in the draft represents, and test the draft by the measurements followed in making it before attempting to cut any material by it. The making of such tests should be kept up until you are absolutely sure of your ability and have no more fear as to your accuracy in doing such work. Then the danger of spoiling material will not be so great.

Time and patience, of course, are necessary at the beginning; and while it may take you 3 or 4 hours to make the first draft, you will be able to make a draft in a much shorter time when you are thoroughly familiar with the lines and points and have in your mind the reasons for their use and the order in which they are generally made to appear in drafts.

DRAFTING MATERIALS AND TERMS

4. Drafting Surface.—Pattern drafting requires a large, smooth surface on which to work. An ordinary sewing table may be used, but a larger table is more convenient. A table with a polished surface should be avoided, as it is frequently necessary to use a tracer, which is likely to injure the finish of such a piece of furniture.

The most convenient and inexpensive drafting and cutting board conceivable is a light-weight board covered on each side with fibrous paper having a smooth surface and known in the trade as *compo board* or *beaver board*. It can be purchased from lumber dealers at a small cost. A good size to select for general home use is 4 feet by 8 feet, as a board of this size is wide enough to accommodate material of average width and long enough, as a rule, to permit you to lay out a suit or a dress length and to place all the patterns on the cloth at one time.

5. Drafting Paper.—For *practice drafts*, the plain wrapping paper that comes to the house may be used. If the pieces are small, they may be pasted or sewed together. Newspapers may be used, but they are not so satisfactory as wrapping paper, because the printing on the paper makes it difficult to distinguish the drafting lines and points.

For *regular drafts*, which you will use again and again, a good quality of medium-weight paper about 32 to 36 inches in width should be employed. It may be white or common manila, or wrapping, paper. Such paper can usually be obtained from local merchants or paper dealers.

Enough paper should be procured to draft the various patterns for oneself and all the members of the family, for as progress is made it will be advisable to practice first on wrapping paper and then to draft patterns by measures that have been taken, so as to have such patterns ready when they are needed to make up any particular garment. Practice and application in drafting will convince any woman of its wonderful possibilities and will create in her the desire to test out and use the drafts given in the various sections.

6. Drafting Pencil.—For making the lines, points, etc., in pattern drafting, a moderately soft lead pencil should always be used. Ink and crayon are not so satisfactory; in fact, their use requires more time and, especially in the case of a beginner, produces less accurate results than does the use of a lead pencil.

7. Terms, Abbreviations, and Letters Used in Drafting.—A *line* in pattern drafting is referred to by the letters between which it lies; for example, the term *line AC* means the line between point *A* and

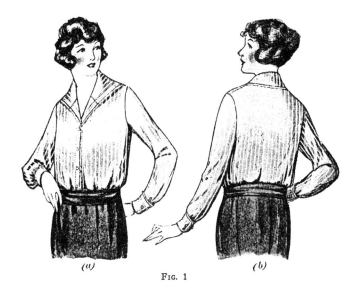

Fig. 1

point *C* on a draft; the *line DE*, the line between two points *D* and *E*; and so on.

It will be well to observe that the letters on the square are small, as *a*, *b*, *c*, etc., and that the letters on the drafts themselves are large, or capitals, as *A*, *B*, *C*, etc. This method of lettering is followed so as to avoid confusion in referring to the drafts and to the Picken square.

The person unfamiliar with *linear measure* should remember that there are 12 inches in 1 foot, and 3 feet, or 36 inches, in 1 yard.

Other abbreviations and terms that relate to the Picken square have already been explained.

DRAFTING A PLAIN FOUNDATION WAIST

PREPARATION FOR DRAFTING

8. Style of Waist.—In Fig. 1 (*a*) is shown the front view and in (*b*) the back view of a blouse developed from a plain-waist pattern. This blouse is plain in construction, having a soft collar that turns back with the waist fronts at the neck line and small soft cuffs at the wrists.

9. Measurements Necessary in Drafting a Waist.—The foundation waist draft, shown in real size in Model I and in reduced size in Fig. 2, is a model for a foundation-waist pattern. The following measurements are used in its construction

	INCHES
Neck	13
Bust	36
Front	21½
Width of chest	14
Width of back	13½
Length of back	15
Center-back depth	7
Armhole	15

10. Studying the Model Draft.—Before attempting to do any drawing, the beginner should carefully read the instructions relating to the making of this draft, and, with the Picken square, go over the model draft, so as to become familiar with the points referred to in the work. For instance, in Model I and in Fig. 2, *AC* is a foundation line, or a line used as a basis or beginning for the draft. In length, *AC* should equal the length of the back. Measure *AC* to make certain that it is the same length as the back; then, measure the bust line; and so on until the entire draft has been tested according to the instructions given.

11. Practicing With the Square.—It is advisable, too, before beginning to draft a pattern with the square, to locate points with the different scales and curves and to draw lines along both the long and the short arm, as well as to draw the long-arm, the short-arm, and the sleeve curves. Fig. 3 serves to show the way in which to hold the square in locating points and making straight and curved lines.

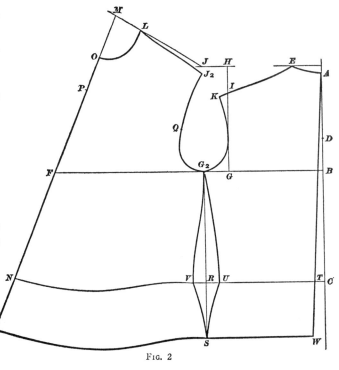

Fig. 2

Thus, view (*a*) illustrates the square in position for locating points along the scale of half inches and for drawing a line along the long arm with the square

13

U. S. up; view (b) shows the square L. S. up and held in position for locating points along the scale of sixths or thirds and for drawing a line along the long arm; and view (c) shows the square U. S. up and in position for drawing a line along the long-arm curve. The position of the hands in each view should be observed and imitated closely, because they show how to hold the square firmly in position while drafting.

12. In Readiness for Drafting.—For drafting this foundation waist, a piece of drafting paper 32

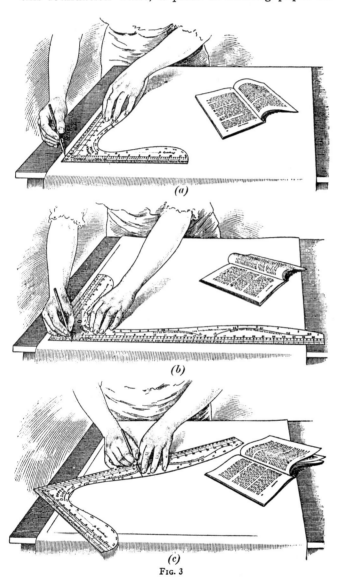

Fig. 3

inches by 36 inches is required. This paper should be laid on the drawing surface so that its short, or 32-inch, edge is next to you. Then, with the Picken square and a lead pencil, and with the model draft at a convenient place for observation, the drawing may be started. The instructions should be read carefully as the work is being done, and reference may be made to the model draft as often as is necessary to establish accurately the position of the various points and lines.

13. Additions to Measurements.—Because a blouse should "set" easy on the figure and be sufficiently loose across the back and through the bust, certain additions are always made for the foundation draft. Therefore, 4 inches is added to the original bust measure, 1 inch to the chest measure, $\frac{1}{2}$ inch to the width-of-back measure, and 1 inch to the original front length.

———

PROCEDURE IN DRAFTING WAIST

14. Drawing the Foundation Center-Back Line. Place the square, U. S. up, so that the long arm is $\frac{1}{2}$ inch from the edge of the paper to your right as you face the paper and the short arm is 9 inches from the top, as shown in position 1, Fig. 4. With the square in this position, draw a light vertical line the full length of the long arm and thus form the *foundation center-back line*.

15. Drawing the Foundation Back-Neck Line. From the top of this foundation center-back line, with the square still in the position described for drawing the foundation back line, draw to the left along the short arm of the square a horizontal line 3 or 4 inches long. This is the *foundation back-neck line*.

16. Locating Construction Points on Foundation Center-Back Line.—Refer to the measurements given in Art. **9** and proceed as shown in Figs. 2 and 4.

Locate:
Point *A*, one end of the back-neck curve, $\frac{1}{2}$ inch below the top of the foundation center-back line.

Point *B*, one end of the foundation bust line, a distance equal to the center-back depth measure below *A*, in this case 7 inches.

Point *C*, one end of the foundation waist line, the length-of-back measure below *A*, in this case 15 inches.

Point *D*, which is used later in determining the foundation front-shoulder line, one-third of the center-back depth above point *B*, in this case one-third of 7 inches, the center-back depth, or opposite 7 on the scale of thirds.

NOTE.—Remember, in using the scale of thirds, that you must place the square, L. S. up, with its corner at *B*. This will bring the long arm of the square still along the foundation center-back line, but pointing away from you rather than toward you.

17. Locating Construction Point *E* for Back-Neck Line.—Before you can draw the back-neck curve, you must locate point *E*, as *E* is one end of the curve, *A*, as already explained, being the other end.

Locate:

Point E one-sixth of the neck measure to the left of the top of the foundation center-back line, placing the square, L. S. up, with the corner resting on the top of the foundation center-back line and the short arm along this line, as shown by position 2. Since in this case the

the width-of-back measure is $13\frac{1}{2}$ inches, to locate G, measure $6\frac{3}{4}$ inches, or $13\frac{1}{2}$ inches on the scale of halves, plus $\frac{1}{4}$ inch, or 7 inches, which is opposite 14 on the scale of halves.

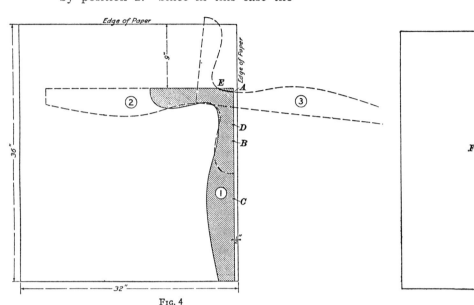

FIG. 4

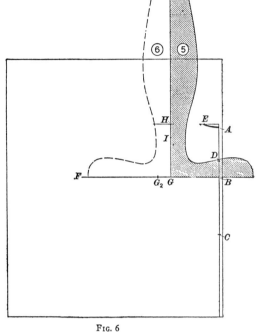

FIG. 6

neck measure is 13 inches, mark point E opposite 13 on the scale of sixths.

18. Drawing the Back-Neck Curve.—Draw curve AE by placing the square so that point j on the curve touches E and the edge of the curve touches A, as in position 3. This is the first pattern line to be drawn.

19. Drawing the Bust Line.—With the U. S. of the square up, the short arm on the foundation line, and the corner of the square at point B, as shown at position 4, Fig. 5, draw a line to the left one-half the length of the bust measure, *plus 2 inches*. The bust measure in this case is 36 inches; therefore, the termination of the bust line would be opposite 36 on the scale of halves, or 18 inches, plus 2 inches, or 20 inches, which is opposite 40 on the scale of halves. Letter this point F.

20. Locating Point G for the Width-of-Back Measure. While the square is in the position for drawing the bust line, locate and mark point G to the left of B one-half the width-of-back measurement, plus $\frac{1}{4}$ inch. Since

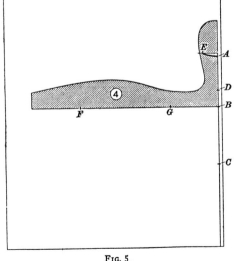

FIG. 5

21. Locating Construction Points for the Back-Shoulder Curve.—Four points must be located before the back-shoulder curve can be drawn.

Locate:

Point H by placing the short arm of the square, U. S. up, on the bust line with its corner at G, as shown in position 5, Fig. 6, and drawing a light line along the straight edge of the long arm the length of one-half the armhole measure. Since the armhole measure in this case is 15 inches, measure $7\frac{1}{2}$ inches, or opposite 15 on the scale of halves.

Point G_2 one-eighth the armhole measure to the left of G, as shown in position 6. As the armhole measure is 15 inches in this case, point G_2 should come opposite 15 on the scale of eighths.

Point I, one-eighth the armhole measure below H, placing the short arm of the square, L. S. up, on line GH, its corner at H,

15

and its long arm extending toward the left, as in position 7, Fig. 7. In this case, as in locating point G_2, mark the point opposite 15 on the scale of eighths.

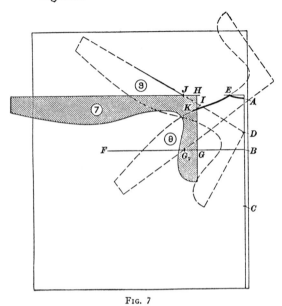

FIG. 7

Point J while the square is still in position 7. Draw a light line 3 or 4 inches to the left of point H, measure on this line one-eighth the armhole measurement from H, and mark J.

22. Drawing the Back-Shoulder Curve.—Place the square, U. S. up, so that mm on the L. A. C. is at E and the edge of the curve touches I, as shown in position 8; then draw a heavy curved line from E through I and about $\frac{3}{4}$ to 1 inch beyond I.

Locate:

Point K, the other extremity of the back-shoulder curve, by measuring to the left of I on the back-shoulder curve $\frac{5}{8}$ inch, using the scale of halves.

23. Drawing the Front-Shoulder Foundation Line. Place the square, L. S. up, so that its corner touches D and the straight edge of the long arm touches J, as shown in position 9, and draw an 8- or a 10-inch light diagonal line up from J as a foundation line upon which the drawing of the front-shoulder curve is based.

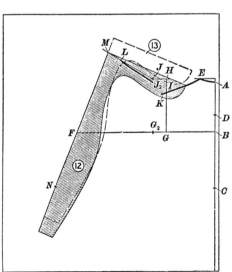

FIG. 9

24. Locating Construction Points for the Front-Shoulder Curve.—Measure the back shoulder from

E to K, and deduct $\frac{1}{2}$ inch from this measurement for the front-shoulder measurement. The front-shoulder curve is made shorter than the back so that the front may be stretched a little during the making of a garment. This produces a better-fitting shoulder curve.

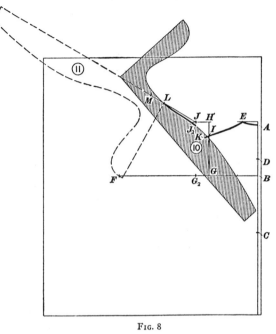

FIG. 8

Locate:

Point L on the front-shoulder foundation line, marking this a distance from J equal to the back-shoulder curve less $\frac{1}{2}$ inch. In this case, the back-shoulder curve is $5\frac{3}{4}$ inches; therefore, the front-shoulder foundation line should be $5\frac{1}{4}$ inches.

Point J_2 $\frac{1}{2}$ inch below J by placing the square so that the corner is at J and the straight-edge touches G_2.

25. Drawing the Front-Shoulder Curve. — Place the square, L. S. up, so that n of the L. A. C. is at L and the curved edge touches J_2, as in position 10, Fig. 8, and connect these points with a heavy full line.

26. Locating Construction Point M for Center-Front Line. Before determining the center-front line and the front-neck curve, it is necessary to locate point M one-sixth of the neck measure to the left of L, both L and M being on the front-shoulder foundation line drawn from J. The neck measure in this case is 13 inches; therefore, with the L. S. of the square up, place the corner of the square at point L, as shown

16

in position 11, and mark point M opposite 13 on the scale of sixths.

27. Drawing the Center-Front Line.—With the L. S. of the square up, the corner on M and the long arm touching F, as shown in position 12, Fig. 9, draw a line from M, through F, the full length of the long arm.

28. Locating Additional Construction Points.—To save time, points N, O, P, and Q, are located in order. Locate:

Point N, the terminus of the front waist line, on the center-front line. Since the front measure was taken from the prominent bone at the back of the neck, point A in the back of the draft representing this bone, it is necessary to deduct the distance from A to E, which is one-sixth the neck measure, from the center-front line. This is done to allow for the part of the back-neck measure that was added originally to find a definite place from which to hold the tape, as explained in Art. **36,** Chapter I. Therefore, since the neck measure in this case is 13 inches, slide the square up so that 13 on the scale of sixths is opposite point M, as shown in position 13; then measure down the length of front, $21\frac{1}{2}$ inches, plus the 1-inch addition for ease, or $22\frac{1}{2}$ inches, and mark point N.

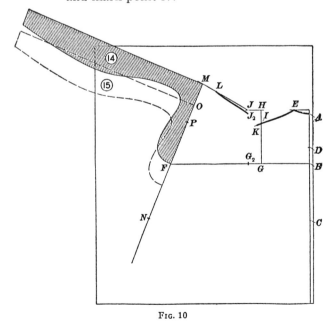

FIG. 10

Point O, the center-front point of the neck curve, by placing the square, L. S. up, so that the short arm rests along the center-front line and the corner is at M, as in position 14, Fig. 10, marking O

one-fourth the neck measure from M, in this case opposite 13 on the scale of fourths.

Point P, a construction point for the front armhole curve, by sliding the square

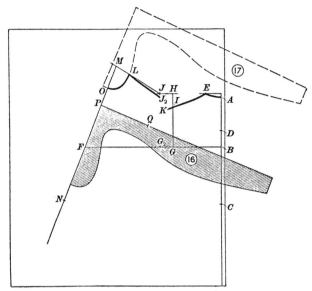

FIG. 11

down until the corner touches O, as in position 15, and marking P $2\frac{1}{2}$ inches below O on the center-front line. *This distance does not vary with different measures.*

Point Q, to be used in drawing the front-armhole curve, by placing the square, U. S. up, so that the short arm rests on the center-front line and the corner is at P, as in position 16, Fig. 11, measuring from P to the right on the long arm of the square to the point indicating one-half the chest measure plus $\frac{1}{2}$ inch. The chest measure in this case is 14 inches; therefore, locate point Q opposite 14 on the scale of halves, plus the $\frac{1}{2}$ inch, or 15 on the scale of halves.

29. Drawing the Front-Neck Curve.—Place the square, U. S. up, so that the arrowhead on the short arm is at point O and the Short Arm Curve touches point L, as shown in position 17, and draw the front-neck curve with a heavy full line from point O to point L.

NOTE.—The drawing of the front-neck curve could be done immediately after locating point O, but as time is saved by locating points P and Q while the square is in position, the plan here given is more satisfactory.

30. Drawing the Front-Armhole Curve.—The drawing of the front-armhole curve consists of connecting, with a heavy full line, points J_2, Q, and G_2. Place the square, U. S. up, as shown in position 18, Fig. 12, adjust it until the three points are touched by the curved edge of the square, and draw the front-armhole curve from J_2 to Q to G_2.

NOTE.—The position of the square varies according to the proportion of the measures used, but when drawing this curve for an average figure jj should be near J_2. If the armhole is small, point jj must be raised; if it is large, point jj must be dropped below J_2.

31. Drawing the Back-Armhole Curve.—Draw the back armhole next, bringing the square around until the arrowhead of the S. A. C. falls on G_2 and adjusting the curve to touch point K, as shown in position 19. Follow the curve from G_2 to K with a heavy full line.

32. Drawing the Foundation Under-Arm Line. Place the square L. S. up, so that its short arm is on the bust line and the corner is at G_2, as shown in position 20, Fig. 13. Then draw a light vertical line

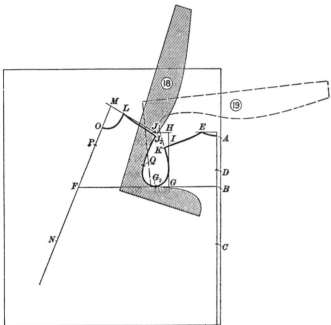

FIG. 12

from G_2 down along the long arm of the square, making it 14 to 16 inches long.

33. Drawing the Back Waist Line.—Place the short arm of the square, L. S. up, on the foundation center-back line so that the corner is at C, as in position 21, and draw along the long arm a light horizontal line that connects point C and the foundation under-arm line.

Locate:

Point R at the intersection of these lines.

34. Locating Construction Points for Under-Arm Curves and Center-Back Line.—Several points must be located so as to give the under-arm curves their proper shape and to determine the center-back line.

Locate:

Point S 4 inches below R on the foundation under-arm line.

Point U 1 inch to the right of R.

Point V 1 inch to the left of R.

Point T $\frac{3}{4}$ inch to the left of C on the back waist line.

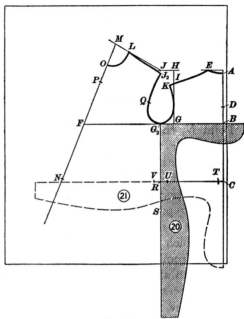

FIG. 13

35. Drawing Upper Parts of Under-Arm Curves. You are now ready to connect points G_2 and V and G_2 and U.

Connect:

Points G_2 and U with a heavy line, placing ff of the L. A. C., U. S. of the square up, on U and the edge of the curve on G_2, (in this case, the point bb is nearly at G_2), as shown in position 22, Fig. 14.

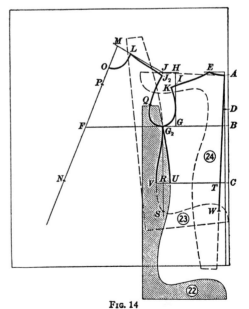

FIG. 14

Points G_2 and V, placing the square so that mm touches V and the edge of the curve touches G_2 (in this case, the point gg is nearly at G_2), as shown in position 23.

18

36. Drawing the Center-Back Line.—Connect points A and T, as shown in position 24, with a heavy straight line, extending it 4 inches below T. Letter its termination W, which will be on the bottom edge of the waist.

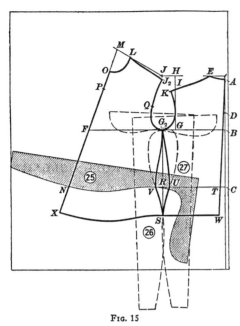

Fig. 15

37. Drawing the Front Waist Line.—With the L. S. of the square up, place point m of the L. A. C. at point V and have the edge of the curve touch N, as shown in position 25, Fig. 15; then draw a light line along this curve.

38. Drawing the Bottom Lines of the Waist. Before the entire bottom line can be drawn, it is necessary to locate one more point.

Locate:

Point X 4 inches below N on the center-front foundation line, as shown in Fig. 15. At the same time, make line OX, which is the center-front line, heavy.

Connect:

Points S and X in the same manner as you connected V and N; that is, with m of the L. A. C. on S and the curve touching X.

Points S and W with a heavy horizontal line.

39. Drawing the Lower Parts of the Under-Arm Curves.—Now connect points V and S and points U and S with heavy curved lines.

Connect:

Points V and S by placing the square, L. S. up, so that q on the L. A. C. touches V and the edge of the curve touches S, as shown in position 26.

Points U and S by placing the square, U. S. up, so that ii touches U and the curved edge touches S, as shown in position 27.

40. Cutting the Draft Apart.—The draft of the waist is now complete and ready to be cut apart.

Cut from S through U to G_2, from G_2 to K; from K, through I, to E; from E to A; from A, through T, to W; and from W to S. This completes the *back* of the waist draft.

For the *front* section, begin at point S and cut through V to G_2; from G_2 through Q, to J_2; from J_2 to L; from L to O; from O, through P, F, and N, to X; from X to S.

If you follow these directions, you will be less likely to tear the draft when cutting it apart.

41. Notching the Armhole.—To mark the arm-hole of the waist so that the seam of the sleeve may be joined to it properly in fitting, measure to the left of G_2 on the front armhole curve one-eighth of the armhole measure and cut a small notch in the pattern.

DRAFTING A ONE-PIECE FOUNDATION SLEEVE

42. Measurements.—The measurements to be used for drafting a plain, one-piece foundation sleeve, shown in reduced size in Fig. 16 are as follows:

	INCHES
Armhole	15
Inside-sleeve length	17
Hand	8

43. Locating Construction Points for Armhole Curves.—To make this draft, first fold a piece of paper about 24 inches by 27 inches through the center lengthwise. Then locate points as follows:

Locate:

Point A on the fold 8 inches from the right-hand edge of the paper.

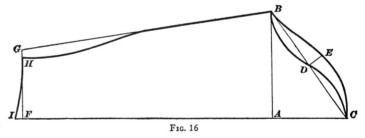

Fig. 16

Point B by placing the square, U. S. up, so that its corner is at A and its short arm is on the fold and drawing a light line along the long arm one-half the armhole measure minus $\frac{1}{2}$ inch. In this case, one-half the armhole measure would be opposite 15. Subtract $\frac{1}{2}$ inch, making B opposite 14 on the scale of halves.

NOTE.—The line AB controls the width of sleeve and of course is determined largely by the armhole measure.

Point C by placing the square, L. S. up, its corner on the fold at A and its short arm on the line AB, and drawing a light line along the fold equal to one-third the armhole measure, in this case, opposite 15 on the scale of thirds.

> NOTE.—Line AC is a very important line, for on its length depends the fitting of the upper portion of the sleeve. If this line is too short, the sleeve will draw out of position at the shoulder point, causing wrinkles under the arm. If it is too long, a puff will be formed in the top of the sleeve.

Connect:

Points B and C with a light diagonal line.

Locate:

Point D on line BC midway between B and C.

Point E with the square L. S. up, placing the corner on D and the long arm along CD and drawing a light line along the short arm one-eighth the length of line BC. In this case, since line BC is $8\frac{3}{4}$ inches, E would be opposite $8\frac{3}{4}$ on the scale of eighths.

44. Drawing the Top Curve.—First, place the square, L. S. up, so that $1A$ of the F. B. C. is at B and the curve touches E, and connect points B and E with a heavy curved line; then, adjust the square so that $3C$ falls on C and the curve touches E, and complete the heavy curved line from E to C.

45. Drawing the Lower Curve.—Adjust the square so that $3C$ of the F. B. C. falls on C and the curve touches D, and connect points C and D with a heavy curved line; then complete the lower curve, turning the square, U. S. up, and placing it so that 1 of the B. C. is at D and the curve touches B.

46. Locating Construction Points for the Lower-Arm Curves.—For the wrist curve and the curve at the lower arm, certain points must be located.

Locate:

Point F the inside sleeve length to the left of A on the fold of paper.

Point G with the short arm of the square, U. S. up, on the fold, the corner at F, and draw a light vertical line the length of one-half the hand measure plus $\frac{1}{2}$ inch. In this case, the hand measure is 8 inches, one-half of which would be opposite 8 on the scale of halves, plus $\frac{1}{2}$ inch, making G opposite 9.

Point H $\frac{1}{4}$ inch below G on line FG.

Point I $\frac{1}{2}$ inch to the left of F.

47. Drawing the Wrist Curve.—Place ll of the L. A. C. of the square, U. S. up, on I and have the edge of the curve, near pp, touch H. Draw a heavy line along this curve.

48. Drawing the Lower-Arm Curve.—Connect G and B with a light diagonal line.

With the L. S. of the square up, place k of the L. A. C. on H and have s touch line BG. Draw a heavy line, following the curve from H to line BG and also make heavy the remainder of the line.

49. Cutting the Draft Apart.—Cut the draft apart by cutting through both thicknesses of paper from C to E; from E to B; from B to H; and from H to I.

Then open the paper out and cut on the curved line, through one thickness of paper, from B to D and from D to C.

DRAFTING A ROLL COLLAR

50. Locating Construction Points.—For drafting a collar, as shown in Fig. 17, a sheet of paper 7 inches wide and 8 inches long is required. Place the paper with one end next to you and locate points A, B, and C for the center-back and points D and E for the front line.

Locate:

Point A 1 inch from the right-hand edge of the paper.

Point B $3\frac{1}{2}$ inches to the left of A.

Point C 1 inch to the left of B.

Point D by placing the square, U. S. up, so that the straight edge of the short arm touches the fold of the paper and the corner of the square is at point C, and then drawing a light vertical line one-half the neck measure above C.

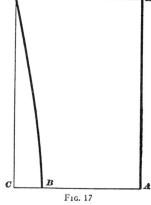

FIG. 17

> EXAMPLE.—The neck measure of the blouse illustrated in Fig. 1 is 13 inches; therefore, point L is opposite 13 on the scale of halves.

Point E by placing the corner of the square at A and drawing a heavy vertical line of the same length as CD.

Form a rectangle by drawing a heavy horizontal line to connect points D and E.

51. Drawing the Neck Curve.—Place the square, U. S. up, so that ff of the L. A. C. touches point B and the edge of the curve, near bb, rests on D. Follow the curve with a heavy pencil mark.

52. Cutting Out the Collar Pattern.—To form the pattern, cut from A to E; from E to D; and from D to B. Then a half section of your roll-collar pattern will be ready for use.

DRAFTING A TURN-BACK CUFF

53. Locating Construction Points.—To draft a cuff, as shown in Fig. 18, fold a piece of paper 5 inches wide and 12 inches long through the center, crosswise. Place the folded edge of the paper next to you in preparation for locating the construction points.

Locate:

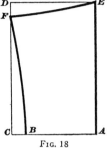

Point *A* on the fold 1 inch from the right-hand edge.

Point *B* 2½ inches to the left of *A*.

Point *C* ½ inch to the left of *B*.

> NOTE.—These points are always the same regardless of the size of the hand measure, which varies in different cases.

FIG. 18

Point *D* by placing the square so that its short arm is on the fold and its corner is at *C* and drawing a light vertical line the length of one-half the hand measure plus ½ inch.

> EXAMPLE.—If the hand measure is 8 inches, as in this case, point *D* is opposite 9 on the scale of halves.

Point *E* by placing the square with its corner at *A* and drawing a heavy vertical line of the same length as *CD*.

Point *F* ½ inch below *D* on line *CD*.

Complete the rectangle by connecting points *D* and *E* with a light line.

54. Drawing the Curves.—Two curves must be drawn for this draft.

Draw:

Curve *BF* by placing the square with *ff* at *B* and the edge of this curve, near *dd*, on *F*, following the curve with a heavy line.

Curve *FE* by placing *ff* on *F* and the edge of the curve, near *dd*, on *E*, following this curve also with a heavy line.

55. Cutting the Draft Apart.—To form the cuff pattern, cut the draft apart as follows, keeping the paper folded: From *A* to *E*; from *E* to *F*; and from *F* to *B*.

DRAFTING A SHIRT-WAIST SLEEVE

56. The shirt-waist sleeve, Figs. 1 and 19, which has the same measurements as the plain sleeve, Fig. 16, differs from the plain sleeve, only in that it has a cuff, a cuff opening, and more fulness at the wrist. So in drafting a pattern for it, the same points are located and the same lines drawn as for a plain one-piece sleeve, until it becomes necessary to locate point *F*.

57. Locating Construction Points for the Lower-Sleeve Section.—The addition of the cuff makes a change in the location of point *F*.

Locate:

Point *F* to the left of *A* on the fold the inside length minus the width of the cuff.

> EXAMPLE.—In this case, the width of the cuff is 2½ inches and the inside-sleeve length is 17 inches. Therefore, 17 inches minus 2½ inches equals 14½ inches, the distance to the left of *A*, at which to locate *F*.

Point *G* by placing the short arm of the square on the fold, with its corner at *F*, and drawing a light vertical line the length of one-half the hand measure plus 1½ inches. In this case, since the hand measure is 8 inches, point *G* would be opposite 11 on the scale of halves.

Point *H* 1 inch below *G* on line *FG*.

Point *I* 1 inch above *F* on line *FG*.

Point *J* with the short arm of the square, U. S. up, on line *FG*, and its corner at *I*, drawing a heavy line parallel with the fold, making it the length of one-half the hand measure plus ½ inch. Since in this case the hand measure is 8 inches, point *J* will be opposite 9 on the scale of halves.

Point *K* by sliding the square up until it touches *B* and *G*, drawing a light diagonal line between these points, and placing *K* ½ inch to the right of *G* on this line.

58. Drawing the Curves of the Lower Sleeve.

Draw:

Curve *FK* by placing *ll* of the L. A. C. on *K* and the edge of the curve, near *hh*, on *F*, and following the curve with a heavy full line.

Curve *BK* by placing *m* of the L. A. C. on *K* and *r* touching line *BG*, and following the curve with a heavy full line which is continued to point *B*.

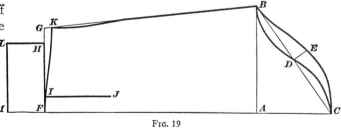

FIG. 19

59. Drafting the Cuff Section.—Additional points must be added for the cuff section.

Locate:

Point *L* by placing the square so that one straight edge is on line *FG* and its corner is at *H*, and drawing a heavy line to the left of H equal in length to the width of the cuff.

Point M the width of the cuff to the left of F.

Draw a heavy vertical line connecting points L and M.

Make heavy the line FH.

60. Cutting the Draft Apart.—To cut the draft apart, proceed as follows: Cut off the *cuff* section by cutting through both thicknesses of the paper from F to H; from H to L; and from L to M.

Cut the *sleeve* through both thicknesses by cutting from C to E; from E to B; from B to K, following the curved line on the right of K; and from K to F.

Open out the draft and cut on the curved line from C to D; from D to B; and, for the *cuff opening*, from I to J.

VARIATIONS IN DRAFTING

PLAIN FOUNDATION-WAIST ALTERATIONS

61. Need of Variations.—Your study of different types of figures has taught you that there are three general types, namely, large, medium, and small, and that under these main classes there are other types that are determined by the peculiarities of the figures, as for example, the short-waisted, the swayed-backed, and the full-hip figure.

For the average figure, a garment cut by the waist draft shown in Fig. 2 fits well, but slight alterations are necessary when this draft is used for figures that are not in correct proportion. The following suggestions will aid you in making alterations in drafting.

62. Altering Shoulder Lines.—*For practically all large figures*, the following method gives very satisfactory shoulder lines:

To alter the back-shoulder line, draw a line at right angles to the center-back line at point A, Fig. 2. Where this line intersects the line drawn from G, locate point H. Then, measure down from this point one-eighth the center-back depth and locate point I. Next, draw the back-shoulder line from E to I as previously directed.

To alter the front-shoulder line, continue the line AH, and on it locate point J one-third the armhole measure from H. Find J_2 in the same manner as described in Art. **24**, and LJ_2 will be the new front-shoulder line.

For the square-shouldered type, draw the front foundation shoulder with the square on a point midway between A and B, Fig. 2, as this will give a line with less slope to it.

For the sloping-shouldered large figure, use point B, Fig. 2, instead of D, in order to draw the front founda-

tion shoulder line, as this will give considerable slope to the line.

If the sloping-shouldered figure has a *small armhole measure*, as is frequently the case, the shoulder line must slant more than is indicated above. To provide for this, draw a line from I parallel to the bust line and locate J on this one-third the armhole measure from I. If the shoulders are very sloping, as sometimes is the case of middle-aged and older women, the front-shoulder line may be slanted still more by locating J_2 $\frac{1}{4}$ to $\frac{3}{4}$ inch below J on the armhole curve.

For the narrow-shouldered figure, it is necessary to shorten the shoulder line. To do this, omit the line KI, Fig. 2, and draw the back armhole line from G_2 to I by placing yy on G_2.

63. Altering Armhole Lines.—In drawing the front-armhole curve after making the shoulder-line changes *for the square-shouldered type*, place the square so that G_2, Q, and J_2, Fig. 2, are connected and rr of the square is on the bust line about 2 inches from G. The bust line will form the under-arm section of the armhole.

No matter to what general type a figure belongs, if it has *large under-arm muscles*, be sure to make G_2 one-sixth the armhole measure; but in the case of *the slender type* always use one-eighth the armhole measure.

64. Altering the Bust Line.—For a large figure, the bust line BF, Fig. 2, may need enlarging. If so, an extra addition of $\frac{1}{2}$ inch, making the total addition $2\frac{1}{2}$ inches more than one-half the bust measure, should be sufficient.

SLEEVE VARIATIONS

65. In the construction of a sleeve draft, there are several points that require very careful consideration, one of the most important of which is to be sure that the top of the sleeve is long enough. Also, to have just the right amount of fulness through the elbow and the upper-arm section to make the wearer comfortable and yet not to have so much fulness that the sleeve appears bunchy and bunglesome, is another point to be watched. Then, too, the length of the entire sleeve must be carefully determined if a satisfactory garment is to result.

66. Alterations Above the Elbow.—In developing or designing a pattern for any type of sleeve you may desire to copy, remember that the length of the shoulder and the size of the armhole of the garment should be carefully determined before the upper part of the sleeve is drafted. Also, keep in mind that there are two lengths to a sleeve, the inside-sleeve length and the length represented in the draft in Fig. 16 as AC. Between the latter and the armhole measure, there is a relationship that is important. When the length of the line AB (one-half the armhole measure minus $\frac{1}{2}$ inch) is reduced, the line AC must be increased, as short, narrow shoulders require a longer, narrower sleeve for that portion above line AB. For most figures, the following proportion is satisfactory:

AB—One-half the armhole measure minus $1\frac{1}{4}$ inches.

AC—Two-fifths of the armhole measure.

67. Drawing the Armhole Curves.—In drawing the curves for the sleeve, locate point D 2 inches from point C on line BC and draw a $\frac{3}{4}$-inch perpendicular line from BC at D, lettering its termination E.

To draw the upper curve, place m at B and allow the curved edge of the square to touch point E. Place $3C$ of the F. B. C. on C and the curve on E. For the lower curve, place m on B and allow the edge to touch point C.

68. Alterations Below the Elbow.—If it is desired to have a sleeve full at the hand, make line FG, Fig. 16, the same or greater in length than line AB and have the wrist and under-arm lines straight.

If a tight-fitting sleeve is wanted, take out the fulness in fitting by putting a dart at the back, extending it from the wrist to a point 2 inches below the elbow.

DRAFTING A MANNISH-SHIRTWAIST PATTERN

DESCRIPTION OF WAIST

69. Style of Waist.—A mannish shirtwaist, the front view of which is shown in Fig. 20 (a) and the back view in (b), is a garment so designed as to follow practically the same lines as those of a man's negligée

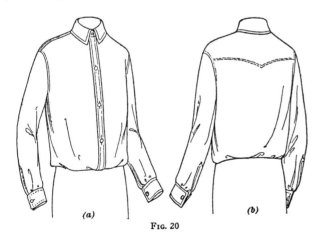

FIG. 20

shirt. Such a garment is intended to fit the figure in a loose manner, with armholes that are larger than those of a plain waist. As compared with a plain waist, the shoulder seams are brought forward for the yoke line, the neck line is arranged in exactly the same

manner as for a man's shirt, and the under-arm seams are brought forward so that the sleeves may be sewed in before their seams and those of the under arms are stitched, thus making it possible to make a very neat flat fell at the armhole and greatly simplifying the construction of the garment.

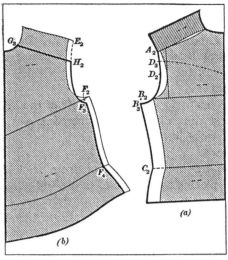

FIG. 21

Sometimes women wish a shirtwaist of this type to wear with knickers for sports wear. It is usually advisable, in such a case, to extend the lines below the waist line, as in a man's shirt.

A mannish-shirtwaist pattern can be developed from a foundation plain-waist pattern with ease. The only necessary changes consist in extending the shoulder line, enlarging the armhole, providing for the yoke line, and adding, at the under arm, $1\frac{1}{2}$ inches to the back portion and taking $\frac{3}{4}$ inch from the front portion to provide for fulness, as well as to permit the under-arm seam to be brought forward. The manner in which these changes are made to produce a pattern for a mannish shirtwaist is shown in Fig. 21.

DRAFTING THE BACK PATTERN SECTION

70. As shown in Fig. 21 (a), pin the back part of the foundation plain-waist pattern to a piece of paper that is 6 inches longer and 3 inches wider than the foundation pattern piece itself, placing it so that its center-back line is along a straight edge of the paper and there is sufficient space above it for the yoke that extends over the front of the waist.

71. Extending the Shoulder and Armhole Lines. First, proceed to locate the necessary construction points.

Locate:

Point A_2 by extending the shoulder line $\frac{1}{4}$ inch to the left of the armhole curve.

Point B_2 by measuring $1\frac{1}{2}$ inches to the left of the intersection of the under-arm line and the bust line. This is a construction point.

Point B_3 $\frac{1}{2}$ inch directly below B_2.

Draw:

The new armhole curve from A_2 to B_3, placing the square so that the arrow point of the S. A. C. is at B_3 and the edge of the curve, near tt, touches A_2.

72. Enlarging the Waist Line and Drawing the Under-Arm Line and Curve.—More width must be added below the armhole point.

Locate:

Point C_2 $1\frac{1}{2}$ inches to the left of the intersection of the under-arm line and the waist line.

Draw:

The new under-arm line from B_3 to C_2, placing the square so that ff of the L. A. C. is at C_2 and the edge of the curve, near bb, touches B_3, and continue this line from point C_2 to the bottom line of the pattern, following the same plan as in drawing this line for the plain-waist pattern, Art. **39**.

DRAWING THE FRONT PATTERN SECTION

73. Pin the front part of the foundation plain waist pattern to a piece of paper that is a trifle larger than it, placing it so that its center front is on one long edge of the paper, as shown in Fig. 21 (*b*).

74. Extending the Shoulder Line and Enlarging the Armhole.—Measure the back-shoulder line from A_2 to the neck curve. Then extend the front-shoulder line until it is the same length.

Locate:

Point E_2 on the right end of the extension thus made.

Point F_2 $\frac{3}{4}$ inch to the left of the armhole curve on the bust line.

Point F_3 $\frac{1}{2}$ inch below F_2, placing the square so that its corner is at F_2 and its short arm is on the bust line.

Draw:

The new armhole curve, placing the square so that rr of the S. A. C. is at F_3 and the edge of the L. A. C., near jj, touches E_2.

NOTE.—In drawing the armhole curve for very large or very small measurements, adjust the square so that the lines of the armhole will be well-balanced and shaped as they would be for an armhole of average measurements.

75. Diminishing the Waist Line and Drawing the Under-Arm Line and Curves.—Width must be subtracted from the part of the front draft below the under-arm point.

Locate:

Point F_4 $\frac{3}{4}$ inch to the left of the under-arm line on the waist line

Connect:

Points F_4 and F_3 and continue the under-arm line from point F_4 to the bottom line, as in drafting the plain-waist pattern, Art. **39**.

DRAFTING THE YOKE SECTION

76. Determining the Yoke Extension.—To provide for the yoke that extends over the front in the mannish shirtwaist:

Locate:

Point G_3 by measuring down on the neck curve one-sixth of the neck measure.

Point H_2 by measuring down on the new armhole curve from E_2 one-sixth of the neck measure, plus $\frac{1}{4}$ inch.

Connect:

Points G_3 and H_2 with a diagonal line.

77. Adding Yoke to Back Waist Section.—It is necessary to transfer that part of the pattern above line G_3H_2 of the front part of the pattern to the back part of the pattern. Therefore, slip a piece of paper underneath this part of the pattern and trace from G_3 to H_2, from H_2 to E_2, and then along the shoulder line of the foundation pattern and the neck curve to G_3.

Cut out this traced part and pin it to the back part of the pattern, as shown; that is, with the shoulder lines together and the neck curves touching. Owing to the difference in the shape of this shoulder line and the bottom of the cut-off piece, there will always be a slight space between them. This, however, will in no way interfere with the development of the pattern. If an angle forms at point A_2, blend the lines to form a graceful curve.

OUTLINING AND CUTTING THE PATTERN PIECES

78. The Front Pattern Section.—Outline the bottom line and the neck curve from the center-front line to G_3 and then trace as follows: On the new shoulder line from G_3 to H_2; on that part of the armhole curve that appears on the plain-waist pattern to F_3; on the under-arm line from F_3, through F_4, to the bottom; and then on the waist line.

Remove the foundation-waist pattern and cut out the required pattern.

79. Outlining the Back Yoke.—If a yoke is desired for the back part of the mannish shirtwaist for which this pattern is to be used, it will be necessary to mark it before cutting out the back part of the pattern. The depth of a yoke at the center back is usually two-thirds of the center-back depth below the back-neck curve; that is, it comes to point D on the shirtwaist pattern.

Locate:

Point D_2 with the short arm of the square on the center-back line and its corner on point D, marking point D_2 on the new armhole curve at the point where the long arm of the square touches it.

Point D_3 $1\frac{1}{2}$ inches above D_2.

Draw the yoke line from D to D_3, placing the square so that w of the L. A. C. is at D and the edge of the curve, near s, touches D_3.

80. The Back Pattern Section.—Trace the yoke line and the waist line, and outline the front portion of the yoke that was pinned to the back, as well as the neck curve of the back portion and the bottom line.

Remove the plain-waist pattern and cut out the back part of the pattern.

Trace off the yoke on a separate sheet of paper, as follows: From D to D_3; from D_3, through A_2, around the front part of the yoke to the top; across the top to the neck line; on the neck line to the center back; and on the center back to D.

With the yoke pattern thus traced, cut it out.

DRAFTING A MANNISH-SHIRTWAIST SLEEVE PATTERN

81. Armhole Measurement.—As the sleeve of a mannish shirtwaist must fit exactly into the armhole of the waist without any fulness whatever, the armhole measure to be used in drafting must be determined by measuring the armhole of the waist pattern; that is, the regular armhole measure should not be used. Therefore, before proceeding to draft the sleeve for a mannish-shirtwaist pattern, measure with a tape line, to insure accuracy, the armhole of both the front and the back part of the mannish-shirtwaist pattern from the shoulder lines to the under-arm lines. In drafting the mannish-shirtwaist sleeve pattern, proceed as shown in Fig. 22.

82. Locating Construction Points for Armhole Curves.—Provide a piece of paper about 24 inches by 27 inches. Fold it lengthwise through the center and place it so that the fold is next to you.

Locate:

Point A 6 inches from the right edge, as in Fig. 22 (a).

Point B by placing the square, U. S. up, so that its corner is at A and its short arm is on the fold and drawing a line along the long arm, making it one-half the mannish-shirtwaist armhole measure, minus 1 inch.

Point C, while the square is in the position for locating point B, by measuring to the right of A with the scale of fifths and marking point C at a point that is one-fifth of the mannish-shirtwaist armhole measure to the right of A.

83. Drawing the Armhole Curves.—The curves at the armhole are drawn thus:

Draw:

The top curve by placing the square so that p of the L. A. C. is at B and the edge of the curve, near u, touches C.

The lower curve by moving the square down until m falls on B and the edge of the curve, near s, touches C.

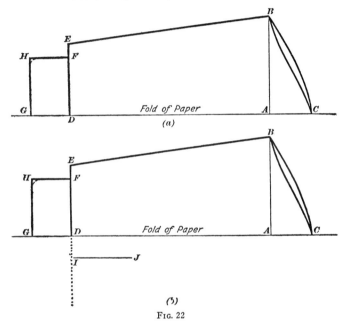

Fig. 22

84. Drafting the Cuff Section.—Subtract the width of the cuff, in this case $2\frac{1}{2}$ inches, from the inside sleeve measure.

Locate:

Point D this distance to the left of A on the fold.

Point E with the short arm of the square on the fold and its corner at D, drawing, along the long arm, a line equal to one-half the hand measure, plus 1 inch, and lettering its termination E.

Connect:

Points B and E with a diagonal line.

Points E and D with a vertical line.

Locate:

Point F on line DE one-half the hand measure above D.

Point G the cuff length to the left of D on the fold, in this case, $2\frac{1}{2}$ inches.

Point H with the corner of the square at G and the short arm on the fold, drawing, along the long arm, a heavy full line equal to one-half the hand measure and lettering its termination *H*.

Connect:

Points *H* and *F* with a heavy straight line, completing the cuff draft.

> NOTE.—If curved lines are desired on the cuff, the corner may be rounded, as is indicated by the dotted line.

85. Drawing the Cuff Opening.—Trace the bottom sleeve line from *D* to *E*, open out the draft, and proceed to mark for the cuff opening, as in Fig. 22 (*b*).

Locate:

Point *I* by measuring down $1\frac{1}{2}$ inches from *D* on the traced line.

Point *J* to the right of *I*, by drawing a line parallel with the creased line formed by the fold, making its length equal to one-half the hand measure, plus $\frac{1}{2}$ inch.

86. Cutting the Sleeve and Cuff Patterns Apart. With the drafting thus completed, fold the paper again and proceed to cut out the pattern for the cuff and for the sleeve.

For the *cuff* portion, cut through both thicknesses of paper from *D* to *F*; from *F* to *H*; from *H* to *G*.

For the *sleeve* portion, cut through both thicknesses of the paper from *C* to *B* on the upper curve; from *B* to *E*; and from *E* to *F*. Then open out the sleeve pattern and cut on the lower curve from *C* to *B*.

> NOTE.—In using the pattern for the mannish shirt waist, join the lower curved edge of the sleeve to the front of the waist, which is the reverse of the usual custom.

For the *cuff opening*, which comes on the back of the sleeve, slash the line from *I* to *J*.

————

DRAFTING A MANNISH-SHIRTWAIST COLLAR PATTERN

87. Locating Construction Points.—To draft a pattern for a collar that will be suitable for wear with a mannish shirtwaist, proceed as shown in Fig. 23. Provide a piece of paper that is 6 inches wide and 20 inches long and fold it crosswise through the center.

With the paper placed so that the fold is to the right of you, draw, $\frac{1}{2}$ inch above the lower edge, rectangle *ABCD*, the sides of which are one-half the neck measure, plus $1\frac{1}{2}$ inches, and the ends as wide as both the turn-over and the stand of the collar are to be, the *stand* portion being that section, *ALMH*, below the line at which the collar turns over.

> NOTE.—A very good width is 5 inches, as it allows $2\frac{1}{2}$ inches for the turn-over, $2\frac{3}{8}$ inches for the stand, and enough in the center for shaping.

Locate:

Point *E* midway between *B* and *C* on line *BC*.

Point *F* midway between *A* and *D* on the fold.

Connect:

Points *E* and *F* with a straight line.

Locate:

Point *G* $\frac{1}{4}$ inch above *F*.

Point *H* $\frac{3}{8}$ inch below *F*.

Point *I* $1\frac{3}{4}$ inches to the right of *E* on line *EF*.

Point *J* $1\frac{1}{2}$ inches to the right of *B* on line *AB*.

Point *K* $1\frac{1}{2}$ inches to the right of *C* on line *CD*.

Connect:

Points *K* and *I* and also points *I* and *J* with diagonal lines.

Locate:

Point *L* $\frac{1}{2}$ inch above *B* on line *BC*.

Point *M* $\frac{7}{8}$ inch to the right of *E* on line *EF*.

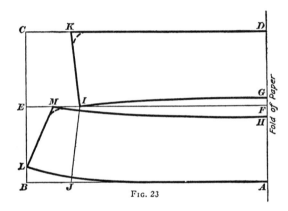

FIG. 23

88. Drawing the Pattern Lines.—Make heavy line *IK*.

Connect:

Points *L* and *M* with a heavy diagonal line.

Point *L* with line *AB* by placing the square so that *gg* is at *L* and the edge of the curve, near *ee*, touches line *AB* where it will.

Points *M* and *H* with a curved line, placing the square so that *aa* of the L. A. C. is at *H* and the edge of the curve, near *ee*, touches *M*.

Points *G* and *I*, placing the square so that *y* is at *G* and letting the edge of the curve, near *v*, touch *I*.

This completes the drafting of the collar, with the exception of rounding the corners of the top of the stand and the lower part of the turn-over. To round the corners, simply draw curves, as shown by the dotted lines in the illustration.

89. Cutting the Draft Apart.—Cut through both thicknesses of the paper.

To cut out the pattern for the *turn-over* part of the

collar, cut from D to K, from K to I, and from I to G, cutting on the dotted line if round corners are desired

To cut out the pattern for the *stand* part of the collar, cut from H to M, from M to L, and from L to A, likewise cutting on the dotted curved line if round corners are wanted.

Finally, trace line IJ, which indicates the center front of the stand.

DRAFTING A MANNISH-SHIRTWAIST NECK-BAND PATTERN

90. So as to provide a means of securing the collar of a mannish shirtwaist, it is necessary to use a neck band, just as in a man's shirt. The pattern for

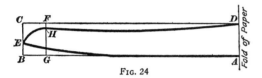

Fig. 24

such a band may be drafted in the manner shown in Fig. 24.

Provide a piece of paper that is 2 inches wide and 18 inches long.

91. Locating Construction Points.—With the paper folded crosswise through the center and placed so that the fold is to the right, draw $\frac{1}{2}$ inch above the lower edge, rectangle $ABCD$, the ends of which are 1 inch and the sides of which are equal to the length of one-half the neck measure, plus $\frac{3}{4}$ inch, this extra amount being the allowance required for the lap of the band.

Locate:

Point E $\frac{3}{8}$ inch above B on line BC.

Point F $\frac{3}{4}$ inch to the right of C on line CD.

Point G $\frac{3}{4}$ inch to the right of B on line AB.

Connect:

Points F and G with a vertical line.

Locate:

Point H $\frac{1}{8}$ inch below F on line FG.

92. Outlining the Neck-Band Pattern.—Three curves must be drawn in outlining the pattern.

Draw:

A curved line from E to meet line AB, placing the square so that gg is at E and the edge of the curve at ee touches line AB where it will.

Another curved line to connect H and D, placing the square so that ff is at H and the edge of the curve, near cc, touches D.

A free-hand curved line from E to H to form the end of the neck band.

93. Cutting the Draft Apart.—With the drafting done, form the pattern by cutting through both thicknesses of the paper from D to H; from H to E; and from E to A

REVIEW QUESTIONS

1. Before beginning to draft a pattern, what necessary equipment should you have?

2. How many measurements are required to make: (*a*) A plain foundation-waist draft? (*b*) A sleeve draft to be used with the plain foundation waist?

3. Why should you measure the model draft before beginning to make a draft?

4. (*a*) What additions are made to the waist measurements when drafting? (*b*) Why are they made?

5. What measurement determines the length of the line AC in the waist draft?

6. Describe the cutting apart of the waist draft.

7. In making a draft for a square-shouldered person, what change in the foundation draft would you make in drawing the foundation front-shoulder line?

8. Make for practice a waist draft according to the following measurements: Neck, 12 inches; bust, 36 inches; front, 20 inches; width-of-chest, 13 inches; width-of-back, 13 inches; length-of-back, $14\frac{1}{2}$ inches; center-back depth, $6\frac{1}{2}$ inches; armhole, 14 inches.

9. Make for practice a plain foundation-sleeve draft according to the following measurements: Armhole, 14 inches; inside length, $16\frac{1}{2}$ inches; hand, 8 inches.

CHAPTER III

FOUNDATION DRAFTS FOR SKIRTS

HELPS TO SKIRT DRAFTING

1. Kinds of Foundation Skirts.—In the drafting of skirts, it is well to remember that there are two general types—the *plain foundation skirt* and the *circular skirt.* The plain skirt is practically straight from the hip line to the hem, while the circular skirt hangs in ripples from the waist line down.

2. Skirt Lines.—The hip line of the skirt is its building line; that is, from this line, the skirt is built up and down. The outside lines of the skirt draft are formed by the waist line, the center-front line, the center-back line, and the bottom line.

3. Definitions.—To avoid any confusion in skirt-pattern drafting, the meaning of the word **dart** should be firmly fixed in mind. As this word is commonly used, it means a portion of material taken out between the waist and the hips to reduce the foundation-draft waist line to exactly one-half the original waist measure;

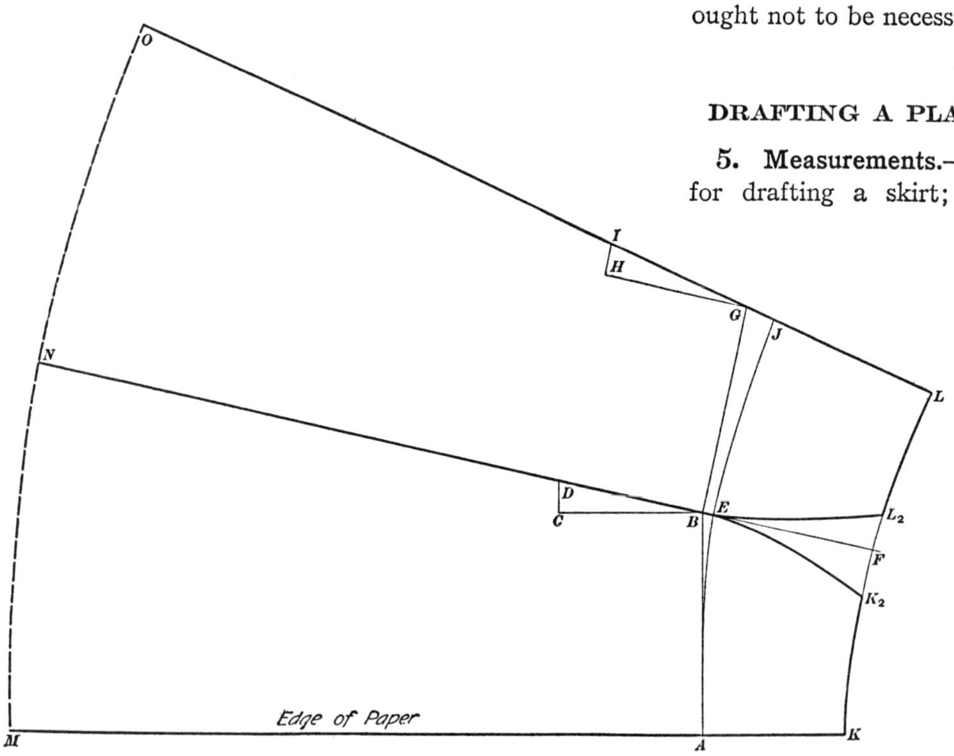

dart is used alone in a list of measurements, it means the side dart.

A **gore** means simply a shaped section of a skirt, each gore being narrower at the top and sometimes tapering so that it forms almost a triangle.

4. Skirt-Drafting Practice.—You will probably wish to practice drafting a skirt pattern several times before making a final draft. Follow the directions carefully just as you did in making the waist drafts and compare your location of every point with the location of the same point in the illustrations. Too much stress cannot be laid on the need of accuracy, for one point incorrectly or inaccurately located may make your pattern so badly proportioned or so small that any garment made from it would be worthless.

The directions for making the skirt drafts are not given in such detail as those for the waist, for after making several waist drafts you will have become so familiar with the square that such detailed information ought not to be necessary.

DRAFTING A PLAIN FOUNDATION SKIRT

5. Measurements.—Six measurements are required for drafting a skirt; namely, the waist, the hip, the dart, the center-front length, the side length, and the back length. The manner in which such measurements are taken has already been explained in detail in Art. **44** to **49** inclusive, in Chapter I.

For the draft illustrated in Fig. 1, the measurements are as follows:

	INCHES
Waist...........	26
Hip.............	40
Dart...........	8
Front length.....	41
Side length......	42
Back length.....	$42\frac{1}{2}$

Fig 1

6. Necessary Materials. For making the plain foundation-skirt draft, a sheet of paper about 54 inches long and 36 inches wide is required. Besides paper and pencil and the Picken square, a yardstick should be on hand for this draft;

sure; but when used with the words *front, side,* and *back* as *front dart, side dart,* and *back dart,* it serves to designate the location of the points that indicate the position of the waist line above the hip line. When however, the yardstick can be dispensed with and merely the Picken square used.

7. Drawing the Front Foundation Hip Line.—Determining the hip line is very important, as it is the basic line in skirt drafting. Using the measurements in Art. **5** and having the long edge of the paper next to you,

Locate:

Point A, measuring in from the right-hand edge about 15 inches and marking A on the edge next to you.

Point B, having the short arm of the square on the edge of the paper next to you, U. S. up, and the corner of the square at A, and drawing a vertical line along the scale of halves the length of one-half of one-half the hip measure, or one-fourth the hip measure, plus $\frac{1}{2}$ inch.

8. Drawing the Center-Side Line.—The center-side line is the first pattern line to be drawn.

Locate:

Point C by placing the long arm of the square, U. S. up, on line AB, with its corner at B, and drawing a line 7 inches long to the left of B along the short arm.

Point D by placing the short arm of the square on line BC, with its corner at C, and drawing a vertical line $1\frac{1}{2}$ inches long above C.

Draw:

The center-side line by placing the square so that the long arm extends 10 or 11 inches to the right of B and touches both B and D, and drawing a line the full length of the square in both directions.

Locate:

Point E on the center-side line $\frac{1}{2}$ inch to the right of B.

Point F the dart length to the right of E on the center-side line.

Note.—*The distances BC, BE, and CD never vary.*

9. Drawing the Back Foundation Hip Line.—It is necessary to locate G in order to determine the back foundation hip line.

Place the short arm of the square on line BF and the corner at B, and draw a line the length of one-half of one-half the hip measure, or one-fourth the hip measure, plus 1 inch, placing G at its termination.

10. Drawing the Center-Back Line.—The second pattern line to be determined is the center-back line.

Locate:

Point H by turning the square so that the long arm of the square, U. S. up, is on line BG and its corner at G, and drawing

a 7-inch line to the left of G along the short arm.

Point I by placing the short arm of the square on line GH and the corner at H, and drawing a vertical line $1\frac{1}{2}$ inches long.

Draw:

The center-back line by placing the square so that the long arm extends 10 or 11 inches to the right of G and touches G and I, and drawing a line the full length of the square in both directions.

11. Drawing the Hip Line.—The third pattern line to be drawn is the hip line.

Locate:

Point J $1\frac{1}{2}$ inches to the right of G on the center-back line.

Draw:

The back hip line by placing the square so that point z of the L. A. C. is on J and the edge of this curve touches E, and drawing a line along this curved edge between J and E.

The front hip line by placing ff of the L. A. C. on E, allowing bb of the L. A. C. to touch line AB where it will, and drawing a line from E that will meet AB.

12. Determining the Length Below the Hip Line.—To obtain the length below the hip line, a definite rule is always followed.

Rule.—Subtract the dart length from the side length and measure on the center-front and the center-back lines this distance below the hip line proper.

EXAMPLE.—When the side length is 42 inches and the side dart is 8 inches, the difference between them equals 34 inches, or the distance from the hip line AEJ to the floor.

Locate:

Point M to the left of A on the center-front line the length below the hip line.

Point N to the left of E on the side line the length below the hip line.

Point O to the left of J on the center-back line the length below the hip line.

13. Drawing the Bottom Curve.—Connect points M, N, and O by a free-hand curve or by using the section of the square between aa and ff and sliding it along.

14. Determining the Front Dart.—The front dart is always determined by means of a definite rule.

Rule.—From the front length, subtract the length below the hip line.

EXAMPLE.—If the front length is 41 inches, as given in Art. **5**, and the length below the hip line is 34 inches, as determined in Art. **12**, then the front-dart length is 7 inches.

Locate:

Point K the front-dart length to the right of A.

15. Determining the Back Dart.—The rule for determining the back dart is as follows:

Rule.—From the back length subtract the length below the hip line.

Example.—When the back length is $42\frac{1}{2}$ inches, as given in Art. **5**, and the length below the hip line is 34 inches, the back-dart length is $8\frac{1}{2}$ inches.

Locate:

Point L the back-dart length to the right of J.

16. Drawing the Waist Line.—Draw the foundation waist-line curve by placing t of the L. A. C. on K with the edge of the curve, near x, touching F, then moving the square so that t is on F and the edge of the curve, near x, is on L.

In order to make the waist line proper equal to one-half the waist measure, it is necessary to take out some of the fulness.

Locate:

Point L_2 by measuring on the foundation waist line from L a distance equal to one-half of one-half, or one-fourth, of the waist measure.

Example.—When the waist measure is 26 inches, find 26 on the scale of halves. Since one-half of one-half the waist measure is used to find L_2, measure from L to 13 on the scale of halves.

17. Drawing the Dart Curves.—Now it is necessary to connect E with L_2 and K_2.

Draw:

Curve EL_2 by placing ff of the L. A. C. on E with the curve, near bb, touching L_2.

Curve EK_2 by placing t of the L. A. C. on E with the curve, near x, touching K_2.

18. Cutting the Draft Apart.—You have completed the making of the plain foundation two-piece skirt draft and, in order to make it into a pattern, you must be very careful to cut only on the pattern lines. These are KK_2, K_2EN, NM, LL_2, LJO, ON, and NEL_2.

DRAFTING A TWO-GORED SKIRT WITH DARTS IN THE BACK

19. A two-piece draft is admirable for a foundation skirt, but it is not practicable for a person having very large hips and a small waist. Such figures should use a two-gored skirt pattern with a dart taken out in the back and in the side, as in Fig. 2. If such a pattern is used, the side seams will be straighter and not so likely to sag.

To draft a two-gored skirt with darts in the back, proceed in the same manner as for drafting the plain foundation skirt just described, up to the point of determining the darts and actual waist line.

20. Determining the Side Dart.—Measure the foundation waist line from K to L. From this amount, subtract one-half the actual waist measure plus 2 inches.

Locate:

Point K_2 one-half this difference below F.

Point L_2 one-half this difference above F.

Note.—The addition of 2 inches to one-half the actual waist measure is to provide for the darts in the back.

Example.—When the distance from K to L, or the length of the foundation waist line, is $16\frac{7}{8}$ inches, and one-half the actual waist measure is 13, plus 2, making 15 inches, the difference is $16\frac{7}{8}$ minus 15 or $1\frac{7}{8}$ inches. Therefore, K_2 is one-half of $1\frac{7}{8}$ inches, or $\frac{15}{16}$ inch, below F, and L_2 is $\frac{15}{16}$ inch above F.

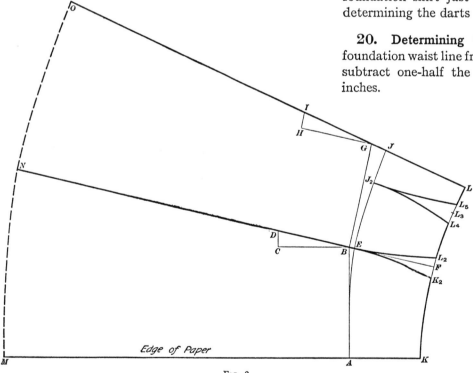

Fig. 2

Point K_2 by placing on K the point of the square equal to one-half the actual waist measure, and measuring back to the point on the square at which you located L_2.

Example.—Place 26 on the scale of halves on K and measure back to 13 on the same scale.

21. Determining the Back Dart.—Measure the hip line from E to J.

Locate:

Point J_2 one-third of the distance from J to E on line EJ.

Point L_3 one-third the length of LL_2 below L.

Point L_4 1 inch below L_3 on the waist line.

Point L_5 1 inch above L_3 on the waist line.

22. Drawing the Dart Curves.—Now you are ready to draw the dart curves.

Connect:

Points L_5 and J_2 as E and L_2 were connected in the plain foundation draft, Art. **17.**

Points L_4 and J_2 as E and K_2 were connected, Art. **17.**

23. Cutting the Draft Apart.—Cut the draft apart in the same way as the plain foundation skirt was cut; then cut the second dart by cutting from L_5 to J_2 and from J_2 to L_4.

___

DRAFTING A CIRCULAR FOUNDATION SKIRT

24. Measurements.—The draft for a circular foundation skirt is shown reduced in size in Fig. 3, it being drafted according to the following measurements:

	INCHES
Waist	25
Hip	38
Dart	8
Front length	41
Side length	42
Back length	$42\frac{1}{2}$

25. Necessary Materials.—For this draft, you will need a sheet of paper 54 inches long and 48 inches wide. As drafting paper is seldom wider than 36 inches, it will be necessary to attach a strip to a full width of paper to make it the proper width. This extra piece may be pasted or sewed, but usually sewing is found more satisfactory.

26. Drawing the Front Foundation Hip Line. Place the long edge of the paper next to you.

Locate:

Point A 16 or 17 inches from the right-hand edge of the paper, as in beginning the draft for the plain foundation skirt.

Point B by drawing a vertical line AB, the length of one-fourth the hip measure plus 1 inch.

27. Drawing the Center-Side Line.—Now you are ready to determine the first pattern line.

Locate:

Point C as in the plain foundation skirt draft, Art. **8.**

Point D on a line perpendicular to line BC, one-fourth the difference between the entire waist and hip measures, from C.

The location of Point D determines the flare at the lower edge.

EXAMPLE.—If the hip measure is 38 inches and the waist measure 25 inches, the difference equals 13 inches. Therefore, locate D opposite 13 on the scale of fourths.

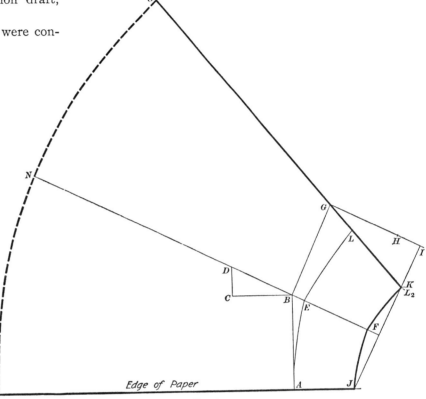

FIG. 3

Connect:

Points B and D and extend the line the full length of the square to the left of D and 10 or 11 inches to the right of B.

28. Locating Construction Points E and F.—Here the method of procedure differs from that in the drafting of a plain foundation skirt, for before you can locate point E you must find the back-dart length. To determine this length, follow the calculations explained in Art. **15** and the example given below.

EXAMPLE.—Using 42 inches for the side length and 8 inches for the side-dart length, subtract 8 inches from 42 inches, which will give 34 inches, or the length below the hip line. Then the back length, $42\frac{1}{2}$ inches, minus 34 inches equals $8\frac{1}{2}$ inches, the back-dart length.

Locate:

Point E one-sixth of the back-dart length to the right of B.

Point F the side-dart length to the right of E.

29. Drawing the Back Foundation Hip Line. Locate point G, so as to complete the foundation hip

31

line, by placing the square with the short arm on line *BF* and its corner at *B*, and drawing a light line along the long arm the length of one-fourth the hip measure plus 1½ inches.

30. Determining the Foundation Waist Line. Three construction points are necessary in order to draw the foundation waist line.

Locate:

Point *H* by placing the square, U. S. up, on line *BG*, its corner touching *G*, and drawing a light line from 12 to 15 inches long to the right, then measuring on this line, from point *G*, the back-dart length.

Point *I* one-third the back-dart length to the right of *H*.

Point *J* the front-dart length to the right of *A* on the center-front line. But before locating *J*, you must determine the front-dart length as explained in Art. **14** and illustrated below.

EXAMPLE.—Using the measurements given in Art. **24**, subtract the dart length, 8 inches, from the side length, 42 inches, which will give 34 inches, the length below the hip line. Then the front length, 41 inches, minus 34 inches equals 7 inches, or the front-dart length.

Connect:

Points *J* and *I* with a light diagonal line.

31. Drawing the Center-Back Line.—The third pattern line to be drawn is the center-back line.

Locate:

Point *K* by measuring up from *J* on line *JI* one-half the waist measure from *J* and marking *K*.

Draw:

The center-back line by placing the square with its corner at *K* and its long arm on *G* and draw a heavy line the full length of the long arm.

32. Drawing the Hip Line.—The hip line is the next pattern line to be drawn.

Locate:

Point *L* one-third the length of line *G I* to the right of *G* on the center-back line.

Draw:

The back hip line by placing the square with *z* at *L* and the edge of the curve,

near *u*, touching *E* and drawing a light line between *L* and *E*.

The front hip line by turning the square so that *ff* of the L. A. C. is at *E* and *bb* touches line *AB* where it will end, drawing a light line between these two points.

33. Drawing the Waist Line.—One more point must be located before the waist line can be drawn.

Locate:

Point *L₂* the back-dart length to the right of *L*.

NOTE.—Points *L₂* and *K* do not necessarily come at the same point. Their location depends on the proportion of the person's other measures.

Draw:

The front waist line by placing the square with *s* on *J* and the edge of the curve, near *v*, touching *F* and drawing a heavy curved line between *J* and *F*.

The back waist line by moving the square so that *t* is at *F* and the edge of the curve, near *w*, touches *L₂* and continuing the heavy curved line to *L₂*.

34. Determining the Bottom Edge.—Locate points *M*, *N*, and *O* and extend the lines below the hip line proper the same as for the plain foundation skirt.

Also, connect them in the same way as was done in marking the previous drafts.

35. Cutting the Draft Apart.—Cut on the pattern lines, *MNO*, *OL₂*, and *L₂FJ*.

***

DRAFTING A CIRCULAR SKIRT WITH RAISED WAIST LINE

36. No special directions are given for drafting a circular skirt with a raised waist line because, as a rule, the waist measure does not have to be increased when a raised waist line is desired. Simply extend the lengthwise lines the required amount. It may seem that the waist line appears too small, but it will generally stretch sufficiently to fit the belting. However, if the waist is unusually high, you may, in drafting, make line *J K* one-half the waist measure plus ½ inch. Then the raised waist line will measure about the same as the normal waist measurement.

***

REVIEW QUESTIONS

1. (*a*) What is the difference between the plain foundation skirt and the circular skirt? (*b*) How many measurements are used in drafting a plain skirt?

2. Why is the hip line called the building line of a skirt?

3. Define: (*a*) A dart. (*b*) A gore.

4. How do you determine the length of lines *A M*, *EN*, and *JO* in the plain foundation-skirt draft?

5. Submit for inspection a plain foundation-skirt draft made according to the following measurements: Waist, 24 inches; hip, 38 inches; dart, 8 inches; front-length, 40 inches; side length, 41 inches; back-length, 41½ inches.

6. Submit for inspection a circular-skirt draft made according to the following measurements: Waist, 24 inches; hip, 38 inches; dart, 8 inches; front, 42 inches; side, 43 inches; and back, 43½ inches.

CHAPTER IV

PATTERNS FOR KIMONO WAISTS

DRAFTING A STANDARD KIMONO WAIST

1. Difference Between Kimono Waist and Plain Waist.—Before starting the actual laying out of the kimono-waist draft, you will understand its construction better if you study Fig. 1, view (*a*), and notice wherein it differs from the draft of the plain foundation waist in Fig. 2, Chapter II. You will notice that the kimono waist has more fulness under the arm and across the back; that the under-arm curve is changed; and that the sleeve is not only of a different shape, but is cut with the waist rather than set in separately.

2. Starting With the Foundation Waist.—To a piece of paper 36 inches wide and 48 inches long, pin the plain foundation waist, so that the front line is at the edge of the paper and the shoulder curves meet at the neck line but are separated $\frac{3}{4}$ inch at the arm-hole.

Fold the paper so that points U and V of the foundation pattern come together, and pin; then crease the paper so that it will appear as shown in view (*b*). As you will notice, the crease does not come on the shoulder line, but a little to the front. Also, it is not horizontal, but has a slight slant.

You are now ready to locate the lines and points for the kimono waist. All the drafting will be done from the back of the pattern and the lines traced through to the front.

3. Adding Fulness to the Back.—Since a kimono waist is not intended to fit snugly, fulness must be added.

  Locate:
    Point A_2 1 inch to the right of T on the continuation of the foundation waist line of the foundation draft.
  Draw:
    The center-back line by connecting A and A_2 and also extending the line $4\frac{1}{2}$ inches below A_2 if a skirt portion is desired. Then letter this point A_4.
  Locate:
    Point A_3 $\frac{1}{2}$ inch below A_2 on the center-back line in preparation for lowering the back waist line.

4. Locating Construction Points for Under-Arm Line.—Several construction points must be located before the under-arm line can be drawn.

Locate:
  Point B_2 $\frac{1}{2}$ inch to the left of U.
  Point C_2 $\frac{1}{2}$ inch to the left of G_2.

Connect:
  Points B_2 and C_2 with a straight line.

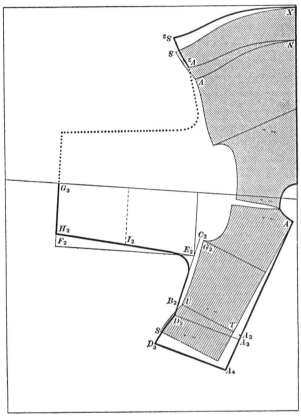

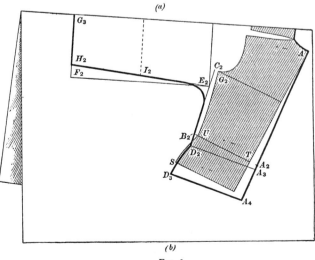

Fig. 1

33

Locate:

Point D_2 $1\frac{1}{2}$ inches below B_2 on an extension of line C_2B_2.

Point D_3 $1\frac{1}{2}$ inches below S by placing the square with its long arm touching points G_2 and S.

Point E_2 by placing the square so that its short arm is on the fold and the long arm touches line C_2D_2 at the point on the square indicating one-half the armhole measure, minus $\frac{1}{2}$ inch. Draw a line along the long arm from the fold to point E_2.

5. Lowering the Back Waist Line and Outlining the Back Skirt Section.—You are now ready to draw some of the pattern lines.

Draw:

Line A_3D_2, the back waist line.

Curve D_2D_3 in the same manner as curve US, in the plain-waist draft, was drawn.

Line D_3A_4 in order to obtain the bottom edge of the skirt.

6. Locating Construction Points for Sleeve.—The sleeve is the next section to be considered.

Locate:

Point F_2 the inside-sleeve length from point E_2, on a line drawn along the long arm of the square when the corner is at E_2 and the long arm is parallel to the fold.

Point G_3 at the intersection of the fold and a line drawn with the corner of the square on F_2 and one arm along line F_2E_2.

Point H_2 one-half the hand measure plus $1\frac{1}{2}$ inches below point G_3 on line F_2G_3.

Draw:

Line H_2E_2 in order to complete the sleeve section.

Locate:

Point I_2 one-half the inside-sleeve length to the left of E_2 on line H_2E_2, if a short sleeve is desired.

Connect:

Point I_2 with the fold by placing the short arm of the square on the fold and drawing a dotted line along the long arm.

7. Drawing Under-Arm Curves.—With l of the L. A. C. touching line H_2E_2 and g of the S. A. C. touching line B_2E_2, follow the curve and connect the two lines with it.

Note.—Ordinarily the curve of the square lies outside the construction lines. However, its position depends to a great extent upon current fashion.

8. Tracing Pattern Lines for the Front Section.—Since all of the drafting has been done on the back

34

portion of the draft, it is necessary to trace the pattern lines through for the front portion. These lines are D_3D_2, D_2H_2, and H_2G_3.

9. Outlining the Front Skirt Section.—Now unfold the pattern in preparation for outlining the front skirt section.

Locate:

Point V_2 on the new front under-arm line at a point corresponding to C_2 on the back waist pattern.

Point S_2 at a point corresponding to D_3.

Draw:

Line V_2S_2 over the lower part of the traced line, making it a heavy pattern line.

Curves NV_2 and XS_2 by following the same lines as the skirt lines in the plain foundation-waist draft.

10. Reducing the Fulness of the Sleeves and Under Arm.—At times Fashion decrees that kimono sleeves be rather close-fitting. When this is the case,

Locate:

Point E_2 one-half the armhole measure minus 1 inch below the fold, and

Point D_2 1 inch below B_2, thus lifting the under-arm seam and the back waist line at the under-arm seam.

Remove the extra fulness at the bottom of the sleeve by taking out a dart at the back from the elbow to the wrist.

11. Tracing and Cutting the Draft.—Open out the draft, trace the new back waist line, the new front waist line, and the neck line, which is the same as the neck line of the plain foundation waist.

Remove the foundation-waist pattern and cut the kimono draft on the pattern lines, as follows: From A_4, through A_3 and A_2, to A, and along the neck curve; then from X to S_2 to V_2; along the traced under-arm and sleeve line to G_3; from G_3 to H_2; from H_2 to I_2 to D_2; and from D_2 to D_3 to A_4.

Note.—If in cutting a waist it is desired to have the center-back as well as the center-front on a fold of the material, the pattern may be slashed on the shoulder line to the bottom of the sleeve, and a seam used here.

DRAFTING THE SHORT-SLEEVED KIMONO WAIST ON A FOLD OF MATERIAL

12. In Fig. 2 (a) is illustrated the way in which to draft a pattern for a short-sleeved kimono waist so that its center front and its center back may be laid on the fold of material and the garment thus cut out in one piece. For this draft, you will need a sheet of paper about 27 inches wide and 45 inches long, as well as your foundation-waist pattern.

The three points to be considered in this pattern are the same as those in the long-sleeved standard kimono-waist pattern; namely, (1) adding fulness in the back; (2) reconstructing the under-arm line; and (3) constructing the sleeve lines.

13.   Placing the Foundation-Waist Pattern on Paper.—Lay the center-front line of the foundation pattern on one long edge of the paper.   Place the back

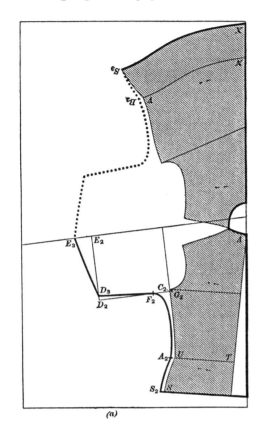

(a)

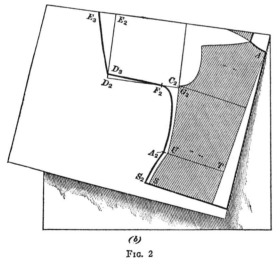

(b)

FIG. 2

of the foundation pattern so that the center back at the waist line is $1\frac{1}{2}$ inches from the edge of the paper. The neck curves must be together at the shoulder. Fig. 2, view (a) shows the position very clearly.

14.   Folding the Paper.—Before you can fold the paper, two points must be located.

Locate:

Point A_2 $\frac{1}{2}$ inch to the left of U on the back section of the waist pattern.

Point B_2 $\frac{1}{2}$ inch to the left of V on the front section of the waist pattern.

Fold the paper so that you can pin these two points together and crease it to show the shoulder line.   The folded paper will appear as in view (b).

15.   Reconstructing the Sleeve Line.—Changes in the sleeve are the first to receive attention.

Locate:

Point C_2 on the under-arm line one-half the armhole measure from the fold of paper, placing the square with the short arm on the fold and the long arm touching the under-arm line of the foundation pattern.

NOTE.—The position of C_2 will vary with different armhole measurements; that is, C_2 will not always fall on a point so near the bust line as in the draft here considered.

Point D_2 one-half the inside-sleeve length from point C_2 on a line drawn parallel to the fold of the paper.

Point E_2 at the intersection of the fold and a line drawn with one arm of the square on line C_2D_2 and the corner of the square on point D_2.

Point D_3 $\frac{1}{2}$ inch above point D_2.

Point E_3 3 inches to the left of point E_2.

Connect:

Points D_3 and E_3 with a straight line.

16.   Reconstructing the Under-Arm Curve.—The under-arm curve is the next to be considered.

Locate:

Point F_2 2 inches to the left of point C_2 on the line C_2D_2.

Draw:

The under-arm curve with rr at F_2 and the edge of the L. A. C. touching A_2.

Connect:

Points D_3 and F_2 with a heavy diagonal line.

Locate:

Point S_2 $\frac{1}{2}$ inch to the left of point S.

Draw:

Curve A_2S_2 the same as curve US in the foundation-waist draft.

17.   Tracing From the Back to the Front.—So as to transfer the pattern lines to the front section, trace the following lines: S_2A_2, A_2F_2, F_2D_3, and D_3E_3.

18.   Drawing the Lower Edges of the Skirt Section. For the lower edge of the back, draw a straight heavy line from S_2 to the edge of the paper, following the bottom line of the foundation pattern.

35

For the front, open out the draft and locate point S_3 at the termination of the traced under-arm line.

Draw:

Line S_3X as SX of the plain foundation waist was drawn.

19. Drawing the Waist Line.—Trace the waist lines from the foundation draft through to the kimono-waist draft, simply extending the lines so that the new front waist line is from N to B_2 and the new back waist line is from A_2 to the edge of the paper.

20. Completing the Draft.—Open out the paper and cut as follows: From X to S_3; along the traced line from S_3, through B_2, to E_3; from E_3 to D_3; from D_3, through F_2 and A_2, to S_2; and from S_2 to the edge. Also follow the original neck curves.

———

CUTTING A KIMONO WAIST WITHOUT PATTERN

21. It is not always necessary to draft a pattern for a kimono waist, for very satisfactory results can be obtained by cutting the garment direct from the material without the aid of a pattern.

The width of the material must be considered in relation to the size of the person for whom the waist is to be made. For a 38-inch bust, 40-inch material will be most satisfactory; for less than a 38-inch bust, 36-inch material is better; while if the bust is less than 34 inches, 32-inch material should be used.

22. Taking the Measurements.—Three measures are required; the blouse length, the hip measure, and a fairly tight armhole measure. These measurements are taken as shown in Fig. 3, and result in a

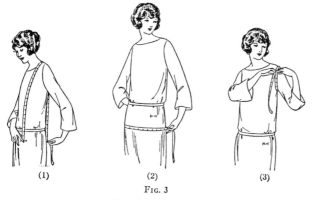

(1)   (2)   (3)

FIG. 3

blouse with the waist line below the normal, which Fashion often favors.

To obtain the length for this long-waisted blouse, put a pin in the dress you have on a little below your normal waist line or in line with the hip bones, to mark the waist line, as shown in (1). If you are rather short, this is usually 2 inches below your normal waist line; if medium tall, 3 inches; if tall, 4 inches. Measure from the pin over the shoulder and down the back to a point opposite the pin.

To obtain the hip measure, hold a tape around the hips at the fullest part, as shown in (2). This measure is taken so that unnecessary fulness may be removed and the blouse made to fit sufficiently snug over the hips.

For the armhole measure, draw a tape around your arm at the shoulder, holding the tape moderately tight, as shown in (3).

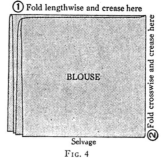

① Fold lengthwise and crease here

BLOUSE

② Fold crosswise and crease here

Selvage

FIG. 4

23. Folding and Creasing the Material.—To prepare the material for cutting, measure the blouse length on the material and cut or tear off the extra amount.

Fold the material lengthwise and crease, as at 1, Fig. 4.

Fold it again crosswise, pulling one end down about 1 inch in order to make the front a little longer than the back, and crease, as at 2.

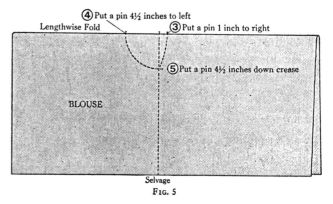

④ Put a pin 4½ inches to left   ③ Put a pin 1 inch to right

Lengthwise Fold

⑤ Put a pin 4½ inches down crease

BLOUSE

Selvage

FIG. 5

Open the crosswise fold and lay the material—still folded lengthwise—on the table in the position shown in Fig. 5.

24. Cutting the Neck Line.—For this waist, directions are given for a boat-shaped neck line, although any desired neck line may be used.

Measure to the right of the crosswise crease—along the folded edge—1 inch, and place a pin, as at 3, Fig. 5.

Measure to the left of the crosswise crease 4½ inches, and place a pin, as at 4.

Measure down the crosswise fold 4½ inches from the folded edge, and place a pin, as at 5.

Cut the neck by cut-

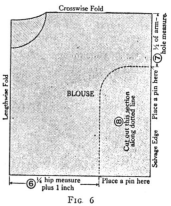

Crosswise Fold

Lengthwise Fold

BLOUSE

Cut out this section along dotted line

⑦ ½ of arm-hole measure

Selvage Edge   Place a pin here

⑥ ¼ hip measure plus 1 inch   Place a pin here

FIG. 6

ting from pin to pin on curved lines, such as the dotted lines show.

25. Shaping the Sleeves.—Fold the material again on the crosswise crease, and lay it on the table in the position shown in Fig. 6.

Measure along the bottom edge one-fourth of the hip measure plus 1 inch and place a pin, as at 6.

EXAMPLE.—If the hip measure is 40 inches, measure off one-fourth of 40 inches, using the scale of fourths on the square. The point is opposite 40. Then add 1 inch and the final point will be opposite 44 on the scale of fourths, or 11 inches.

Measure down from the crosswise fold on the selvage one-half the armhole measure and place a pin, as at 7.

Cut from pin to pin on a curve such as the dotted line shows, removing from the waist the section of material indicated by 8.

Open out the crosswise fold and shape the lower edge of the back, slanting it so that it is about ½ inch shorter at the under-arm seam than at the center back. Then, in order to make the under-arm seams of the front and the back the same length, cut off the front about 1½ inches at the under arm and taper off the lower edge to nothing, about 5 inches from the under arm.

This completes the cutting of the kimono waist.

NOTE.—For short figures, the sleeves may need to be shortened, especially if 40-inch material is used. Erect figures with full bust may need to shorten the back of the waist from 1 to 2 inches at the center back, shaping in a slanting line from the center back around toward the front to give a correct balance to the blouse.

REVIEW QUESTIONS

(1) In what three ways does a kimono waist differ from a plain waist?

(2) Make for practice a draft for a standard kimono waist, using the following measurements for the plain foundation-waist draft: Neck, 12 inches; bust, 36 inches; front, 20 inches; width-of-chest, 13 inches; width-of-back, 13 inches; length-of-back, 14½ inches; center-back depth, 6½ inches; armhole, 14 inches.

(3) How may the sleeve of the long-sleeve kimono waist be made to fit well at the lower edge?

(4) Name the measurements required to cut a kimono waist without a pattern and tell how to take them.

(5) Describe how to cut a kimono waist from measurements without a pattern.

CHAPTER V

PATTERNS FOR CLOSE-FITTING GARMENTS

DRAFTING A TIGHT-FITTING FOUNDATION WAIST WITH A TWO-PIECE BACK

1. The drafting of the tight-fitting waist pattern is a piece of work requiring accuracy and care, a fact that you will appreciate fully when you realize that every one of its lines must closely and smoothly fit every line of the figure above the hip line.

The drafting of this pattern begins as for a plain foundation draft, but certain changes are made in order to produce a waist that will be tight-fitting. In general, these changes are as follows:

(1) No additions are made to the actual measurements, for a tight-fitting garment must fit closely.

(2) Material is taken out in darts at the waist line in order to give a close-fitting waist line.

NOTE.—If a semifitting garment is desired, add 2 inches to the original bust measure, 1 inch to the waist measure, and 1 inch to the hip measure; also, take out less material in the darts at the waist line than for a tight-fitting garment.

2. Measurements.—The measurements for the tight-fitting foundation waist with a two-piece back, as shown in reduced size in Fig. 1, are as follows:

	INCHES
Neck	13
Bust	38
Front	$21\frac{1}{2}$
Chest	14
Width of back	$13\frac{1}{2}$
Length of back	15
Center-back depth	7
Armhole	15
Waist	25
Hip	38
Dart	8

3. Necessary Materials.—To draft a pattern for the tight waist, you will need a sheet of paper of the same size as that used in drafting the plain foundation-waist pattern; that is, 32 inches by 36 inches.

Make a draft, according to the directions given for the plain foundation-waist draft, until point Q is located and the armhole curves are drawn, but make no additions to the original bust, width-of-back, or front measures.

4. Drawing the Front Waist Line.—Place the square so that its corner is at N and its short arm is on the center-front line below N, and draw a light

diagonal line 5 or 6 inches in length along the long arm.

Locate:

Point N_2 to the right of N, one-third the bust line from F to G_2.

EXAMPLE.—Using the measurements in Art. **2**, measure the bust line from F to G_2, obtaining in this case $10\frac{3}{8}$ inches. Placing the corner of the square on N and the short arm on the center-front line above N, locate N_2 to the right of N opposite $10\frac{3}{8}$ on the scale of thirds.

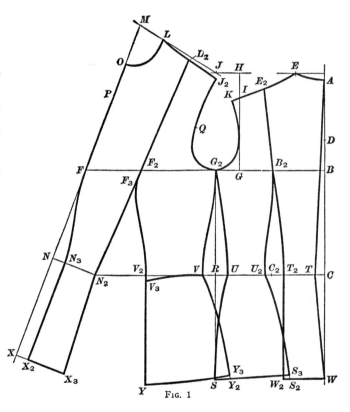

FIG. 1

Point N_3 by keeping the square in the same position as in locating N_2, and measuring 1 inch to the right of N.

5. Drawing the Side Line of the Front Section.
Locate:

Point L_2 midway between points L and J_2.

Connect:

Points L_2 and N_2 with a heavy diagonal line.

Locate:

Point F_2 at the intersection of line L_2N_2 and the bust line.

Point F_3 1 inch below F_2 on line L_2N_2.

6. Drawing the Front Curve.—Place the square so that n is at point N_3 and the edge of the curve, near t, touches F and draw line N_3F.

Note.—By using the front curve N_3F, a better-fitting front section and side line are obtained than when a straight front line is used.

7. Completing the Foundation Waist Line.—Line N_3N_2 has already been drawn. To complete the foundation waist line, place the corner of the square at N_2 and the straight edge touching C on the foundation back line; then draw a straight line connecting these points.

8. Drawing the Foundation Under-Arm Line. Draw the under-arm line as directed in making the plain foundation-waist draft, Art. **32,** Chapter II, extending it the dart length below the waist line.

Locate:
Point R at the intersection of the waist and under-arm lines.

9. Locating Construction Points for Back Darts. To locate points T, V, and U, follow the directions given in the making of the plain foundation waist, Art. **34,** Chapter II.

Locate:
Point C_2 midway between points C and R on the waist line.
Point T_2 1 inch to the right of C_2.
Point U_2 $\frac{1}{2}$ inch to the left of C_2.

10. Drawing the Upper Back-Dart Line.—The upper back-dart line must be drawn before the back-dart curves.

Locate:
Point E_2 midway between K and E on the back-shoulder line.
Draw:
The upper back-dart line by laying the straight edge of the square on E_2 and T_2 and drawing a line from E_2 to the bust line.
Locate:
Point B_2 at the intersection of these lines.

11. Drawing the Back-Dart Curves.—Now you are ready to draw the back-dart curves.
Draw:
Curve B_2T_2 by placing ff of the L. A. C. at T_2 and the edge of the curve, near bb, at B_2.
Curve B_2U_2 by placing mm of the L. A. C. at U_2 and the edge of the curve, near gg, at B_2.
Curve G_2U by connecting points G_2 and U with a heavy curved line as in drafting the plain foundation waist, Art. **35,** Chapter II.

Curve G_2V by connecting G_2 and V as B_2 and U_2 were connected.

12. Continuing the Waist Line.—To locate point V_2, it will be necessary to measure each section of the foundation waist line drafted thus far, that is, from N_3 to N_2, from T_2 to T, and from U to U_2, using the scale of halves, and subtract the sum obtained from one-half the waist measure, as follows:

With the corner of the square at N_3, measure from N_3 to N_2, placing your left thumb on the square at the point where N_2 is located.

With your thumb still on this point on the square, pick up the square and place this point of the square on T_2, and measure to T. Place your thumb on that point on the square and slide the square back until your thumb is at U; then measure to U_2.

Place your thumb on the square as before and move the square back until the point on the square that indicates one-half the waist measure is at point V: then the point at which your thumb is will be V_2.

A careful study of Fig. 1 and the following example will make this clear to you.

Example.—From N_3 to N_2 equals $2\frac{1}{2}$ inches. Place the $2\frac{1}{2}$-inch mark of the square on point T_2, measure to point T, and the reading is $4\frac{7}{8}$ inches. Place the $4\frac{7}{8}$-inch mark on U. Measure to U_2, and the reading is $7\frac{7}{8}$ inches. Slide the square back until the point indicating one-half the waist measure, in this case 25 on scale of halves, is on V, and V_2 will be where the $7\frac{7}{8}$-inch mark touches line N_2C.

Locate:
Point V_3 by placing the corner of the square on F_3 and its straight edge on V_2, marking V_3 the length of line N_2F_3 minus $\frac{1}{4}$ inch.
Example.—Since N_2F_3 is $7\frac{7}{8}$ inches, V_3 will be $7\frac{7}{8}$ minus $\frac{1}{4}$ or $7\frac{5}{8}$ inches below F_3.

13. Drawing the Front Curve of the Side-Front Section.—Draw curve V_3F_3 with m of the L. A. C. at V_3 and the edge of the L. A. C., near s, touching F_3.

Blend the curves at F_3 by moving the square until $3C$ of the F. B. C. falls on F_2 and adjusting the curve to touch the line F_3V_3 from $\frac{1}{2}$ to 1 inch below point F_3.

14. Completing the Waist Line.—The waist line of this draft has a curved section. To draw this curve, place m of the L. A. C. touching V and the edge of the L. A. C., near q, at V_3, and connect the two points with a heavy line.

15. Drafting the Back Skirt Section.—The dart length figures in drafting the skirt sections.
Locate:
Point W by measuring down the dart length on line AC. Then connect points T and W with a heavy diagonal line.
Point W_2 by placing the straight edge of the short arm of the square along the bust line with the straight edge of the long arm touching T_2 and marking W_2 the dart length below T_2.

Draw:

Line T_2W_2 by connecting T_2 and W_2 with a heavy line.

Line WW_2 by connecting W and W_2 with a heavy line.

16. Drafting the Side-Back Skirt Section.—Now determine the side-back skirt section.

Locate:

Point S the dart length below R on the foundation under-arm line.

Point S_2 $\frac{1}{2}$ inch to the right of W_2.

Point S_3 the dart length below U_2, by placing the straight edge of the square on points U_2 and S_2.

Draw:

Curve U_2S_3 by placing s of the L. A. C. on U_2 and the edge of the L. A. C., near w, on S_3 and connecting U_2 and S_3 with a heavy curved line.

Curve US by placing gg of the L. A. C. on point U and the edge of the L. A. C., near cc, on S, and connecting points U and S with a heavy curved line.

Line SS_3 by connecting points S and S_3 with a heavy diagonal line.

17. Drafting the Front Skirt Section.—Next proceed to draft the front skirt section.

Locate:

Point X by extending the center-front line the dart length below N.

Point X_2 1 inch to the right of X, placing the square with its corner at X and its short arm on the foundation center-front line.

Point X_3 $\frac{1}{2}$ inch farther from X_2 than N_2 is from N_3, placing the square in the same position as in locating point X_2.

Connect:

Points N_3 and X_2, X_2 and X_3, and X_3 and N_2 with heavy diagonal lines.

18. Drafting the Side-Front Skirt Section.—The last section to draft is the side-front skirt section.

Locate:

Point Y by placing the square with its short arm along the bust line and its long arm touching point V_3, marking Y, the dart length below V_3 and connecting V_3 and Y with a heavy line.

Point Y_2 in the same manner as given for the locating of point V_2 on the waist line, Art. **12**.

Point Y_3 by placing the straight edge of the square on V and Y_2 and marking point Y_3 the dart length below V.

Draw:

Line VY_3 by placing the square so that s of the L. A. C. is at V and the edge of this curve, near w, is at Y_3, and connecting V and Y_3 with a heavy curved line.

Line YY_3 by placing y of the L. A. C. at point Y of the draft and the edge of the curve, near v, touching Y_3, and connecting these points.

19. Cutting the Draft Apart.—Before cutting apart the draft for the tight-fitting foundation waist, machine stitch or paste a piece of paper 8 or 10 inches square across the back hip section at the waist line only, so that there will be two thicknesses of paper from the waist line to the hip line of the two back sections. The purpose of this extra paper is to take care of the side-back section that overlaps the back and the side-front sections.

With this extra piece of paper in place, trace with a tracing wheel from U to S; from S to S_3; and from S_3 to U_2. Then proceed to cut apart the sections of the pattern as follows:

Cut the *center-back section* from W, through T, to A; from A to E to E_2; from E_2 to B_2 to T_2 to W_2; and from W_2 to W. In cutting from T_2 to W_2, lift the paper so as not to cut the piece of paper that has been added to the side-back section.

Cut the *side-back section* on the traced line from S_3 to U_2; from U_2 to B_2; from E_2, through I, to K; from K to G_2; from G_2 to U; from U on the traced line underneath the original line to S; from S to S_3 on the traced line.

Cut the *side-front section* from Y_3 to V; from V to G_2; from G_2, through Q, to J_2; from J_2 to L_2; from L_2, through F_2 and V_3, to Y; and from Y to Y_3.

Cut the *front section* from X_3 to N_2; from N_2 to F_3; then from L_2 to L; from L on the front-neck curve to O; from O, through P, F, and N_3, to X_2; and from X_2 to X_3.

20. Importance of Practice.—With the completion of the draft for the tight-fitting foundation waist, you will realize that you have completed a rather intricate piece of work. In order that all the lines and methods of locating the points may be fixed firmly in your mind, it would be well for you to make another draft from the same measurements at once. While this draft is not difficult, it involves the locating of numerous points; so making the draft several times will be excellent practice that will be of great help in making other tight-waist drafts. Also, this practice will increase your ability to draft a given pattern without more than one or two references to your textbook. Practice and accuracy are the two essentials in drafting.

DRAFTING A TIGHT-FITTING WAIST WITH A THREE-PIECE BACK

21. The tight-fitting foundation-waist draft with a two-piece back makes a well-balanced pattern for the small and medium-sized figure, but for the large woman having a bust measure of 42 inches or more, the three-piece back is much better for two reasons:

> The front side section is more easily fitted to the figure.
>
> The pattern sections are kept in a more even proportion.

The chief difference in appearance between these two drafts is that the three-piece-back waist draft has two under-arm lines, one at each side of the armhole, instead of one line, as in the two-piece-back draft.

22. Measurements.—The following model measurements for a woman having a bust larger than 42 inches will serve as a check in making drafts for three-piece-back waists. It is from these measurements that the original of the draft shown in Fig. 2 was constructed.

	INCHES
Neck	$14\frac{1}{2}$
Bust	44
Front	23
Chest	16
Width of back	$15\frac{1}{2}$
Length of back	$15\frac{1}{2}$
Center-back depth	$7\frac{1}{2}$
Armhole	17
Waist	31
Hip	44
Dart	9

23. Locating Original Construction Points.—In drafting the three-piece-back, tight-waist pattern, the rules for the two-piece-back draft are used in laying out the construction lines with this exception: 1 inch is added to the bust line of this draft, whereas in the two-piece-back draft nothing is added to any of the measurements.

24. Drawing the Under-Arm Foundation Lines.
Locate:
> Point G_3 $\frac{1}{2}$ inch to the left of G on the bust line.
> Point F_4 one-fifth of the distance between G_2 and F to the left of G_2.

Draw:
> The back under-arm line down from G_3.
> The front under-arm line at right angles down from F_4.

25. Locating Additional Construction Points.
Many additional points must be located before more lines can be drawn.

Locate:
> Point F_3 $1\frac{1}{2}$ inches below F_2 on the line L_2N_2.
> Point R_3 at the intersection of the front under-arm line and line CN_2, the foundation waist line.
> Point R_4 $\frac{1}{2}$ inch to the right of R_3.
> Point V $\frac{1}{2}$ inch to the left of R_3.
> Point R at the intersection of the foundation waist line and the back under-arm line.
> Point U $\frac{1}{2}$ inch to the right of R.
> Point R_2 $\frac{1}{2}$ inch to the left of R.
> Point C_2 midway between points U and T on the waist line.
> Point T_2 $\frac{1}{2}$ inch to the right of C_2.
> Point U_2 $\frac{3}{4}$ inch to the left of C_2.

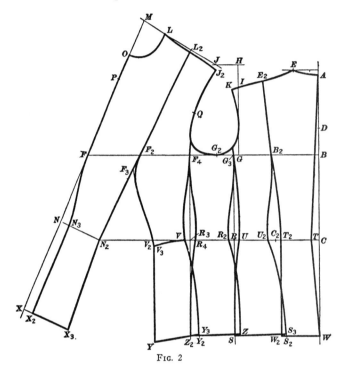

FIG. 2

26. Drawing the Dart Lines Above the Waist Line.
Draw the dart lines above the waist line the same as the corresponding lines in the two-piece-back, tight-fitting waist, with the exception of lines F_4R_4 and F_4V, the curves from G_3 being drawn in the same manner as those from G_2, Art. **11.**

Draw:
> Curve F_4R_4 by placing m on R_4 and the edge, near s, on F_4, extending the line above F_4 to the armhole.
> Curve F_4V by placing the square so that nn is at V and the edge, near hh, is at F_4.

27. Drafting the Front, Back, and Side-Back Skirt Sections.—Locate points X, X_2, and X_3 and draw lines N_2X_3, X_3X_2 and N_3X_2, following the directions given in connection with the two-piece-back, tight-fitting waist, Art. **17.**

According to the directions given in Art. **15** and **16,** draw lines TW, T_2W_2, U_2S_3, and US and the straight connecting lines at the bottom.

28. Drafting the Under-Arm Skirt Section.—The dart length is used in drafting this skirt section.

Locate:

Point Z by measuring $\frac{1}{2}$ inch to the right of S.

Point Z_2 the dart length below R_3 on the front under-arm foundation line.

Draw:

Curve R_2Z by placing the square so that s of the L. A. C. is at R_2 and the edge of the curve, near w, is at Z.

Curve R_4Z_2 by placing the square so that ff of the L. A. C. is at R_4 and the edge of the curve, near bb, touches Z_2.

Line Z_2Z by connecting Z_2 and Z with a straight line.

29. Drafting the Side-Front Skirt Section.—Now proceed to the side-front skirt section.

Locate:

Point V_2 by measuring the waist-line sections as in Art. **12.**

Point V_3 below F_3 a distance equal to the length of F_3N_2 minus $\frac{1}{4}$ inch.

Draw:

Line V_3Y as in drafting the two-piece-back tight-fitting pattern, locating point Y the dart length below V_3, as explained in Art. **18.**

Locate:

Point Y_2 by measuring all the sections at the hip line, following the same method as described for locating point V_2 on the waist line, Art. **12.**

Point Y_3 as described for locating point V_3Y_3, in Art. **18.**

Draw:

Line VY_3 by connecting V and Y_3 when s of the L. A. C. is at V and the edge of the curve, near w, is at Y_3.

Line YY_3 by connecting Y and Y_3 with a slightly curved free-hand line or by placing the square so that the arrow-head of the L. A. C. is at Y_3 and the edge of the curve, near cc, is at Y.

30. Cutting the Draft Apart.—In cutting this draft apart to form the parts of the pattern, follow the same general directions given for cutting the preceding draft apart, and to accommodate the extra section of the three-piece back below the waist line be sure to use a piece of paper of the proper size.

DRAFTING A STOCK COLLAR

31. Measurements.—To draft a stock collar, two measurements are required—the neck measurement, taken around the base of the neck, and a measurement taken from the base of the neck in front to a point where the chin joins the neck.

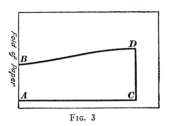

Fig. 3

For the draft shown in Fig. 3, the following measurements were used: Neck, 14 inches, and front measurement, $2\frac{1}{4}$ inches.

The paper needed should be 6 inches wide and 18 inches long and folded through the center crosswise.

32. Locating Construction Points.—All of the construction points can be located in succession.

Locate:

Point A, with the fold to the left, measuring up $\frac{1}{2}$ inch from the lower edge.

Point B from A a distance equal to the front measurement.

Point C by placing the short arm of the square on the fold and the corner at A, and drawing a line along the long arm equal to one-half the neck measurement plus $\frac{1}{2}$ inch.

Point D by placing the square on line AC, its corner at C, and drawing along the long arm a line 1 inch longer than AB.

33. Drawing the Neck Curve.—To complete the draft, place the middle point of the curve between m and n on point B and the edge of the curve, near t, on D and draw curve BD.

34. Cutting the Draft Apart.—Cut from A to C, from C to D and from D to B.

———

DRAFTING A FOUNDATION, PLAIN, TWO-PIECE SLEEVE

35. Measurements.—A draft for a foundation two-piece sleeve is shown reduced in size in Fig. 4. The measurements followed in making this draft are:

	INCHES
Armhole	15
Inside sleeve length	17
Hand	8

The paper necessary should be 27 inches square and folded once through the center.

36. Locating Construction Points.—Draw a foundation line the full length of the long arm of the square, placing the square so that its short arm is along the right edge of the paper and its long arm is 1 inch above the fold.

Locate:
> Point *A* 2 inches to the left of the right edge of the paper.
> Point *B* one-fourth the armhole measure to the left of *A*.
> Point *C* midway between *A* and *B*.
> Point *D* the inside-sleeve measure to the left of *B*.
> Point *E* 1¼ inches to the left of *D*.
> Point *F* midway between *B* and *D*.

37. Drawing the Armhole-Curve Construction Lines.—Certain construction lines are necessary in order to draw the armhole curves.

Locate:
> Point *G* with the straight edge of one arm of the square on the foundation line *EA* and its corner at *A*, drawing a vertical line along the other arm equal in length to one-fourth the armhole measure.

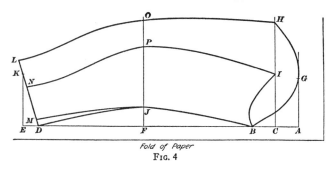

Fig. 4

> Point *H* with the corner of the square at *C*, and its short arm resting on the foundation line *EA*, drawing a vertical line the length of one-half the armhole measure plus ½ inch.
> Point *I* midway between points *C* and *H*.

38. Drawing the Elbow Line.—Place the corner of the square at *F* and allow one arm to rest on the line *EA*. Draw the elbow line the full width of the folded paper.

Locate:
> Point *J* 1½ inches above *F* on the elbow line.

39. Drawing the Wrist Line.—The wrist line is the first pattern line to be drawn.

Locate:
> Point *K* by placing the corner of the square at *E* and the short arm on line *AE*, and drawing a vertical line the length of one-half the hand measure.
> Point *L* by placing the corner of the square on point *D* and a straight edge touching point *K*, and drawing a heavy diagonal line from *D*, through *K*, the length of two-thirds of the hand measure.

> Point *M* ½ inch above *D* on line *DL*.
> Point *N* one-third the hand measure above *M*.

40. Drawing the Outside-Seam Curves.—Next consider the outside-seam curves.

Draw:
> Curve *LH* with *m* at *L* and the edge of the curve, near *z*, touching *H*, using a heavy line. For a long sleeve, the square may be too short to reach to point *H*. In such a case, the line should be extended by moving the end of the square to the right after the first part of the outside line has been drawn and connecting this line with point *H*.

Locate:
> Point *O* at the intersection of the line *LH* and the elbow line.
> Point *P* 2 inches below point *O* on the elbow line.

Draw:
> Curve *NP* by placing *l* on *N* and having the edge of the curve, near *t*, touch *P*.
> Curve *PI* by placing *s* on *P* with the edge of the curve, near *x*, touching *I*.

41. Drawing the Inside-Seam Curves.—Proceed now to the inside-seam curves.

Draw:
> Line *BJ* by placing *u* on point *J* with the edge of the curve, near *y*, touching *B*.
> Curve *JD* by placing *ff* on *J* with the edge of the curve, near *bb*, on *D*.
> Curve *JM* by placing *ff* on *J*, with the edge of the curve, near *bb*, on *M*.

42. Drawing the Armhole Curves.—With the seam curves drawn, the armhole curves may be put in.

Draw:
> The top-armhole curve by placing 2*E* of the R. F. C. at point *G* and the curve, near 4*G*, touching *B*, also by placing 4 of the F.C. on point *G* and the curve, near 2, touching *H*.
> The under-armhole curve by placing the square so that *rr* of the S. A. C. touches *B*, and the edge of the L. A. C., near *mm*, touches *I*.

43. Tracing the Pattern and Cutting Apart.—Trace the part of the pattern to be used for the *under part* of the sleeve from *B* to *I*; through *P*, to *N*; from *N* to *M*; from *M*, through *J*, to *B*; and, since the elbow line should be indicated on both sections, trace from *J* to *P*.

Unfold the paper and cut the pattern for the *under part* on all the traced lines, with the exception of the elbow line.

Next cut the *top part* of the sleeve as follows: From B to G to H; from H, through O, to L; from L, through K, N and M to D; and from D, through J, to B.

DRAFTING A PRINCESSE PATTERN

44. When close-fitting basques and dresses are in vogue, the princesse slip is almost a necessity. Since these styles return at intervals, you will find it helpful to know just how the patterns for them are made. In brief, the pattern for the princesse slip, Fig. 5,

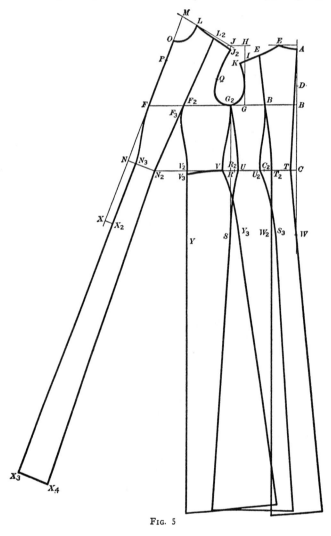

FIG. 5

is made by extending the dart lines of either of the tight-waist drafts the length required for a petticoat. For the draft shown here, the two-piece-back draft was used. The neck line may be made in a V shape or cut round following the directions given for a blouse.

45. Drafting the Center-Back Extension.—To obtain the center-back skirt section,

Extend:
> Line TW by placing the corner of the square on point T and its long arm along line TW, drawing a heavy line the length of the back-skirt length.

Line T_2W_2 straight down from W_2 in the same manner as the center-back line was drawn.

Draw:
> The bottom line of the center-back section by connecting the extensions of lines TW and T_2W_2 with a straight line.

46. Drafting the Side-Back Extension.—For the side-back skirt section,

Extend:
> Line U_2S_3 by placing the corner of the square on T_2, and, with the straight edge on S_3, drawing the line until it is the back-skirt length below U_2.

Locate:
> Point R_2 midway between R and U on line CR.

Extend:
> Line US by placing the corner of the square on R_2 and the straight edge of the long arm on S, and drawing it to equal the side-skirt length.

Draw:
> The bottom line of the side-back section by connecting the extensions at the bottom with a straight line.

47. Drafting the Side-Front Extension.—In order to draft the side-front skirt section,

Extend:
> Line VY_3 by placing the corner of the square on R and the straight edge of the long arm on Y_3, making the line the side-skirt length.
> Line V_3Y straight down from Y, making it the same length as the extended VY_3.

Draw:
> The bottom line of the side-front section by connecting the extremities of the two lines with a straight line.

48. Drafting the Front Extension.—To extend the front skirt section,

Locate:
> Point X_3 by extending the line N_3X_2 until it is the front-skirt length.
> Point X_4 by placing the corner of the square at X_3 and its short arm along N_3X_3 and drawing a line along the long arm from point X_3 the length of N_3N_2 plus $1\frac{1}{2}$ inches.

Draw:
> Line N_2X_4 by connecting points N_2 and X_4.

49. Cutting the Draft Apart.—To form the pattern for the princesse slip from this draft, proceed as explained in connection with the tight-fitting waist drafts, using, of course, paper of the proper size to accommodate the extensions below the waist line.

CLOSE-FITTING PATTERNS FOR FIGURES OUT OF PROPORTION

50. Up to this time, sufficient study and practice have been had to permit a few suggestions to be made about the drafting of close-fitting patterns for figures that are out of proportion, such as those with rounding shoulders, backs that are full between the neck and the shoulders, very wide backs and narrow chests, and so on. The woman who has thoroughly mastered the drafting up to this point will enjoy working out drafts whose measurements do not correspond with the average, for the plan of proportioning on which all drafts are built makes it possible, with a little study and practice, to make a perfect-fitting pattern for any figure.

51. There is one measurement, namely, the center-back depth, that must always be considered in drafting patterns for persons out of proportion. It will readily be seen how the length of the center-back depth will affect the height of the shoulder, and as line GH of the draft in Figs. 1 and 2 is governed by the armhole measure it is necessary sometimes, especially in extreme cases where the shoulders are rounding, to use a center-back-depth measure that corresponds with the armhole measure, which may be determined from the table of measurements given in Art. **50,** Chap. I.

FIG. 6

52. Alterations for Round Shoulders.—If in taking the measurements of a person, it is found that the center-back-depth measure is too long and gives a shoulder line that has a very decided slope, use a measure that corresponds with the armhole measure, and then from the original length-of-back measure in drafting subtract the difference between the original center-back-depth measure and the one used for drafting, thus avoiding the making of the back length too long. For instance, if the person's center-back depth is 8 inches, her length of back $15\frac{1}{2}$ inches, and her armhole 16 inches, a center-back depth of $7\frac{1}{2}$ inches should be used. The difference between 8 inches and $7\frac{1}{2}$ inches is $\frac{1}{2}$ inch. This should be subtracted from the length-of-back measure. Thus, $15\frac{1}{2}-\frac{1}{2}$ $=15$ inches.

Then, before cutting out the material, slash the pattern from D on the draft to line GH, so that it may be separated in placing the pattern on the material, as shown in Fig. 6, to give the necessary length to the back, especially over the rounding part of the shoulders where a garment cut over this pattern might draw if such a precaution were not taken.

It should be remembered that such an alteration in the pattern is not necessary unless the round shoulders are very pronounced, when it will rarely be necessary to separate the pattern more than $\frac{3}{4}$ to 1 inch at point D, as shown at a.

53. Alterations for Narrow Chests.—For very narrow chests, where the width-of-back measure is wide in proportion to the chest measure, $\frac{1}{2}$ to 1 inch should be added to the original chest measure in order to give better lines to the draft. A pattern so drafted will help to overcome the appearance of narrow chests.

54. Alterations for Enlarged Neck at Back.—Sometimes a figure with a roll of flesh just below the prominent bone at the back of the neck is encountered. This flesh takes up the material so much that it is well, in such cases, to slash the pattern from 1 to 2 inches below A on line AC of the draft and separate it $\frac{1}{8}$ to $\frac{1}{2}$ inch in order to allow additional width.

55. Alterations for Back Out of Proportion.—Very wide backs and small bust measurements may be adjusted to give better lines to both the draft and the figure if the width-of-back measure is reduced $\frac{1}{8}$ to $\frac{1}{2}$ inch so that the draft may be kept in better proportion.

Very narrow backs and wide chests may be made to show less difference if the width-of-back measure is increased $\frac{1}{8}$ to $\frac{1}{2}$ inch in drafting.

56. Alterations for Large Waist Line.—A change in the drafting of a tight-waist draft, Fig. 1, that is sometimes advisable for a figure having a large waist line in proportion to the hip measure is in the locating of points V and U each $\frac{1}{2}$ inch from R, and U_2 $\frac{1}{4}$ inch and T_2 $\frac{1}{2}$ inch from C_2. This gives a more evenly balanced waist line and permits line V_3F_3 to be more graceful. In extreme cases, line X_2F may be omitted; then the straight line from F to X is used instead of the curve.

Another method of taking care of this is to make a plain foundation waist without any additions to the actual measurements and then to fit the fulness at the waist line in the front to the figure with darts.

REVIEW QUESTIONS

(1) Why is it necessary to be very accurate and careful when drafting a tight-waist draft?

(2) What general changes are made in the plain foundation-waist draft when making a tight-fitting waist draft?

(3) When is a tight-fitting waist with a three-piece back necessary?

(4) What are the advantages of the additional under arm piece in the three-piece-back waist?

(5) When is the princesse pattern a necessity?

(6) What particular measurement must always be considered in the drafting of patterns for figures that are out of proportion?

(7) In drafting a tight-waist pattern for a very round-shouldered figure, how may the center-back depth be adjusted without unbalancing the pattern?

(8) What changes are advisable in drafting for figures with: (a) A narrow chest? (b) An enlarged neck at the back?

(9) Submit a draft of a two-piece-back, tight-waist pattern made according to the following measurements: Neck, 12 inches; bust, 36 inches; front, 20½ inches; chest, 13 inches; width-of-back, 13 inches; length-of-back, 14 inches; center-back depth, 6¾ inches; armhole, 14½ inches; waist, 23 inches; hip, 36 inches; dart, 7 inches.

(10) Submit a draft of a plain two-piece sleeve pattern made according to the following measurements: Armhole, 14 inches; inside sleeve length, 16 inches; hand, 8 inches.

CHAPTER VI

PATTERNS FOR UNDERWEAR AND LINGERIE

MERITS AND ADVANTAGES

1. Consideration of the development of undergarments usually brings to mind not so much the cut of the garment as the material of which it is to be made and the manner in which it is to be trimmed. Both of these features are of decided importance, for unless the material and trimming are of the proper quality they almost invariably have an ill effect on the appearance of the costume under which the lingerie is worn. But it is, after all, the cut of the undergarment that is of primary importance, for this, more than any other factor, has a decided influence on the costume as a whole, and unless the pattern has the correct lines and the proper amount of fulness and is made according to accurate measurements, the undergarments made with its aid are certain not to prove entirely satisfactory.

2. Just as in making patterns for outer garments, there are distinct advantages in the drafting of patterns for undergarments. A pattern drafted carefully to a correctly taken and balanced set of measurements is bound to give extreme satisfaction so far as the fitting of the garment is concerned. Then, too, there is the added advantage of being able to copy any exclusive design, or the still greater advantage of a means of expression or of development of original ideas.

Lingerie designing, although it does not cover nearly so broad a field as the designing of outer garments, involves practically the same principles as dress designing, but because it is somewhat simpler than advanced dress designing, you may use it as a stepping-stone to more extensive achievements and thus gain valuable experience.

Many sources of inspiration for lingerie designing are available. You will probably find showings in high-grade specialty shops of the most interest, although you may gain excellent ideas, also, from lingerie displays in almost any shop or department store or from fashion magazines and even from ready-to-wear garment catalogs.

3. As fashion changes do not have so decided an effect on lingerie designs as on dress styles, you will find it worth while to preserve carefully any lingerie patterns you may develop, for you will undoubtedly find use for them many times. It is especially advisable to save any foundation underwear patterns that you make according to the instructions given in this lesson, for you will need them as a basis for any unusual designs you may wish to develop. By outlining on these patterns any new designing features you wish to apply and tracing the new pattern to another piece of paper, you will be able to use the foundation pattern a great many times.

4. If you intend to make patterns for others, you will find that a great many women, especially those of generous proportions, will be as eager to have lingerie patterns made according to their individual measurements as to have dress patterns designed for them. The well-dressed woman realizes the intrinsic value of well-cut underwear and will appreciate any cooperation on your part in the planning of a foundation for her outer garments.

BRASSIÈRES

PLAIN BRASSIÈRE

5. In the development of a pattern for a plain brassière, such as that illustrated in Fig. 1, use the foundation tight-waist draft prepared with a two-piece or a three-piece back, but omit the back darts.

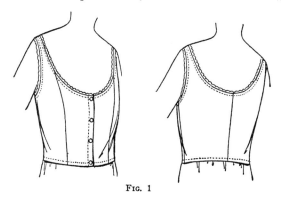

FIG. 1

Fig. 2 illustrates the method of making the plain-brassière pattern. The neck lines may be marked as high or as low as you desire. To determine the position of the neck lines, measure up on the center front, as well as on the center back, of the pattern to a point that indicates just where the upper edge of the brassière should terminate. Many women prefer to have a brassière come up to within 6 inches of the neck in front and to within 5 inches of the neck in back, and others like to have it lower. It is well, though, in making a plain brassière, to have it come just high enough to cover the undervest and still be low enough in case a daintier cover is to be worn over it.

6. Determining the Width of the Shoulder Pieces.
If lace edging or a binding is to be used, the shoulder pieces need be only $1\frac{1}{4}$ inches wide at the shoulder, but if just a hem is to be used to finish the neck and the armholes, make the shoulder pieces $1\frac{3}{4}$ inches wide, so that they will hold their shape well.

7. Drawing the Neck Lines.—In order to form the neck curve, connect with an arc the front shoulder-piece line and the center-front point; also draw an arc from the back shoulder-piece line to about 1 inch from the center-back point. Fig. 2 shows the general shape that these arcs will take.

The position of each point, or center, from which to swing each arc that forms a neck line of the brassière pattern will have to be determined by trial. In locating such points as these, always bear in mind that the

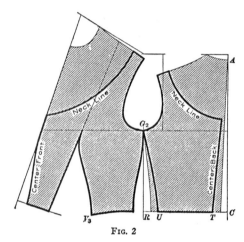

FIG. 2

distance from one end of an arc to the center must always be the same as the distance from the other end to the center and that the curvature of the arc depends on the location of the point.

8. Drawing the Center-Back Line.—Points A and C have already been located on the foundation waist draft, as in Art. **16,** Chapter II.

Locate:
> Point T $1\frac{3}{4}$ inches to the left of C on the back waist line.

Draw:
> The center-back line by placing the corner of the square on A and the straight edge touching T, and drawing a straight line connecting T with the back-neck line.

9. Completing the Back Section.—In order to decrease the width of the back section at the under arm,

Locate:
> Point U $1\frac{1}{2}$ inches to the right of R.

Draw:
> Line UT, the back waist line, by connecting points U and T with a straight line.

Curve UG_2 by placing ff at U and the edge of the curve, near bb, at G_2, and connecting points U and G_2.

10. Drawing the Waist-Line Curve.—Test the waist line and locate point V_3, following the same directions as for locating point V_3 and drawing this curve in the tight-waist draft, Art. **12,** Chapter V.

11. Completing the Pattern Lines.—For the remainder of the brassière pattern lines, follow the lines above the waist line of the tight-waist draft.

12. Tracing the Pattern Lines and Cutting the Draft Apart.—Place a sheet of paper under the tight-waist pattern and trace all the brassière-pattern lines on it, including the side-front seams from the bust point to the neck edge. Cut the draft apart on these traced lines.

VARIATIONS OF PLAIN BRASSIÈRE

13. Using Side-Front Darts.—If you wish to use the plain-brassière pattern for cutting a brassière having darts that extend from the bust point at the side front instead of seams that are continued to the neck edge, do not cut the side-front seam line from the bust point to the neck edge. Rather, keep the side and center-front sections in one piece and depend entirely on the dart for the fitting.

14. Changing Position of Seam Lines.—To make a pattern for a brassière having seam lines that are in a different position from those of the plain-brassière pattern, you will find muslin modeling the easiest method. For cutting the muslin model, you may use as a guide the pattern suggested for cutting a brassière with darts in front, but do not cut away the dart allowance. Also, as a precaution, leave extra material below the waist line.

In fitting the muslin model, pin seam lines or darts at any points you desire to have them. For instance, if you wish to take out the surplus fulness at the front waist line by means of horizontal darts placed at the under arm, fold the material in at the under arm an amount sufficient to make the brassière close-fitting. If necessary, piece the material at the lower end of the front under-arm seam to make this of the same length as the back under arm.

15. Using Bands of Insertion.—The most satisfactory method of making a brassière entirely of bands of insertion is to model this on the dress form or figure, arranging the insertion just as you desire and drawing it sufficiently close to give the required support.

Another method is that of basting the insertion, with the edges overlapping, to the brassière pattern and, when all are basted, stitching the rows of insertion to the paper pattern with the sewing machine. The pattern must then be torn from the lace.

CORSET COVERS

PLAIN CORSET COVER

16. A pattern for a plain corset cover like that shown in Fig. 3 may be very easily and quickly developed from the plain foundation-waist draft, as shown in Fig. 4, for, as the illustration indicates, only the upper portion of this pattern requires any change.

The depth of the neck line may be made to suit the desire of the person for whom it is intended. To be most pleasing, the corset cover should not be too high, yet it should be made high enough to cover the undervest completely.

FIG. 3

17. General Rule for Length of Back and Front. A corset cover should usually measure two-thirds of the original back length or a trifle less from the waist line at the center back to the finished edge of the trimming. For the front, a measurement should be taken from the waist line to the top of the breast bone in the center front and the corset cover finished to measure about two-thirds of this length.

18. Drawing the Back-Neck Line.—Before the arc indicating the neck line can be drawn,

Locate:

Point A_2 on the center-back line of the plain foundation-waist draft by measuring up from the center-back waist line, or point T, two-thirds of the length-of-back measurement, minus 1 inch.

Point E_2 2 inches from the back armhole line on the shoulder.

Connect:

Points A_2 and E_2 with an arc.

19. Drawing the Front-Neck Line.—B_2 and F_2 must first be located as the termination points of the neck line.

Locate:

Point B_2 by measuring from the center-front waist line two-thirds of the distance from the waist line to the neck line, minus 1 inch.

NOTE.—The reason for subtracting 1 inch in locating A_2 and B_2 is to allow for trimming.

Point F_2 2 inches from the front armhole line on the shoulder line.

Connect:

Points B_2 and F_2 with an arc.

20. Drawing the Armhole Curves.—Two points, C_2 and D_2, are necessary for the armhole curves.

Locate:

Point C_2 1 inch from the back-armhole line on the shoulder.

Point D_2 1 inch from the front-armhole line on the shoulder.

Redraw the armholes, using curves similar to those in the plain foundation waist, Art. **30** and **31**, Chapter II.

21. Cutting the Draft Apart.—Form the corset-cover pattern by cutting on the heavy lines shown in the illustration, omitting the portion below the waist line, as a corset cover is generally finished with a band, a casing, or a fitted peplum.

22. Adding Fulness to the Plain Corset Cover. As you remember, 4 inches is added to the bust line of the plain foundation-waist pattern in its development, so if you desire more fulness than this in the corset cover, make provision for it in the cutting of the material.

Generally, sufficient fulness is provided by allowing $2\frac{1}{2}$ inches beyond the center-front line of the pattern, 1 inch of this being for the hem finish. However, as outer garments for very slender persons are usually made with more fulness than those for the average figure, more than $2\frac{1}{2}$ inches may be allowed for a slender person.

If you wish to add considerable fulness to the front, slash it lengthwise through the center and separate the pieces an amount sufficient to give the fulness you desire. Then blend the neck-line curve.

23. Developing the Sleeve-Cap Pattern.—To form a pattern for the sleeve cap, use the plain founda-

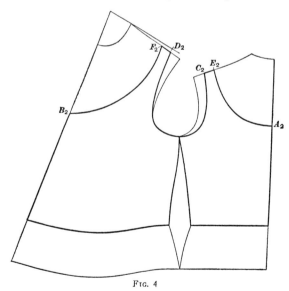

FIG. 4

tion-sleeve pattern, but add beyond the upper curve of the sleeve the amount you took from the shoulder length, or 1 inch, in developing the corset-cover pattern. Then cut off the lower portion to make the sleeve cap of the length you desire.

24. Very small women or women who are narrow through the chest and the shoulders derive much satisfaction from corset covers whose shoulder portions are extended. When worn under waists made of sheer material, a corset cover of this kind gives to the wearer the appearance of greater width.

Corset covers with extended shoulders may be made in the same manner as the plain corset cover,

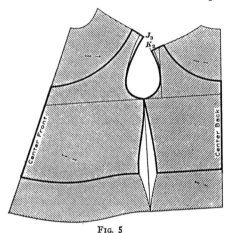

FIG. 5

but the pattern must first be worked out to suit the person who is to wear the garment, so that the width may be obtained across the shoulders and yet a correct-fitting armhole secured, which will aid in holding the corset cover in position on the shoulder.

25. Extending the Shoulder Portions.—To extend the shoulder lines,

Locate:

Point J_3, Fig. 5, $\frac{1}{2}$ inch to the right of J_2 of the plain foundation waist.

Point K_2, $\frac{1}{4}$ inch to the left of K of the same draft.

26. Drawing the Armhole Curves.—New armhole curves must then be drawn.

Draw:

The front curve by connecting point J_3 and the original curve, placing kk at J_3 and allowing the edge of the curve, near oo, to touch the original armhole where it will.

The back curve by placing uu at K_2 and allowing the edge of the curve at ww to touch the original armhole line where it will.

NOTE.—Preparing the pattern in this way will cause the armholes of the garment, when made, to be a trifle smaller than those of the plain corset cover, but the garment will extend over the end of each shoulder of the wearer and thus prove very comfortable.

27. Drawing the Neck Lines.—First, measure from points K_2 and J_3 the width desired for the shoulder straps, usually $1\frac{1}{2}$ inches. Then connect the points just located with the center-front and center-back lines by means of arcs, being very careful to locate the centers for these arcs correctly.

28. Cutting Out the Pattern.—To form the pattern, trace on the heavy lines, remove the plain foundation-waist pattern, and cut on the traced lines.

PLAIN CORSET COVER WITH PEPLUM

29. Preparing the Peplum Pattern.—Instead of a corset cover with a band or a casing for elastic at the waist line, some women prefer to have one with a *peplum*, or small skirt-like effect below the waist line. In such a case, it will be necessary to prepare for the peplum a pattern that may be used in connection with the corset-cover pattern.

To prepare a peplum pattern, measure down $3\frac{1}{2}$ inches on the center front of a circular foundation-skirt pattern, 3 inches on the side line, and $2\frac{1}{2}$ inches at the center back, and mark these points. Then connect these points by placing the square in the same manner as for drawing the waist line of the circular foundation-skirt pattern, so that the bottom line of the peplum pattern thus marked will correspond with the curve at the waist line.

Place a piece of paper of suitable size underneath the part that outlines the peplum, trace off the pattern, and cut on the traced lines.

TWO-PIECE EMBROIDERY CORSET COVER

30. A two-piece embroidery corset cover, as shown in Fig. 6, may have its pattern formed by changing the plain foundation-waist pattern in the manner shown in Fig. 7.

There are two points to be considered in marking the plain-waist pattern for this corset cover: (1) the length of the back and the front, and (2) the locating of points to guide in placing the waist pattern on the paper on which the corset-cover pattern is to be drafted.

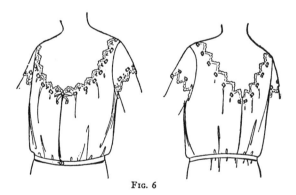

FIG. 6

31. Locating Construction Points for Neck Line.

Locate:

Points A_2 and B_2 the same as in the plain corset-cover draft.

Point C_2 1 inch to the right of the armhole curve on the back-shoulder line.

Point D_2 1 inch to the left of the armhole curve on the front-shoulder line.

32. Pinning the Foundation Pattern to the Paper. Use a paper 36 inches long and 18 inches wide. Pin the back part of the waist pattern on this paper so that the intersection of the waist line and the center-

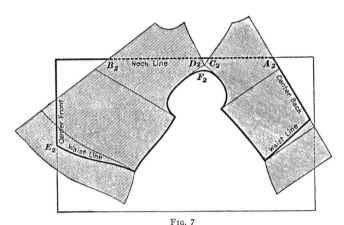

FIG. 7

back line is at the right edge of the paper and points A_2 and C_2 touch the top edge of the paper, as shown.

Pin the front part so that points B_2 and D_2 touch the top edge of the paper and the shoulder lines of the waist-pattern parts touch at the shoulder points near the armhole.

33. Raising the Back Waist Line.—Measure 1 inch above the original waist line along the center-back line. Draw the new waist line from this point to connect with the original waist line at the under arm, using a diagonal line for this purpose.

34. Drawing the Center-Back Line.—Make heavy the original center-back line from A_2, as far down as its intersection with the new waist line.

35. Determining the Front Length.—Locate a point on the waist line 2 inches to the right of the center-front line.

Determine the length of the corset cover in front by measuring on the center-front line from point B_2 to the waist line of the foundation-waist pattern.

NOTE.—In this draft, the center-front line falls on the edge of the paper. If the center-front measure were less, it would fall inside of the edge, and in case of a greater center-front measure, a larger sheet of paper would be necessary.

Place the square so that its short arm is even with the top edge of the paper and the straight edge of the long arm touches the point located on the waist line, and draw a line along the long arm of the square.
Locate:
Point E_2 on this line a distance below the top edge of the paper equal to the front measurement just determined.

36. Lowering the Front Waist Line.—Draw the front waist line of the corset cover in the regular way,

connecting point E_2 with the intersection of the original waist line and the under-arm line of the waist pattern.

37. Drawing the Shoulder Strap.—You may make the strap that is to go over the shoulder any width you wish, but the usual width is $1\frac{1}{2}$ inches.
Locate:
Point F_2 by measuring down $1\frac{1}{2}$ inches from the top edge of the paper at the point where the shoulder points touch.

38. Drawing the Armhole Curve.—Draw the top of the armhole, or one side of the shoulder strap, by placing the square so that the arrowhead of the S. A. C. touches the back-armhole curve, *uu* touches the front-armhole curve, and the edge of the curve, between *ww* and *xx*, touches point F_2.

Complete the armhole for the corset-cover pattern by drawing around both the back and the front of the waist pattern to the under-arm lines.

39. Drawing the Under-Arm Lines.—Draw the under-arm lines to the waist lines, using the under-arm lines of the waist pattern as a guide.

40. Tracing the Pattern and Cutting It Apart.—To form the pattern, first trace the new center-back, center-front, and waist lines; then remove the plain foundation-waist pattern and cut on the traced lines and also on the marked armhole and under-arm lines.

41. Drafting the Sleeve Cap.—For the sleeve cap, use a plain foundation-sleeve pattern and cut it the length you desire.

SLIP-OVER CORSET COVER

42. In preparing the pattern for the slip-over corset cover shown in Fig. 8, use the pattern drafted for the plain corset cover and a sheet of paper 40 inches long and 22 inches wide.

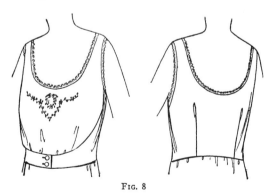

FIG. 8

43. Pinning the Foundation Pattern in Position. Follow the plan illustrated in Fig. 9. At the right end of the paper, place the front part of the pattern so that its center-front line is on the long edge and at the left end of the paper, place the back part of the pattern so that its center-back line is on the long edge and the inside point of its shoulder strap touches the inside point of the shoulder strap of the front part of the pattern.

44. Drafting the Back Section and Front Belt. Place the square so that its short arm rests on the center-back line and its long arm on the waist line of the back part of the pattern, and draw a line along the long arm, making it 17 or 18 inches in length.

Locate:

Point A on this line, measuring up from the under-arm line one-fourth of the waist measure, plus 3 inches.

Point B by placing the square so that its corner is at A and its long arm rests on the line just drawn, and drawing to the left on the short arm, a line 3 inches long, lettering its termination B.

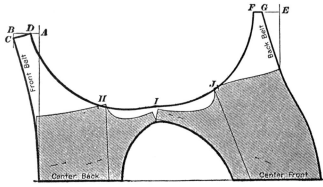

FIG. 9

Point C by placing the square with its short arm on line AB and its corner at B and drawing a 2- or 3-inch line along the long arm, placing point C $\frac{1}{2}$ inch below B.

Point D 2 inches to the right of B on line AB.

Form the end of the front belt by connecting C and D with a diagonal line.

Draw:

The bottom line by placing the square with the arrowhead of the L. A. C. at point C and the edge of the curve, near gg, touching the waist line of the pattern, continuing the curve until it touches the center-back line.

45. Drafting the Front Section and Back Belt. Place the square with its short arm on the center-front line of the pattern and the straight edge of the long arm touching the intersection of the under-arm and waist lines. Draw a line along the long arm from the under-arm line, making it 7 to 8 inches long.

Locate:

Point E by measuring up on this line, from the under-arm line one-fourth of the waist measure.

Point F with the short arm of the square on the line just drawn, and its corner at E, drawing a 3-inch line along the long arm and lettering its termination F.

Point G 1 inch to the right of F on line EF.

Draw the back belt from G, making a line to connect with the waist line of the pattern, first placing the square with z at G and the edge of the curve, near v, touching the waist line of the pattern.

46. Locating Construction Points for the Armhole.—Three points must be located before the armhole can be drawn.

Locate:

Point H on the back part of the pattern, placing it 1 inch to the left of the armhole curve on the under-arm line.

Point I the width you wish the shoulder strap to be above the inside of the strap directly above where the shoulder straps meet. A good width for the shoulder strap is 2 inches.

Point J on the front of the pattern, placing it $\frac{1}{2}$ inch to the right of the armhole curve on the under-arm line.

47. Swinging Arcs for the Armhole Lines.—Swing an arc from F to I and another from I to D, first locating the center for each of the arcs by trial. These arcs need not exactly touch point J or H, but they should come within $\frac{1}{8}$ to $\frac{1}{2}$ inch of each point.

With the arcs drawn, blend the lines that form the shoulder straps at the shoulder points, so that the pattern for the slip-over corset cover will not appear pointed at the shoulder.

48. Tracing the Draft and Cutting It Apart. Outline the rest of the front waist line and the neck line, following the plain corset-cover pattern as a guide, and trace the lines that appear on this pattern at the under-arm lines.

Remove the plain corset-cover pattern, and then cut out the slip-over corset-cover pattern by cutting the paper on both the drawn and the traced lines.

SURPLICE CORSET COVER

49. The plain foundation-waist pattern should be used as a guide in preparing the pattern for the surplice corset-cover shown in Fig. 10, the work being done in the manner shown in Fig. 11.

50. Drafting the Front Section.—The size of the paper should be 24 to 27 inches wide and equal in length to the waist pattern.

Pin the front of the foundation pattern to the paper after placing the center-front line about $6\frac{1}{2}$ inches, or one-fourth of the waist measure, to the left of the short edge of the paper, as shown in view (*a*). This allowance is made so as to provide for the lap of the corset cover at the waist line.

Locate:

> Point A_2 one-fourth of the original waist measure to the left of the center-front line at the waist line.

> Point B_2 one-third of the distance between the neck curve and the waist line on the center-front line, measuring down from the neck line.
>
> Point C_2 $\frac{1}{2}$ inch to the left of the armhole curve on the shoulder line.

Fig. 10

Draw:

> The front-neck line by connecting C_2 and B_2 with a curved line, placing the square with *aa* at C_2 and the edge of the curve, near *ff*, touching B_2.

Complete the front surplice by connecting A_2 and B_2 with a diagonal line.

Locate:

> Point D_2 by measuring one-sixth of one-half of the waist measure to the right of the under-arm line at the waist line, placing the straight edge of the square so that it touches the waist line at the center front and at the under-arm seam.
>
> Point E_2 1 inch above D_2.

Draw:

> The under-arm line by connecting points E_2 and C_2 with a curved line, placing the square so that *kk* is at C_2 and the edge of the curve, near *cc*, is at E_2.
>
> The front waist line by drawing first the part from E_2 to the center-front line, placing the square with *m* at E_2 and the edge of the curve, near *x*, touching the center-front line of the waist pattern at the waist line; then complete the waist line from the center-front line to A_2, keeping the square in the same position, but moving the end so that it touches A_2.

51. Tracing and Cutting the Front Section. Trace the lines from B_2 to C_2 to E_2; also, trace the waist line from E_2 to the center-front line.

Remove the foundation-waist pattern from the paper and cut out the front part of the corset-cover pattern, following the traced and marked lines.

52. Drafting the Back Section.—The size of paper necessary for the back section is from 18 inches to 22 inches wide and as long as the foundation pattern piece.

Pin the back of the foundation pattern to the paper, as shown in Fig. 11 (*b*), leaving a space that is one-fourth the waist measure, minus 1 inch, to the right of the center-back line.

Locate:

> Point F_2 by placing the square with its short arm along the center-back line of the pattern and its corner at the waist line, and marking F_2 at the point where the long arm touches the edge of the paper.
>
> Point G_3 $\frac{1}{2}$ inch to the right of the arm-hole curve on the shoulder line.

Draw:

> The back-neck line and surplice by connecting G_3 and F_2 with a curved and a diagonal line.
>
> For the curved line, place the square with the arrowhead of the L. A. C. at G_3 and the edge of the curve, near *ee*, touching the center-back line at the bust line.
>
> Continue by drawing a diagonal line from this point to F_2.

Locate:

> Point H_2 by measuring one-fourth of one-half the waist measure to the left of the under-arm line at the waist line.

Draw:

> The under-arm line by connecting H_2 and G_3 with a curved line, placing the square with *p* at G_3 and the edge of the curve, near *y*, at H_2.
>
> The waist line by drawing a straight line between F_2 and H_2.

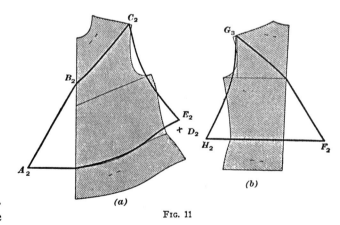

Fig. 11

53. Tracing and Cutting the Back Section.—Trace the waist line, the line from G_3 to the center-back line, and the under-arm line from G_3 to H_2.

Remove the waist pattern from the paper and cut out the pattern for the back part of the surplice corset cover, following the traced and marked lines.

PETTICOATS

54. Kinds of Petticoats.—As regular foundation-skirt patterns are generally used in the development of petticoats, the drafting of such patterns is not considered here. The different styles are discussed, however, so that you may become familiar with them.

Petticoats are seldom made with a great number of gores. Even when closely fitted or many-gored outside skirts are in favor, petticoats are generally made with as few seam lines as will permit their proper cutting and fitting so that they will not mar the appearance of the outside skirt.

55. The **two-piece petticoat** seems to be the most favored of all styles, except at times when very full skirts are in vogue, undoubtedly because of the simplicity of its construction and the small amount of material required for developing it. The seam lines at the sides permit of a closely fitted effect for the average figure, and if the waist measurement is small in proportion to the hips, darts may be placed in the back to assist in the fitting.

When outside skirts are made with fulness at the waist line, the two-piece petticoat may likewise have fulness. Provide for this fulness as you would in making a pattern for an outside skirt; that is, instead of shaping the side seam line above the hip line, leave this straight, and then slash the pattern lengthwise in two or more places and separate the pieces the desired distance.

You may lay these pieces directly on the material when you are cutting out the garment or place them on a piece of paper large enough to accommodate the new skirt pattern. Also, in placing the pieces, you may separate them merely at the waist line, if you wish no extra fulness at the lower edge of the skirt, or, if you prefer a skirt even narrower than the foundation pattern, you may overlap the pieces at the lower edge enough to take out the surplus width.

56. The **three-piece petticoat** may be cut almost as economically as a two-piece skirt. This style has the advantage of an extra seam line at the back, which is slightly or decidedly bias, according to the width at the lower edge, and thus causes the skirt to fit into the figure more closely than it would if it were cut on a lengthwise fold of the material.

57. A **double-front petticoat**, which is desirable for wear under summer dresses, may be made with either a two- or a three-piece skirt pattern by cutting two front gores of exactly the same shape and size.

58. A **four-gored petticoat** is desirable when material less than half the width that the petticoat is to be made must be used in its development, for such a skirt may be cut from narrower material without piecing.

54

When flared skirts are in vogue, a four-gored pattern that will provide side-front and side-back seams rather than center-front, center-back. and side seams is preferable. Such a pattern permits the placing of each gore with its lengthwise center over a lengthwise thread of the material, thus making the seam lines of a uniform bias rather than one seam line much more decidedly bias than the other, and therefore avoiding any marked sagging tendency.

59. A **five-gored petticoat** made with a panel front and seams at the sides and center back is used only when flaring skirts are in vogue or the extra seam lines are required for a very close-fitting effect over the hips.

60. Flounce Patterns.—The general rule for making a petticoat-flounce pattern is to make this straight of the desired depth and one and one-half times as wide as the skirt to which it is to be applied.

If you wish to make a circular flounce, first outline a pattern on the lower edge of the skirt pattern with which you intend to use it, measuring up from the bottom the desired width all the way around the skirt pattern and then tracing the portion outlined for the flouncing. Slash the flounce pattern at comparatively close intervals from the lower edge almost to the top; then, to form the circular effect, pin this pattern to another piece of paper, separating the slashed edges an equal amount at the lower edge.

Fig. 12

NIGHTGOWNS

KIMONO NIGHTGOWN

61. To prepare the pattern for a kimono nightgown like that shown in Fig. 12, use the front part of the plain foundation-waist pattern. Either a pattern may be made or pattern lines may be drawn on the material. If a pattern is to be drafted, use a piece of paper 25 inches wide and $3\frac{1}{3}$ yards long, and do the work in the manner illustrated in Fig. 13. If paper is to be used, fold it through the center crosswise, keeping the long straight edges together; if the lines are to be made on the material, fold it first lengthwise through the center and then crosswise.

62. Pinning on the Foundation Pattern.—After the paper or the material has been folded, place it in front of you so that a long edge is next to you and the crosswise fold is to the left. This is a preparatory step in pinning the foundation pattern to the paper.

Pin the front of the plain-waist pattern at the left end, near the fold, as shown; that is, with the neck curve at the shoulder on the fold and the neck curve at the center-front line on the long edge of the paper, and also with the waist line at the center-front line 1 inch above the long edge of the paper, as shown in the illustration.

of the S. A. C. is at *B* and the edge of the L. A. C., near *m*, touches *C*.

NOTE.—This curve in some cases may appear a trifle pronounced, but it works out satisfactorily if the under-arm seam is stayed in making.

64. Determining the Length of the Nightgown. Determine the length that the gown is to be by measuring from the shoulder to the length you desire, and then, this distance from the fold of the paper, locate

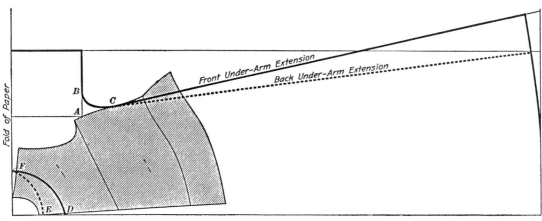

FIG. 13

63. Drafting the Sleeve.—To determine the sleeve width,

Locate:

 Point *A* by placing the square so that its short arm is on the crosswise fold of the paper or the material and the straight edge of the long arm touches the underarm line of the waist pattern at a point indicating one-half of the armhole measure, plus ½ inch, and marking point *A*. Before moving the square,

Draw:

 A vertical foundation line along the long arm to point *A*.

To determine the sleeve length,

Draw:

 A horizontal foundation line, placing the corner of the square at *A*, and its short arm on the line just drawn, extending the horizontal line usually to the edge of the paper or material. Then,

Locate:

 Point *B* while the square is still in the position for determining the sleeve length by measuring 2½ inches above *A*.

 Point *C* by measuring the under-arm line of the waist pattern from point *A* to the waist line and locating point *C* midway between these two points.

Draw:

 The under-arm curve, connecting points *B* and *C*, by placing the square so that *h*

a point on the lengthwise edge of the paper or the material.

From this point, draw a line that will be perpendicular to the lengthwise edge of the paper and serve as a foundation bottom line.

65. Determining the Width of the Nightgown. For small, slender figures, 36-inch material will give a width that is almost 2 yards at the lower edge and that will generally be sufficient. Therefore, for such a figure, it is necessary to draw the line for only the back skirt portion of the gown and then use this same line in cutting the front.

For a figure whose bust measure is more than 36 inches, a wider gown is desirable. Such a gown, however, does not really require any more material, because the material cut out at the armhole in goring the back portion will serve to piece the front width very nicely.

To complete the back of the gown, measure up from the lower right corner of the paper or the material, at the point indicating the length of the gown, one-half the width of the back of the gown.

Draw the back seam line, or back under-arm extension, by connecting this point and point *C* of the under-arm line with a diagonal line, in this case, the dotted line shown.

If the gown is to be wider in front than in back, then, to allow for addition of width, determine the width of the front by measuring up from the same point as for the back, or at the lower right corner of the paper or the material.

Since the width of the gown at the bottom is 2¼

yards, subtract the width of the back of the gown, which is the width of the material, in this case 36 inches, from the entire width of the gown; then, for the front, measure out one-half of the remainder of this

FIG. 14

distance, or $22\frac{1}{2}$ inches in this case, from the lower right corner of the paper or the material.

Draw the front seam line, or front under-arm extension, by connecting this point also with point C of the under-arm.

66. Making the Bottom Line Even.—Measure 1 inch to the left of the bottom on the back under-arm line, and then shorten the front under-arm line to make it the same in length as that for the back.

Connect these points with the foundation bottom line by means of a free-hand curve.

67. Drawing the Neck Lines.—Both the front- and the back-neck curves are drawn at this time.

Locate:

Point D 6 inches to the right of the fold.
Point E $3\frac{1}{2}$ inches to the right of the fold.
Point F 3 inches above the neck curve on the fold.

Draw:

The front-neck line by connecting points F and D with an arc, locating the center by trial.
The back-neck line by connecting points F and E with an arc. Fig. 13 illustrates the usual curves formed by these arcs.

68. Use the standard kimono-waist pattern as a foundation in developing the pattern for a raglan-sleeve nightgown like that shown in Fig. 14, unless you desire a very loose effect through the shoulder and armhole portion, when you may use the kimono-waist pattern that may be cut on a fold of the material. Fig. 15 illustrates the changes that must be made in the standard kimono pattern in order to develop the raglan-sleeve nightgown pattern.

69. Drafting the New Neck Line.—A lower neck line is used, so a new neck line must be drawn.

Locate:

Point A_2 on the center-back line $2\frac{1}{4}$ inches below the neck line.
Point B_2 on the center-front line 3 inches above the neck line.
Point C_2 on the fold that was made at the shoulder in the development of the original pattern, placing this point $2\frac{1}{2}$ inches from the neck line.

Draw:

Curve A_2C_2 by placing the square so that 5 of the F. C. is over C_2 and the curve, between 2 and 3, touches A_2.

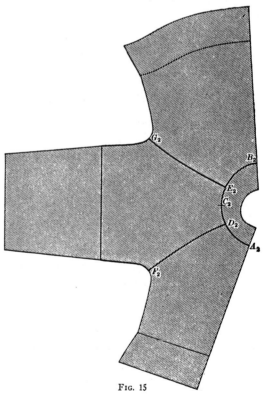

FIG. 15

Curve C_2B_2 by placing 5 of the F. C. over B_2 and letting the curve, near 2, touch C_2. If necessary, blend the curves at C_2 in order to make them pleasing.

NOTE.—The neck curves just drawn are satisfactory for a neck line of average depth. Either a higher or a lower neck line can be made by the use of parallel curves.

70. Drawing the Raglan Lines.—Two lines are drawn from the neck line to the under-arm curves.

Locate:

Points D_2 and E_2 on the new neck line, each 2 or $2\frac{1}{4}$ inches from C_2.

Points F_2 and G_2 in the center of the back and front under-arm curves, respectively, as shown.

Connect:

Points D_2 and F_2 by placing the square, with gg touching D_2 and the edge of the curve, beyond bb, touching F_2.

Points E_2 and G_2 by placing the square so that bb touches E_2 and the edge of the curve, beyond gg, touches point G_2.

71. Marking the Sleeve Length and Cutting the Draft Apart.—Mark the sleeve length as short as desired, and then form the pattern for the upper portion of the nightgown by cutting on all the new lines.

72. Making the Under-arm Extensions.—Make the under-arm extensions by pinning the pattern to a long piece of paper or directly to the material and drawing the lines and providing the skirt portion in practically the same manner as in forming the skirt portion of the kimono-nightgown pattern. In this case, however, make the front and the back portion separate.

LONG-SLEEVED NIGHTGOWN

73. For cutting a long-sleeved nightgown, use a plain-waist pattern as a foundation, deepen the armhole a trifle at the under arm, make large seam allowances at the armhole and under-arm edges, and extend the under-arm lines in much the same manner as directed for the development of the kimono nightgown, in Art. **63.**

In making the nightgown, take up only a normal allowance in the seams, thus leaving the remainder of the allowance to give necessary freedom, for a garment of this kind should fit looser than a shirtwaist.

For cutting the sleeves, use a one-piece sleeve pattern drafted to the measurement of the deepened armhole of the nightgown. The directions given for the shirt-waist sleeve in Art. **81,** Chapter II, will help you in drafting this sleeve. Make it with fulness at the wrist edge and at the armhole also, if you wish.

A nightgown having set-in sleeves is often made with a yoke effect. To provide this feature, outline a yoke of the depth you desire on the foundation pattern. This suggestion applies likewise to any other features you wish to embody in the nightgown. Simply outlining them on the foundation pattern, you will find to be an easy method of designing.

DRAWERS

PLAIN DRAWERS

74. Measurements.—In the drafting of the pattern for plain drawers with an embroidery ruffle, as shown in Fig. 16, only three measurements are used—

the waist, the hip, and the side length. The work is done in the manner shown in Fig. 17, the original draft being made according to the following measurements:

FIG. 16

	INCHES
Waist	26
Hip	38
Side length	22

75. To draft a pattern like this, procure a sheet of paper 30 inches wide and 44 inches long, fold it through the center crosswise, and then, with the folded edge next to you, proceed as follows:

76. Drawing Rectangle ABFE.—A rectangle must be drawn before this pattern is drafted.

Locate:

Point A 2 inches from the right edge of the paper, on the fold.

Point B one-half the hip measure minus 3 inches above A, placing the square with the short arm on the fold.

Point E the side length plus one-sixth the difference between the waist and the hip measures to the left of A.

Point F the same distance above E that B is above A.

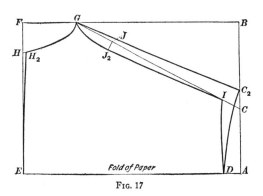

FIG. 17

77. Locating Construction Points for Back Waist Line.—Three points must be located for the back waist line.

Locate:

Point C one-fourth the waist measure above A.

Point C_2 2 inches above C on the line AB.

Point D on the fold one-sixth the difference between the waist and the hip measures to the left of A.

78. Drawing the Leg Portion and Lower Edge. To save time, both the leg portion and the bottom edge can be outlined at the same time.

Locate:

Point G one-fourth the length of line BF to the right of F.

Point H one-fifth the length of EF below F.

Connect:

Points G and H by placing the square so that the midway point between qq and rr is at G and the edge of the curve, near kk, is at H.

Locate:

Point H_2 $\frac{1}{2}$ inch to the right of point H on this curve.

Connect:

Points E and H_2 with a gradually curved free-hand line.

79. Drawing the Center-Back and Center-Front Lines.—The drawing of the center-back line forms the next step.

Connect:

Points C_2 and G with a heavy diagonal line.

To draw the center-front line, it is first necessary to connect points C and G with a light diagonal line.

Locate:

Point I to the left of C the same distance that A is from D plus $\frac{1}{2}$ inch.

Note.—If you are making the pattern for a person having prominent hips, it will be advisable to add $\frac{3}{4}$ to 1 inch to the length of line AD in order to locate point I. For a person having a comparatively straight figure, add only $\frac{1}{4}$ inch to the length of this line.

Point J one-fourth the length of GI on line GI to the right of G.

Point J_2 by placing the short arm of the square on line JI with its corner at J, and drawing a light line from J 1 inch long, lettering its termination J_2.

Connect:

Points J_2 and I with a heavy diagonal line and J_2 and G with a heavy curved line, placing the square with the point midway between i and j at G and the edge of the curve, near n, at J_2.

80. Drawing the Waist Line Curves.—Two different curves form the waist line.

Draw:

The back waist line by placing the square with gg at C_2 and the edge of the curve, near bb, at D, and connecting D and C_2 with a curved line.

The front waist line by placing the square with ff at I and the edge of the curve,

near bb, at D, and connecting D and I with a curved line.

Note.—When drafting to extremely large measurements, you will find it necessary to extend the waist-line curves slightly, moving the square along to give the proper curve.

81. Cutting the Draft Apart.—Without unfolding the paper, cut the draft from D to C_2; from C_2 to G; from G to H_2; and from H_2 to E.

Open out the draft and cut from D to I, and from I, through J_2, to G, in this instance cutting through only the one thickness of the paper on which the lines are marked.

82. Removing Fulness.—The pattern for plain drawers provides for a little fulness at the waist line. In most cases, such fulness is desirable, but if a fitted effect at the waist line is preferred, the extra fulness may be taken out by means of darts.

In order to place the dart in correct position for the individual figure, hold the pattern up to the figure and fit out the fulness by means of merely a back dart, if this will suffice. When the hips are very large, another dart, either at the center side or at the side front, will be found of aid in fitting out the fulness.

If preferred, the placing of darts may be postponed until during the fitting of the garment. In this case, the dart or darts on one side of the drawers should be carefully pinned and the darts on the other side afterwards placed in the same relative position and made of the same depth. An exception to this method is advisable if the hips are larger on one side than on the other, for this difference would necessitate variance in the depth of the darts, according to the degree of prominence of the hips at one side.

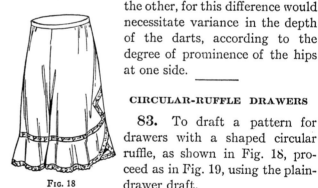

Fig. 18

CIRCULAR-RUFFLE DRAWERS

83. To draft a pattern for drawers with a shaped circular ruffle, as shown in Fig. 18, proceed as in Fig. 19, using the plain-drawer draft.

84. Outlining the Circular Ruffle.—In preparing the circular ruffle, certain points must be located.

Locate:

Point K on line EH_2 one-third the length of EH_2 above E.

Point L with the corner of the square at K, and the straight edge of the short arm along line KH_2 and measuring out on the long arm $3\frac{1}{2}$ inches, or the width that the ruffle is to be.

Point M 4 inches to the right of E on the fold of the paper.

Point N 3 inches to the right of M, also on the fold.

Point O 3½ inches to the right of H_2, placing the square so that the corner is at H_2, and its short arm is along KH_2, and then measuring out on the long arm.

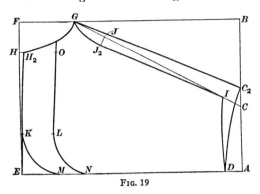

FIG. 19

85. Drawing the Curves.—To complete the outline of the ruffle,

Connect:

Points K and M with a curved line, placing the square so that 5 of the F. C. is at K and the portion of the curve between 2 and 3 touches M.

Points L and N in the same manner.

Points L and O with a diagonal line, extending it up to line H_2G.

86. Cutting the Draft Apart.—Cut off the ruffle-pattern portion, cutting through the double thickness of paper from N to L to O and on to line H_2G; then to H_2, and from H_2, through K, to M.

87. Making a Shaped Circular Ruffle.—Slash the ruffle pattern at close intervals from the lower edge almost to the upper edge, and, as shown in Fig. 20, pin the slashed ruffle portion to a piece of paper several inches larger than the ruffle pattern, separating the pieces at the lower edge to give the amount of flare you desire and keeping the upper edge intact in order that the top of the ruffle will be of exactly the same length as the lower edge of the drawers.

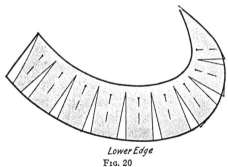

Lower Edge
FIG. 20

Then form the shaped circular-ruffle pattern by outlining the new lower edge with a smooth curved line to connect the sections, and cutting on the heavy lines that are illustrated.

88. Making a Plain Circular Ruffle.—To make a pattern for a plain circular ruffle, measure up from H_2 on line H_2G and to the right of E on line AE the width of the ruffle desired. Then connect these points with a straight line and cut the pattern off on this line.

Slash this ruffle portion, as directed for the shaped circular ruffle, separate the pieces at the lower edge to provide the amount of flare you desire, and cut out the circular ruffle.

––––––––

CIRCULAR DRAWERS

89. Slashing and Overlapping the Pattern.—To make a pattern for a pair of circular drawers, it is necessary simply to slash the plain-drawer pattern and then pin the slashed pattern to a sheet of paper, arranging the slashed pattern so as to obtain a circular effect.

With the pattern folded as it is drafted, divide the waist line and the bottom line, or line EH_2 of the plain-drawer pattern, into two equal parts.

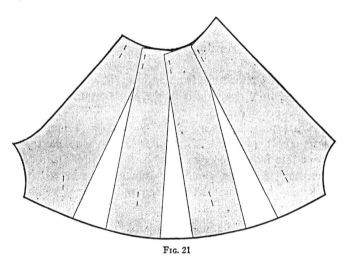

FIG. 21

Connect with a diagonal line the point thus made on the waist line and the point on the bottom line, and then trace on this new line.

Open the pattern and slash on the fold and then on the traced lines.

To form the circular effect, pin the pattern pieces to a sheet of paper in the manner shown in Fig. 21, separating the pieces at the lower edge from 3 to 5 inches, according to the amount of flare desired, and overlapping them at the waist line, provided you wish to remove some of the fulness here.

90. To determine the correct amount for the overlapping of the pieces at the waist line, measure the waist line of the pattern and subtract from this amount ¾ inch more than one-half the waist measurement according to which the pattern was developed. The ¾-inch fulness is advisable so that the bias edge may be slightly eased when it is applied to the waist-line band and thus prevent drawing or puckering of the material. If the amount of separation or overlapping of the pattern pieces is very great, the angles

59

that form at the waist line should be eliminated by blending the lines, thus forming a gradual curve, as in Fig. 21.

91. Cutting the Pattern.—After the pattern is pinned to the paper in the manner explained, form the pattern for the circular drawers by cutting on the regular pattern lines of the plain-drawer pattern, continuing the cutting in an even line from one slash to another along the entire lower edge.

YOKE PATTERN FOR DRAWERS

92. Drafting the Pattern.—In many cases, drawers must be provided with a yoke in order to fit smooth at the waist and hips and to overcome excessive fulness.

To make a yoke pattern for a pair of drawers, use the top of the circular-skirt pattern as a guide.

On the center-front line of this pattern, measure down from the waist line the depth of yoke desired in front, which is usually 3 to $3\frac{1}{2}$ inches, and on the center-back line measure down from the waist line the depth of yoke desired at the back, which, as a rule, is 2 inches.

Connect the point in front and that at the back with a curved line, drawing it in the same manner as the waist line was drawn.

Slip a piece of paper of the correct size under the skirt draft and trace as follows: On the center-front line from the yoke depth in the center front to the waist line; on the waist line and down to the yoke depth at the back; and then on the new yoke line to the yoke depth at the front.

93. Cutting the Pattern.—Form the yoke pattern by cutting on the traced line. Then, to make it possible to add the yoke to a pair of drawers without giving additional length to them, place the yoke pattern on the top of the drawer pattern, fold in the fulness until the top of the drawer pattern is just the same in size as the yoke pattern, and then cut the drawer pattern off at this point, being careful to obtain an even, unbroken line.

Fig. 22

KNICKERBOCKERS, OR BLOOMERS

94. Making the Pattern.—The plain-drawer pattern is used also in the development of a pattern for knickerbockers, or bloomers, which are illustrated in Fig. 22.

To make such a pattern, mark lines for slashing in the same manner as for the development of a pattern for circular drawers. Pin the pattern sections to another sheet of paper, as in Fig. 23, separating them their entire length an amount sufficient to provide the fulness desired.

95. Determining the Amount of Fulness.—The amount of fulness should be regulated to a certain extent by the material that is to be used and the purpose for which the garment is intended. Knickerbockers of jersey, or glove, silk are generally made

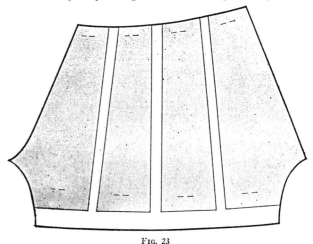

Fig. 23

with less fulness than those of more firmly woven materials. In no case are knickerbockers that are intended for wear in the place of drawers made with a great deal of fulness. However, bloomers intended for athletic or sports wear are generally made with considerable fulness laid in plaits at the waist line.

96. Securing the Blouse Effect of the Knee. Another point that must be considered in the development of a pattern for knickerbockers, or bloomers, is the extension of the length in order to provide a bloused effect at the knee. Make this extension, as shown in the illustration, by measuring down the desired amount from the lower edge of the leg portion. An extension of 2 inches is sufficient for a slightly bloused effect, but for athletic bloomers much more length is necessary. In any event, the amount of the extension should be gauged by the same factors that govern the amount of fulness.

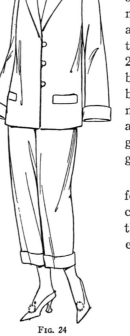

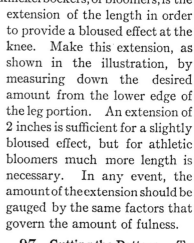

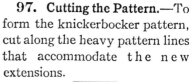

Fig. 24

97. Cutting the Pattern.—To form the knickerbocker pattern, cut along the heavy pattern lines that accommodate the new extensions.

PAJAMAS

FOUNDATION PATTERNS

98. Variation in pajama styles is generally afforded by the trimming rather than by any marked difference in cut. For this reason, in most cases, a plain-pajama pattern with few, if any, changes may be used for cutting such garments. The complete pattern for pajamas of the kind shown in Fig. 24 consists of trousers, coat, sleeve, and collar portions. The making of each of these pattern portions is considered in turn.

TROUSERS

99. The development of a pattern for the trousers, as shown in Fig. 25, is similar to the making of a pattern for plain drawers. In addition to the measurements required for a plain-drawer pattern, the length, at the side, from the waist line to the ankle is needed for pajamas.

100. Size of Paper.—Provide a piece of paper $1\frac{1}{4}$ to $1\frac{1}{2}$ yards long for this pattern. A width of 36 inches is sufficient for average measurements, but when the hip measurement is greater than 40 inches, more width is required. This width may be obtained by piecing, if necessary.

101. Locating Construction Points for Upper Portion.—Fold the paper through the center lengthwise, and then, with the folded edge next to you, proceed as in making the plain-drawer draft, locating all the points as directed for this draft, with the exception of point C, and omit the location of point H_2, for this is unnecessary in a pajama pattern.

Locate:

Point C, one-fourth the waist measurement, plus $2\frac{1}{2}$ inches, above point A instead of merely one-fourth the waist measurement above A.

> NOTE.—This allowance will provide more fulness through the waist and hip portions and thus make the pattern more desirable for a sleeping garment.

102. Drawing the Waist-Line Curves.—Draw the waist-line curves C_2D and ID in practically the same manner as in the development of the drawer pattern, even though point C and, consequently, point C_2, which is located 2 inches above C on line AB, are changed.

For large measurements, however, you will find it possible to draw only a part of each curve with the square in the positions suggested, for the curves of the square which are mentioned are not sufficiently long to extend to point D on the draft. In this case, complete the waist-line curves by moving the square along and blending the lines together in order to form a continuous and smoothly curved line for the waist line.

103. Drawing the Leg Portion.—For the extended leg portion in this pattern, two new points must be located.

Locate:

Point K on the fold to the left of point D a distance equal to the measurement that was taken from the waist line, at the side, to the ankle, or according to any other desired length.

Point L next. Measure the distance from point E to H on the draft, place the square with its short arm along the fold and its corner at K, and to form the lower edge of the leg portion, draw a line along the long arm equal in length to line EH, minus 2 inches, and letter its termination L.

Complete the draft by connecting L and H with a straight line.

104. Cutting the Draft Apart.—Form the pattern by cutting the draft through both thicknesses of the paper from D to C_2; from C_2 to G; from G, through H, to L; and from L to K.

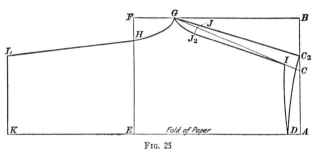

FIG. 25

Open out the draft and, as directed for forming the plain-drawer pattern, cut from D to I, and from I, through J_2, to G, in this instance cutting through only the one thickness of paper on which the lines are marked.

105. Providing the Trouser Cuffs.—The cuffs, which are used to finish the lower edge of the trousers, are merely straight pieces. If you wish to make a pattern for these, cut it about 2 inches wide and equal in length to the measurement of the lower edge of the leg portion.

THE COAT

106. A pattern for the coat portion of pajamas may be developed with the aid of the plain foundation-waist pattern, only a few simple changes being required in this pattern to make it entirely suitable.

Any kind of sleeping garment is, as a rule, made larger than other garments. It is especially necessary that the armhole be made larger and, for this reason, the sleeve seam may be made continuous with that of the under arm, and thus the construction of the garment simplified. It is only with a closely fitted armhole that you must use a sleeve having its curves so arranged that the seam must be placed in front of the under-arm seam of the waist.

107. Drafting the Back Section.—Pin the back section of the plain foundation-waist pattern to a piece of paper 5 or 6 inches wider and 9 to 12 inches longer than the pattern itself. Place the center back so that, at the neck line, it touches one lengthwise edge of the paper, as shown in Fig. 26, and at the waist line it is $\frac{3}{4}$ inch from the edge of the paper, thus supplying the fulness that was removed at the center back in the development of the plain foundation-

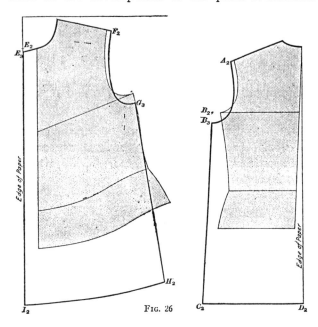

FIG. 26

waist pattern. Let the surplus length of paper extend below the foundation pattern.

Locate:

Point A_2 by extending the back-shoulder line $\frac{1}{2}$ inch.

Point B_2 1 inch to the left of the intersection of the bust and under-arm lines. This will give more fulness in the back.

Point B_3 1 inch below B_2, as a larger armhole is provided by using this point.

Draw:

The new armhole curve from A_2 to B_3, placing the square so that the arrow point of the S. A. C. is at B_3 and the edge of the curve, near tt, touches A_2.

The under-arm line, a straight line, flaring this from point B_3 an amount sufficient to produce the desired width at the lower edge and extending it below the waist line to give the desired length.

Locate:

Point C_2 by lettering the termination of this line C_2.

NOTE.—As a rule, the width at the lower edge in the back portion of a pattern of this kind is made 2 to 4 inches greater than the length of the bust line of the back portion of the foundation pattern. The length is usually made from 9 to 13 inches below the waist line and is extended on an even line all around the figure.

Point D_2 by measuring below the waist line at the center back the same distance that point C_2 was located below the waist line at the side. At the same time, draw the center-back line.

Draw:

The lower edge of the pattern by connecting C_2 and D_2 with a straight line.

108. Drafting the Front Section.—Pin the front section of the plain foundation-waist pattern to a piece of paper that is from 6 to 9 inches wider than the length of the bust line on the draft and 6 to 9 inches longer than the pattern itself.

To provide for an overlap at the center front, place the center front of the pattern $1\frac{1}{2}$ inches from the left lengthwise edge of the paper and exactly parallel with this edge; let the surplus length extend below the foundation pattern.

109. To draw the new neck line, points E_2 and E_3 must be located.

Locate:

Point E_2 by placing the square with its long arm along the center front of the foundation pattern and its corner at the intersection of the neck and center-front lines, and placing E_2 where the edge of the short arm crosses the edge of the paper.

Point E_3 $\frac{3}{8}$ inch below E_2.

Draw:

The neck line by connecting point E_3 and the intersection of the neck and center-front lines with a slightly curved line.

110. To draw the new armhole line, points F_2 and G_3 must be located:

Locate:

Point F_2 $\frac{1}{2}$ inch to the right of J_2 on the foundation draft.

Point G_3 1 inch below the intersection of the bust line and under-arm line.

Draw:

The front-armhole curve by placing the square so that tt is at G_3 and the edge of the curve, near jj, touches F_2.

111. To draw the under-arm line, point H_2 must be located.

Locate:

Point H_2 by flaring the under-arm line from point G_3 an amount sufficient to give the desired width at the lower edge. Make this line the same in length as line B_3C_2 of the back portion and letter its termination H_2.

NOTE.—As a rule, the width at the lower edge is made 3 to 7 inches greater than the length of the bust line of the front portion of the foundation pattern, this amount including the extension at the center front.

112. To determine the center-front length, point I_2 must be located.

Determine the distance below the waist line that the pattern should extend at the center front, subtracting 1 to 2 inches from the distance that C_2 of the back portion was located below the waist line at the side.

You will readily understand the reason for subtracting from the side length when you consider that 1 inch was added to the front measurement in the drafting of the plain foundation-waist pattern in order to provide for a slightly bloused effect which, of course, is unnecessary for a coat effect that is intended to hang straight without any blouse. Then, too, additional length may be taken from the front if the hips are at all prominent, for most figures have a difference of 1 inch or more between the side and the front dart lengths.

Locate:

Point I_2 on the left edge of the paper the distance you determine it should be below the waist line.

Draw:

The bottom curve by connecting I_2 and H_2 with a smooth curved line.

113. Tracing and Cutting the Draft Apart.—Trace the pattern lines of the coat draft, which are drawn directly on the foundation pattern, and outline the center-front line and the shoulder and the neck lines of the front and back foundation-pattern portions.

Remove the foundation patterns and cut the *back*, starting at the center-back neck line and cutting along the shoulder line to A_2, from A_2 along the armhole curve to B_3, from B_3 to C_2, and from C_2 to D_2.

Cut the *front* portion from I_2 to H_2, from H_2 to G_3, from G_3 along the armhole curve to F_2, from F_2 along the shoulder line, and then following the neck curve and on to E_3.

---

114. New Measurements Necessary.—As the sleeve of the coat portion of the pajamas should fit exactly into the armhole without any fulness whatever, the armhole measurement to be used in drafting the sleeve pattern must be determined by measuring the armhole of the coat pattern; that is, the regular armhole measurement should not be used. Therefore, before you start to draft the sleeve pattern, to insure accuracy, measure with a tape line the armhole of both the front and the back part of the coat pattern from the shoulder to the under-arm lines. Then proceed with the drafting, being guided by Fig. 27.

The size of paper to use is 24 inches wide and 27 inches long.

115. Drawing the Top of the Sleeve.—Before the armhole curves can be drawn, a number of points must be located.

Locate:

Point A 6 inches from the right edge of the fold when the paper is folded lengthwise through the center and placed so that the fold is next to you.

Point B by placing the square so that its corner is at A and its short arm is on the fold, and drawing a light line along the long arm, making it one-half the armhole measurement of the coat, minus 1 inch.

Point C one-fifth the armhole measurement of the coat, plus $\frac{1}{2}$ inch, to the right of point A, using the scale of fifths for this purpose.

Point D by connecting points C and B with a light diagonal line and finding the point midway between these points.

Point E by placing the square with its corner at D and its short arm along line BC and drawing a light line $\frac{1}{2}$ inch long out from D.

Draw:

The upper armhole curve of the sleeve next, placing the square so that r of the L. A.

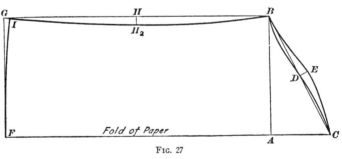

Fig. 27

C. is at E and the edge of the curve, near t, touches C; then move the square until n of the L. A. C. is at B and the edge, near r, touches E, and connect B and E.

The lower armhole curve by placing j of the L. A. C. at B and letting the edge of the curve, near o, touch D. Then move the square until q of the L. A. C. is at D and the edge of the curve, near t, is at C and connect D and C.

116. Drawing the Lower Sleeve Portion.—This includes the seam and wrist curves.

Locate:

Point F on the fold the inside sleeve length to the left of A.

Point G, with the corner of the square at point B and the short arm along line AB, drawing a line along the long arm equal

63

in length to the inside sleeve measurement, or the distance from A to F.

Point H midway between G and B.

Point H_2 $\frac{1}{2}$ inch directly below H.

Draw:

The inside curve by placing the square with u of the L. A. C at B and the curve, beyond y, touching H_2 and connecting B and H_2; then by moving the square until u is at H_2 and the curve, beyond y, touches G and connecting points H_2 and G.

Locate:

Point I $\frac{1}{2}$ inch to the right of G on line GH_2.

Draw:

The wrist curve by placing u of the L. A. C. at F and letting the edge of the curve, near y, touch I.

117. Cutting the Sleeve Draft Apart.—Form the pattern by cutting the draft through both thicknesses of the paper from C to E to B; from B, through H_2, to I; and from I to F. Then open out the pattern and cut through only one thickness of the paper on the lower armhole curve from C to D to B.

This lower curve should join the front of the coat, which is just the reverse of the manner of placing the plain foundation sleeve in the armhole. You will do well to keep this fact in mind so that no difficulty will be encountered in the construction of the garment.

118. The Sleeve Cuffs.—The sleeve cuffs, like those of the trousers, are straight. Cut the pattern for these about 2 inches wide; that is, the same width as the pattern for the trouser cuffs, and of a length that corresponds to the measurement of the lower edge of the sleeve.

COLLAR

119. Drafting a Sailor Collar.—An ordinary type of sailor collar is frequently used on pajamas. To make the pattern for such a collar, which may be joined so as to turn back with the fronts, follow the method illustrated in Fig. 28. The size of paper necessary is 20 inches long and 12 inches wide.

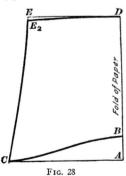

Fig. 28

120. Determining the Neck Line.—Fold the paper crosswise through the center and place the edge at the right.

Locate:

Point A at the lower right-hand corner.

Point B $1\frac{1}{2}$ inches above A on the fold.

Point C with the corner of the square at B, adjusting it until a point on the long arm indicating one-half the neck measure, plus $1\frac{1}{2}$ inches, or the width of the extension made beyond the center front of the coat pattern, touches the lower edge of the paper.

Draw:

The neck line by placing the square with m of the L. A. C. at B and the edge of the curve, near t, touching C.

121. Drawing the Outline of the Collar.—This includes the side and back edges.

Locate:

Point D on the fold the desired depth of the collar, in this case 8 inches above point B.

Point E with the short arm of the square on the fold and the corner at point D, drawing a line along the long arm equal in length to one-half the width-of-back measure, minus $\frac{1}{2}$ inch.

Connect:

Points E and C by placing the square with z of the L. A. C. at C and the edge of the curve, near u, touching E.

Locate:

Point E_2 $\frac{1}{4}$ inch below E on line EC.

Connect:

Points E_2 and D by placing the square with aa of the L. A. C. at E_2 and letting the edge of the curve, near dd, touch point D.

122. Cutting the Draft Apart.—Form the pattern by cutting the draft through both thicknesses of paper from B to C, from C to E_2, and from E_2 to D.

123. Drafting a Roll Collar.—A roll-collar pattern in round or pointed outline may be formed in much the same manner as a sailor collar, it being necessary merely to change the outline; the original neck line, that is, line BC, may be retained.

COMBINATION SUITS

ENVELOPE CHEMISE

124. The only real difference between the simple chemise and the envelope chemise, which is shown in Fig. 29, lies in the lower part of the garment, the simple chemise being open and the envelope chemise having a flap that fastens at the front and thus serves to close the garment, as shown. The drafting of patterns for both is therefore considered at one time.

125. Size of Paper for Back Portion.—To draft the pattern for the usual type of chemise, which may be made plain or with an extension at the bottom for the envelope style, the size of paper necessary is 54 inches, or $1\frac{1}{2}$ yards long and 20 inches wide.

126. Determining Construction Points for Back Armhole and Neck Curve.—A number of construction points are required for these curves.

Locate:

Point *A* with one long edge of the paper toward you, as shown in Fig. 30, measuring in 3 inches from its right edge and up 4 inches from its bottom edge.

Point *B* with the corner of the square at *A*, and its short arm parallel to the long edge of the paper that is toward you, drawing along the long arm a line equal in length to one-half the width-of-back measure plus $2\frac{1}{2}$ inches.

Point *C* one-fourth the width-of-back measure below *B*.

Point *D* $1\frac{1}{2}$ inches below *C*.

Point *E* with the corner of the square at *A*, and its short arm on line *AB*, drawing along the long arm a line that is equal in length to one-half the armhole measure minus $\frac{1}{2}$ inch.

Point *F* with the short arm of the square on the line *AE*, drawing along the long arm a vertical line of the same length as line *AB*, or one-half the width-of-back measure plus $2\frac{1}{2}$ inches.

Connect:

Points *F* and *B* with a horizontal line.

Draw:

Curve *FC*, placing the square so that *h* of the S. A. C. is at *F* and the edge of the L. A. C., near *q*, touches *C*.

Curve *ED* by swinging an arc, locating the center for the arc by trial and at a point below *A*.

127. Drawing the Back Under-Arm Line.—For a chemise without a cap,

Locate:

Point *G* with the corner of the square at *A*, and its long arm on line *AE*, marking *G* at the point that is the length-of-back measure to the left of *A*.

Point *H* with the corner of the square at *G* and its long arm resting on line *AG*, drawing along the short arm a line that is equal in length to one-fourth the waist measure plus 2 inches.

Draw:

The under-arm line by placing the square so that *ff* of the L. A. C. is at *H* and the edge of the curve, near *bb*, touches *F*.

128. Back Extension for Armhole Cap.—If an armhole cap is desired,

Locate:

Point F_2 by extending line *EF* $1\frac{1}{2}$ inches above *F*.

Draw:

A new armhole curve, shown dotted, from F_2 to *C*, placing the square so that *hh* of the L. A. C. is at F_2 and the edge of the curve, near *dd*, touches *C*.

A new under-arm line, shown dotted, placing the square so that *qq* of the S. A. C. is at F_2 and the edge of the L. A. C., near *ii*, touches *H*.

129. Drawing the Center-Back Line.—Some of the fulness is first removed from the center back.

Locate:

Point G_2 by measuring $\frac{1}{2}$ inch above point *G*.

Connect:

Points G_2 and *E* with a diagonal line.

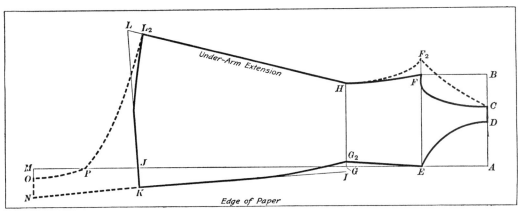

FIG. 30

130. Drafting the Lower Center-Back Line.—Additional width is provided in the lower back section, necessitating a change in the center-back line.

Locate:

Point *I* $\frac{1}{2}$ inch below *G*.

Point J to the left of G a distance equal to the side-length measurement, placing the corner of the square at G and its short arm on line GH, and then drawing a line of the required length along the long arm.

Point K 2 inches below J.

Draw:

The center-back line by connecting points K and G_2 with a diagonal line and a curve. For this curve, place the square so that aa of the L. A. C. is at G_2 and the edge of the curve, near ee, touches line IK, and connect G_2 and line IK with a curved line.

131. Drawing Bottom Line and Under-Arm Extension.—It is necessary first to locate a construction point.

Locate:

Point L with the corner of the square at K and its short arm on line KI, drawing along the long arm a line equal to one-fourth the desired width at the bottom, and lettering its termination L.

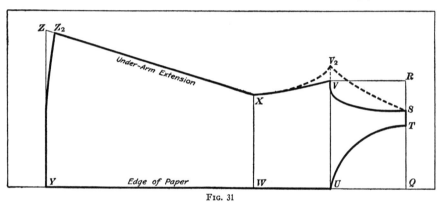

FIG. 31

Connect:

Points L and H with a diagonal line.

Locate:

Point L_2 by measuring on line HL the side length to the left of H.

Connect:

Point L_2 and line KL with a curved line, placing the square so that z of the L. A. C. is at L_2 and letting the edge of the curve, near v, touch line KL.

132. Drafting the Envelope Extension.—In a chemise of this kind, an extension must be made at the bottom.

Locate:

Point M by extending line GJ 11 inches to the left of J.

Point N 3 inches below M, placing the corner of the square at M and its short arm on line JM, and then drawing a 3-inch line along the long arm.

Connect:

Points N and K with a diagonal line.

Locate:

Point O 2 inches above N on line MN.

Point P midway between M and J, on line MJ.

Connect:

Points L_2 and P with a curved line, placing the square so that aa of the L. A. C. is at L_2 and the edge of the curve, near ii, touches P.

Points P and O in a similar way, adjusting the square so that ff touches P and the edge of the curve, near ii, touches O.

133. Cutting the Draft Apart.—Cut from E to D, from D to C, from C to F, and from F to H; or, if the sleeve cap is to be used, cut from C to F_2 and from F_2 to H.

Then, for the envelope chemise, cut from H to L_2; from L_2, through P, to O; from O to N; from N, through K, to G_2; and from G_2 to E.

If the chemise is to be made without the extension, simply cut from H to L_2; from L_2, through J, to K; from K to G_2; and from G_2 to E.

Also, if you desire to make the chemise without a seam in the center back of the portion below the waist line, cut from K on the straight line to I, rather than on the curve to G_2, and cut straight across from I to G_2. Then, in laying the pattern on the material, lay the edge corresponding to line NI on a lengthwise fold.

If you do not object to fulness at the waist line, you need not cut away the material from I to G_2; if you do cut it away, fold under the fulness at IG_2 to make an inverted plait.

134. Size of Paper for the Front Section.—Provide a sheet of paper 18 inches wide and 45 inches long.

135. Determining the Front-Armhole and-Neck Curves.—Before drawing the front-armhole and-neck curves,

Locate:

Point Q by placing the paper so that one long edge is next to you, as shown in Fig. 31, and measuring in 3 inches from the right end of the paper.

Point R with one straight edge of the square on the long edge of the paper and its corner at Q, drawing a vertical line from Q and making it one-fourth the bust measure, plus 2 inches.

Point S one-fourth the chest measure, minus $\frac{1}{2}$ inch, below R on line QR.

Point T $1\frac{1}{2}$ inches below S.

Point U one-half the armhole measure, plus $\frac{1}{2}$ inch, to the left of Q.

Point V by placing the corner of the square on U and drawing a line above this point at a right angle to line QU, making it one-fourth the bust measure, plus 2 inches. It may be well to bear in mind that lines QR and UV must be the same length.

Connect:

Points V and R with a horizontal line.

Draw:

Curve VS, the armhole curve, by placing the square so that h of the S. A. C. is at V and the edge of the L. A. C., near r, touches S.

Curve UT, by swinging an arc, locating the center of the arc by trial and at a point below point Q.

136. Drawing the Under-Arm Line.—Two points must first be located.

Locate:

Point W on the edge of the paper to the left of U, placing it the same distance from U that G is from E on the back portion of the pattern.

Point X directly above W by drawing a line at right angles to W equal to one-fourth the waist measure, plus 3 inches.

NOTE.—For a person having a prominent bust, you will find it advisable to drop point W from $\frac{1}{2}$ to 1 inch after locating point X and then connect the new point W and X with a smoothly curved line. This method will provide extra length in the upper front portion.

Draw:

The under-arm line by placing the square so that ff of the L. A. C. is at X and the edge of the curve, near bb, touches V.

137. Front-Armhole Extension for Cap.—If a cap is desired on the armhole of the chemise, extend line UV $1\frac{1}{2}$ inches above V to locate point V_2, and then

Draw:

A new armhole curve, as shown by the dotted line, from V_2 to S, placing the square so that hh of the L. A. C. is at point V_2 and the edge of the curve, near cc, touches point S.

A new under-arm line, shown dotted, from V_2 to X, placing the square, still U. S. up, so that qq of the S. A. C. is at V_2 and the edge of the L. A. C., near ii, touches X.

138. Drafting the Lower Section of the Chemise.

Locate:

Point Y on the long edge of the paper, measuring to the left of W a distance equal to the side length, or the length that the chemise is to be below the waist line.

Point Z directly above Y by drawing a line at a right angle to line WY equal to one-fourth the width of the chemise at the bottom.

Connect:

Points Z and X with a diagonal line.

Locate:

Point Z_2 by measuring to the left of X on line XZ the side length.

Connect:

Point Z_2 and line YZ with a curve, placing the square so that z of the L. A. C. is at Z_2 and letting the edge of the curve, near u, touch line YZ.

139. Cutting the Draft Apart.—Form the pattern by cutting from U to T; from T to S; from S to V; from V to X; from X to Z_2; and from Z_2 to Y.

If the sleeve cap is to be used, cut from S to V_2 and from V_2 to X.

_____

SEMIFITTED PRINCESSE COMBINATION SUIT

140. In the preparation of the pattern for the combination suit shown in Fig. 32, which is moderately close-fitting, and has, in addition to under-arm seams, center-front, center-back, side-front, and side-back seams, the semi-fitting princesse foundation draft, Fig. 5, Chapter V, must be used.

141. Preparing the Paper. To begin, paste on both the back and the front of the princesse pattern, a piece of paper that is 10 or 12 inches wide and as long as the side measure. The lines for the drawers are made as shown in Fig. 33.

142. Drafting the Back Extension.—The back section is the first to be drafted.

FIG. 32

Locate:

Point A_2, placing the square so that its corner is at C and its long arm is on the foundation back line and drawing an 8- or a 10-inch line along the short arm to the right of C. Then, using the scale of fourths, measure on this line one-fourth of the original waist measure for A_2.

Point B_2 with the corner of the square at A_2, and its short arm on line CA_2, drawing along the long arm a line equal in length to the length of the side measure.

Point C_2 on line T_2W_2, or the line directly below T_2, measuring down the side length and locating point C_2.

Connect:

Points B_2 and C_2 with a straight line.

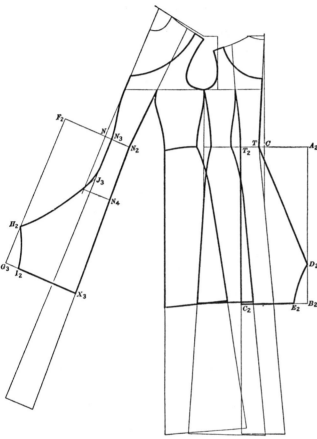

FIG. 33

Locate:

Point D_2 on line A_2B_2 one-fourth the side length from B_2.

Point E_2 2 inches to the left of B_2 on the line B_2C_2.

Connect:

Points D_2 and E_2 with a curved line, placing the square so that jj of the L. A. C. is at D_2 and the edge of the curve, between gg and ff, is at E_2.

Points T and D_2 with a diagonal line.

143. Drawing the Side-Back and Side-Front Sections.—Measure down on the extension of lines U_2S_2, US, VY_2, and V_3Y a distance equal to the side length and connect the corresponding lines at the bottom.

144. Determining the Front Section.—The front section of the drawers is to be drawn in practically the same manner as the back section. Therefore,

extend the waist line 8 to 10 inches to the left of N, placing the square so that the straight edge of the long arm is on the waist line already drawn.

Locate:

Point F_2, on the extended waist line, one-fourth of the waist measure to the left of N.

Point G_3 by turning the square around, placing its corner at F_2 and its short arm on line NF_2 and drawing along the long arm a line equal in length to the length of the side measure.

Point X_3 by measuring down on line N_2N_4 the side length below N_2.

Connect:

Points G_3 and X_3 with a diagonal line.

Locate:

Point H_2 one-fourth of the side measure from G_3 on line G_3F_2.

Point I_2 2 inches to the right of G_3 on line G_3X_3.

Connect:

Points H_2 and I_2 with a curved line, placing the square so that r of the L. A. C. is at H_2 and the edge of the square, near u, is at I_2.

145. Drawing the Center-Front Curve.

Locate:

Point J_3 by measuring down 6 inches on line N_3X_2, or the center-front line of the draft.

Connect:

Points H_2 and J_3 with a curve, placing the square so that aa is at J_3 and the edge of the curve, near gg, touches H_2.

To ease the curve just drawn a trifle, measure 2 inches above J_3 on line N_3J_3 and 2 inches below J_3 on curve H_2J_3 and connect these two points with a curved line, placing the square so that gg of the L. A. C. is at a point below J_3 and the edge of the curve, near ee, is at a point above J_3.

146. Cutting the Draft Apart.—Form the pattern by cutting from I_2 to H_2 to N_3; from I_2 to X_3; and from X_3 to N_2. Paste an extra piece of paper under the side-back section, letting it extend to the bottom of the draft; then trace this section and continue to cut the draft apart. Cut the back from E_2 to D_2 to T and then from E_2 to C_2 and from C_2 to T_2.

Cut the waist portion according to the directions previously given for cutting the tight-fitting waist.

———

SEMIFITTING PRINCESSE SLIP

147. Changes in Foundation Princesse Measurements.—The foundation princesse pattern without any change is suitable for cutting only a princesse garment that you wish to be very close-fitting. If you desire a semifitting garment, such as the princesse slip illustrated in Fig. 34, make provision in drafting the pattern; that is, to provide freedom through the body part of the garment, add 2 inches to the original bust measure, 1 inch to the waist measure, and 1 inch to the hip measure.

If you prefer to have the slip still looser, add a sufficient amount to the bust, waist, and hip measures to provide for the desired fulness.

If you wish to have the garment less full around its lower edge, decrease each gore from $\frac{1}{2}$ to $2\frac{1}{2}$ inches on its outside lower edge, making the decrease proportionately on each one, so as to keep the gores well balanced.

148. Cutting the Semifitting Draft Apart.—In cutting the semifitting princesse draft apart, do not shape the pattern in at the waist line in the center front and center back; rather, cut it on the foundation lines, so that the center front and the

FIG. 34

center back of the pattern may be placed on the fold of the material and made without a seam.

149. Varying the Semifitting Pattern.—When comparatively narrow skirts are in vogue, semifitting princesse slips are sometimes made with the front in one piece and darts running from the bust point to the lower edge of the skirt, and the back with a seam at the center back rather than with seams at each side back.

In forming the pattern for such a style, follow the general principles for developing a semifitting princesse pattern, but omit the side-back seams. Mark the front dart line on the pattern, following the line suggested for the side-front seam line of the center-front section, and bring the front under-arm seam in as close as you desire.

PRINCESSE SLIP WITH THREE-PIECE BACK

150. Extending the Lines.—It is seldom necessary to fit a princesse slip so close that the three-piece-back, close-fitting pattern must be used in its development. In case you wish to make such a pattern, however, you may be guided by the rules given for extending lines TW, T_2W_2, U_2S_3, V_3Y, N_2X_3, and N_3X_2, in the princesse pattern just considered, and then follow these instructions for extending the remainder of the lines.

Extend:

Line R_2Z by first locating a point midway between R and U and then placing the square with its corner at this point and the straight edge of the long arm touching point Z and drawing a line of the required length beyond point Z.

Line US by placing the square so that its corner is at the point located between R and U and its straight edge touches point S and drawing a line of the required length.

Line R_4Z_2 by placing the square with its corner at point R_4 and the straight edge touching point Z_2 and then drawing a line of the desired length.

Line VY_3 by placing the square with its corner at point R_3 and the long edge touching point Y_3 and drawing a line of the required length.

NOTE.—In extending any of these lines, you need not follow instructions precisely; instead, extend the lines in the manner that seems to blend best with the curves above the hip line and also gives the amount of flare you desire in the skirt portion.

REVIEW QUESTIONS

(1) What general advantages of drafting apply to the making of patterns for undergarments?

(2) How is it possible to gain ideas for lingerie designing?

(3) What is the advantage of preserving foundation underwear patterns?

(4) What foundation draft is used in the development of a plain corset-cover pattern?

(5) What sort of sleeve pattern should be used in the cutting of a long-sleeve nightgown?

(6) How may fulness at the waist line of plain drawers be eliminated?

(7) How may a yoke pattern for drawers be formed?

(8) Tell briefly the procedure in the development of a pattern for knickerbockers or bloomers.

(9) Why may the sleeve seam of pajamas be made continuous with that of the under arm?

(10) What precautions in regard to the armhole measurement must be taken to insure a correct sleeve pattern for pajamas?

CHAPTER VII

PATTERNS FOR APRONS AND CAPS

APRON-PATTERN DESIGNING

1. Apron-pattern designing, although it is not nearly so intricate and does not include so many possibilities as dress-pattern designing, is nevertheless a fascinating subject, principally because of the practical appeal of aprons and the happiness and pride that almost every woman feels in the development of something that is a bit novel in a domestic need. Also, as apron-pattern designing provides an outlet for original ideas, it is of much value, not only because of the immediate results it accomplishes, but also because of the broadened training and the self-assurance that it gives in designing.

2. **Applying Apron Instructions.**—In this chapter, you will find explicit directions for various types of house and fancy aprons and caps. As these are all very practical styles, you may find that they fit into your needs particularly well and think that it is, therefore, not necessary for you to experiment in the development of other styles. It is advisable for you to study carefully the principles involved in the development of these patterns and to try out the instructions so as to gain a better understanding of the reasons for locating the various points.

In addition, however, you should gain just as much experience as possible in applying these drafting and designing principles in the development of other styles of aprons. Following detailed instructions will impress the principles on your mind, but applying these instructions in working out designs different from those which are illustrated will give you the self-confidence and the broad knowledge that are essential to successful designing.

3. **Acquiring Apron Ideas.**—As to apron ideas, you will find them on every side. Many fashion publications, catalogs, and advertisements illustrate styles that should prove of help and inspiration to you; besides, you may gain ideas from many dress designs and adapt them to the purpose for which you wish to use them. Do not consider lightly a suggestion that a friend or a neighbor may have to offer. Ideas that come from the home woman are frequently of decided value, for they are usually a result of the experience she has had in wearing aprons and are therefore of a very practical nature.

Keep ever in mind the thought of practicability in the development of apron patterns. Originality is,

of course, a very worth-while aim, but only when it is worked out in a practical way is it a real asset in apron development.

4. **Value of Muslin or Paper Models.**—In designing apron patterns, you need not rely upon flat designing, or the use of the square, alone. Rather, you will find that you can best develop some styles by modeling with muslin or soft, yielding paper that does not tear readily, oftentimes using a foundation waist pattern or one of the apron patterns illustrated in this chapter as a basis for forming the new pattern.

Muslin is somewhat more satisfactory than paper for modeling, but unless a number of aprons are to be made from the pattern, the cost of the muslin is hardly justified except for the experience it gives. After you have developed a muslin or a paper model, you will find that the square will help you to work out rules for drafting the same design according to any set of measurements.

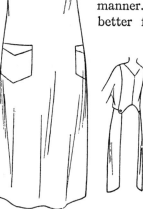

Fig. 1

5. **Selling Apron Patterns.**—If you wish to make a business of developing patterns or to take orders merely for apron patterns, you will find it a good plan to have on display an apron of each of the designs you have to offer made up in attractive material and trimmed in an unusual manner. A customer can always tell better from a completed garment than from the pattern whether or not it is one she would like to have.

SERVICE APRONS

ONE-PIECE, COVER-ALL APRON

6. The apron shown in Fig. 1 is a practical slip-over model that "sets" especially well on the figure without any tendency to slip up in the front, provided it is developed over a correctly fitting foundation pattern. A seam joins the center-back edges and extensions lap over the corners of the skirt portion of the apron. Patch pockets with a turn-over section may be applied if desired.

70

7. Altering Foundation Patterns.—As a foundation for developing a pattern for this apron, use a plain-waist pattern that is correct in every detail for the person for whom the apron is intended. If the front portion of the waist pattern seems very broad at the waist line, fold a dart from the lower edge almost to the shoulder line, as shown in Fig. 2, removing from 1 to $2\frac{1}{2}$ inches in this dart. This precaution is advisable for all figures except those having a compara-

Curve V_3G_3 with qq at V_3, and adjusting the square until the edge of the L. A. C., near ii, is at G_3.

Curve G_3K_2 by placing z of the L. A. C. at K_2, with the edge of the curve, near v, touching G_3.

Curve K_2B_2 by placing the square so that ee of the L. A. C. is at K_2 and the edge, near hh, touches B_2.

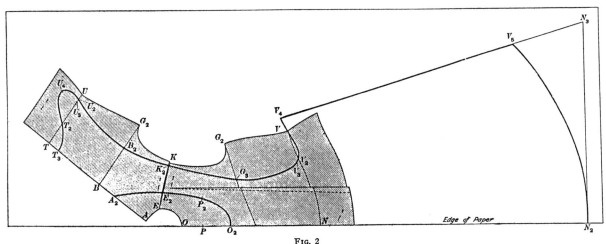

FIG. 2

tively flat bust, as it prevents the skirt portion from falling out from the figure at the center front.

With the dart folded in position and one long edge of the paper toward you, pin the pattern pieces, as shown, to a sheet of paper 2 to $2\frac{1}{4}$ yards long and 1 yard wide, placing the center front along one edge of the paper a skirt length from the right-hand end, and the back so that its shoulder line meets the front shoulder line and the neck edges are even. If it is not convenient for you to obtain one sheet of paper large enough for the development of this pattern, paste or sew several pieces of wrapping paper together to form a sheet of sufficient size.

8. Outlining the Outer Edge of the Bib Portions. A number of points must be located before the curves can be drawn.

Locate:

Point V_2 on the front waist line 4 inches below V of the foundation pattern.

Point V_3 $\frac{3}{8}$ inch to the left of V_2.

Point G_3 on the bust line one-eighth the bust measure below G_2.

Point K_2 on the shoulder line $\frac{3}{8}$ inch below K.

Point B_2 on the bust line one-half the width-of-back measure minus $1\frac{1}{2}$ inches above B.

Point U_2 on the waist line $\frac{5}{8}$ inch below U.

Draw:

Curve VV_3 by placing the square so that qq of the L. A. C. is at V_3 and the edge of the curve, near uu, touches V.

Curve B_2U_2 by sliding the square along until ee is at B_2 and the edge of the curve, near ii, is at U_2.

9. Outlining the Tab Portion.—Four points must be located and three curves drawn for the tab portion in the back.

Locate:

Point U_3 on the waist line 1 inch below point U.

Point U_4 $2\frac{1}{4}$ inches to the left of U_3, placing the square with its corner at point U_3 and its straight edge along the waist line.

Point T_2 on the waist line one-sixth the width-of-back measure, plus $\frac{1}{2}$ inch, or, for very large figures, 1 or $1\frac{1}{2}$ inches, above T.

Point T_3 on the center-back line $1\frac{1}{2}$ inches to the right of T.

Draw:

Curve U_2U_4, placing the square with rr of the S. A. C. at U_4 and the edge of the curve, near pp, at U_2.

Curve U_4T_2 by sliding the square around until qq is at U_4 and the edge of the curve, near uu, touches T_2.

Curve T_2T_3 by sliding the square back until xx of the S. A. C. is at T_3 and the edge of the curve, near uu, is at T_2.

10. Drawing the Neck Line.—For the deep oval neck line in this apron,

Locate:

Point A_2 on the center-back line 5 inches to the left of point A.

Point E_2 on the shoulder line 2 inches above point E.

Point P_2 one-fourth the chest measurement directly above point P of the foundation pattern.

Point O_2 on the center-front line 6 inches to the right of point O.

Draw:

Curve A_2E_2 by placing the square so that dd of the L. A. C. is at A_2 and the edge of the curve, near gg, touches E_2.

Curve E_2P_2 by sliding the square along until ff is at P_2 and the edge of the curve, near cc, touches E_2.

Curve P_2O_2 by placing yy of the S. A. C. at O_2 and letting the edge of the curve, near uu, touch P_2.

11. Outlining the Skirt Portion.—At the waist line, draw a straight line out from point V, extending it, as shown, in the general direction of the curve drawn from V_3 to V.

Locate:

Point V_4 on this line 2 inches above point V, or for large hip measurements, 3 or 4 inches.

Point N_2 on the front edge of the paper the desired apron length, usually the prevalent skirt length, to the right of point N.

Point N_3 with the corner of the square at point N_2 and its short arm along the front edge of the paper, drawing a line along the long arm equal in length to one-half the hip measure, plus from 4 to 7 inches, according to the flare you desire at the lower edge.

Draw:

Line V_4N_3 by connecting V_4 and N_3 with a straight line.

Locate:

Point V_5 to the right of V_4, on line V_4N_3, the distance from point N to N_2 minus 3 inches.

Points for the lower edge by measuring the skirt length from the waist line down at one or two points near the center front and measuring on around to the back, gradually decreasing the length until it corresponds with the length of line V_4V_5.

Draw:

Line V_5N_2, a smoothly curved, free-hand line, or follow the directions for drawing the lower edge of the plain foundation-

skirt pattern, as given in Art. **13**, Chapter III.

12. Tracing and Cutting the Pattern.—Trace the lines marked on the waist pattern so that it will not be necessary to cut this. Start the tracing at point V and continue it through V_3, G_3, K_2, B_2, U_2, U_4, T_2, and T_3; then trace along the center-back line from T_3 to A_2, and from this point trace the neck line through points E_2, P_2, and O_2.

After tracing, remove the waist pattern and form the apron pattern by cutting first on the traced lines and then from V to V_4, V_4 to V_5, and V_5 to N_2.

13. Varying Instructions for One-Piece, Cover-All Apron Pattern.—In making a one-piece, cover-all apron pattern according to odd or extreme measurements, you may find it advisable to vary the instructions slightly in order to work out a well-balanced draft. This is true especially in regard to curves that may sometimes meet in a point. In case the curved lines seem "easy" and graceful in appearance, except where they meet in points, blend the curves with a free-hand line or by following the curved edge of the square. In extreme cases, it may be necessary to vary the entire curve.

Also, in apron-pattern designing, as in the designing of patterns for other garments, do not hesitate to change the location of a point if you feel that this will make the apron more becoming or more suitable for a certain type of figure. One precaution to observe in the changing of the location of a point is to see that the balance or the fit of the pattern or garment is maintained.

14. The instructions given for the making of this apron pattern should suggest the manner in which patterns for many other apron designs can be formed. In almost every case, you will find that the pattern for an apron that extends over the shoulders can be very easily and quickly developed by using a plain-waist pattern as a foundation and outlining the upper portion of the apron on this, as directed for the one-piece, cover-all apron.

If you prefer, you may make the one-piece, cover-all apron in separate front and back sections, providing shoulder seams and laying the center back of the waist portion on a fold of the material, in order to avoid a seam at the center back. Cutting in this manner will effect a saving in material.

BODICE APRON

15. Drafting the Bodice Portion.—In the development of a pattern for the bodice apron shown in Fig. 3, the front of a plain-waist pattern is required as a foundation for the bodice, or waist portion.

Remove fulness at the waist line of the plain-waist

pattern so as to give practically straight lines, by laying a fold through the lengthwise center, making this about 1 inch or a trifle more in width at the lower edge of the pattern and tapering it to nothing at the shoulder seam, as shown in the one-piece, cover-all apron.

Outline the deep oval neck line and deep armhole curve and either cut the pattern on the marked lines or trace these lines to another piece of paper, or better still, to a piece of muslin, and cut on the traced lines.

Provide the extension from the under arm by holding the front portion up to the figure and pinning a piece of paper or muslin to the pattern. Shape this extension as you desire across the back, letting it reach to the center back. Mark the waist line of any depth you desire, taking care to make this line even and sufficiently loose to fit comfortably.

FIG. 3

16. Portions Cut Without Patterns.—It is not necessary to make patterns for the straps, skirt portions, strings, and pockets.

For the straps, use straight pieces about 16 inches long and $3\frac{1}{2}$ inches wide. Slant the ends of the straps in order to make them fit in position properly, but do not slant them until the apron is being fitted; then they may be cut in the manner that makes them fit most comfortably.

For the skirt portion of the apron, cut three straight sections, the center one about 36 inches wide and the side sections 9 or 10 inches wide.

For the pockets, provide oblong pieces about 7 inches long and 9 inches wide, and for the strings straight strips about 24 inches long and 5 inches wide.

LONG-SLEEVED APRON

17. To cut out a long-sleeved apron like that shown in Figs. 4 and 5, it is not necessary to draft a pattern, as the plain foundation-waist pattern may be placed on the material in the manner shown in Fig. 6 (a) and (b) and lines for the skirt parts of the apron extended and drawn directly on the material. Of course, if you prefer, you may make a full-length pattern of paper so that it may be preserved for future use.

18. Obtaining the Front Dart.—Make provision for a lengthwise dart between the shoulder and the bust line so that the apron will hang straight down from the bust and yet be loose enough not to draw across the bust.

Form the dart by measuring the front shoulder line, locating a point midway on this line, and from this point drawing a line parallel to the center-front line, extending it to within 2 inches of the bust line.

Slash the pattern on the line thus drawn and then lap the pattern at the waist line so that it will spread apart about $1\frac{1}{2}$ inches at the shoulder, as shown in Fig. 6 (a), or more than this, if you are making the pattern for a person having a very prominent bust.

19. Obtaining the Under-Arm Line.—With the waist pattern thus prepared, fold the material lengthwise through the center and lay it out on a flat surface so that the folded edge is next to you. If you are making a pattern, however, it is not necessary to fold the paper; merely place the long, straight edge next to you.

Lay the waist pattern as just prepared on the material (or on the paper if you are making a pattern), with the center-front line on the fold or edge and the waist line a distance from the cut end equal to the

FIG. 4   FIG. 5

skirt length you desire to make the apron, plus allowance for a hem, and pin it securely in position.

Locate:

Point G_3 by measuring out from G_2 $\frac{1}{4}$ inch, plus any seam allowance you wish to make.

Point V_2 by measuring out $\frac{1}{2}$ to 2 inches from the waist line at V, gauging this distance by the amount of flare you wish in the skirt portion.

Draw:

The under-arm line from G_3, through V_2, the full length of the long arm of the square; extending it until it is the side skirt length, plus a hem allowance, if this is desired, below V_2.

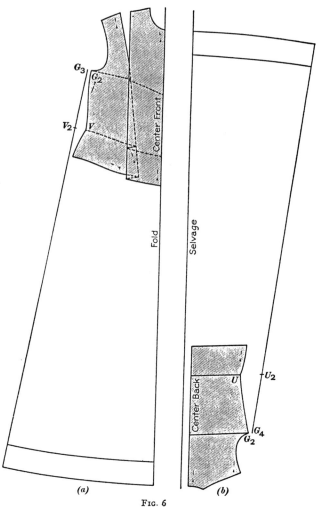

FIG. 6

20. Forming the Lower Edge of the Front. Locate a point at the center front measured the front skirt length, minus 1 inch, from the center-front waist line, with additional allowance for a hem, if this is desired. The reason for taking 1 inch from the center front is to subtract the allowance made beyond the front measurement in the drafting of the foundation-waist pattern, for, as this apron hangs straight from the bust line at the front, no provision for a bloused effect is necessary.

Connect the point on the under-arm line with the point at the center front by a gradually curved line.

21. Outlining the Back.—Pin the back of the foundation-waist pattern on the material or the paper,

making the same provision for the skirt portion as suggested for the front section of the pattern and, if you are outlining the pattern directly on the material, placing the center-back line $1\frac{1}{2}$ inches from the selvage, thus allowing for hems.

Locate:

Point G_4 by measuring out from the under-arm point G_2 the same distance you measured to locate point G_3.

Point U_2 on the back waist line 2 to 4 inches from U.

Draw:

The back under-arm line from G_4 through U_2, making this line of the same length as the front under-arm line.

22. Forming the Lower Edge of the Back.—Draw a gradually curved line from the termination of the under-arm line to a point at the center back which is measuring the back skirt length from the waist line, with additional allowance for a hem, if this is desired.

23. Outlining the Dutch Collar.—To draft the pattern for a Dutch collar having a natural neck line rather than the one shown on this apron, proceed as follows, using Fig. 7 as a guide:

First, pin the front and the back of the plain foundation-waist pattern with the shoulder lines together on a piece of paper about 10 inches by 14 inches and place the center front of the pattern 1 inch from the long edge of the paper and the shoulder point midway of the length of the paper, as shown.

Locate:

Point A_2 on the center-back line the width of the collar from point A. Usually 3 inches is satisfactory.

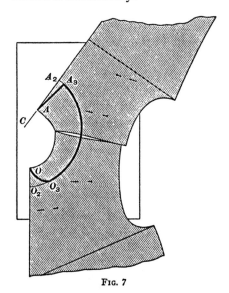

FIG. 7

Point O_2 on the center-front line the width of the collar from point O. Usually $1\frac{1}{2}$ inches is satisfactory.

Point C $1\frac{3}{4}$ inches from A on an extension of the center-back line.

Swing arc A_2O_2 using C as a center, for the outer edge of the collar.

Locate:

Point A_3 on curve A_2O_2 $\frac{1}{2}$ inch from A_2.

Point O_3 on line O_2A_2 $1\frac{1}{2}$ inches from O_2.

Draw:

Line AA_3 by connecting A and A_3 with a diagonal line.

Curve OO_3 free-hand to shape the front of the collar, or by placing the square so that j of the L. A. C. is at point O_3 and the edge of the S. A. C., near h, touches O.

24. Forming the Dutch-Collar Pattern.—Trace the pattern on the piece of paper to which the front and the back foundation-pattern pieces are pinned, by tracing from O to O_3, from O_3 to A_3, from A_3 to A, and from A to O, following the original neck line of the front- and back-pattern portions. Remove the waist pattern from the paper and cut the collar pattern thus drafted by cutting on the traced lines.

25. Outlining Other Varieties of Collars.—Many other attractive flat-collar patterns, such as those with square corners or points on the shoulders, may be obtained by placing the shoulder lines of the pattern together and tracing the outside line to conform with the style desired.

If the front and the back are cut in one and the shoulder seam is omitted, the outlining of the collar may be done in practically the same manner. In either case, the neck line of the collar should correspond exactly with that of the pattern on which it is outlined.

26. Cutting Sleeves, Cuffs, and Belt.—For this apron, the shirtwaist sleeve and cuff patterns are suitable. Cut the sleeve with a little extra allowance at the upper end of the inside seam line so as to make the armhole measurement of the sleeve sufficiently large for that of the waist.

For the belt, cut a straight piece 2 or 3 inches wide and equal in length to the width-of-back measurement.

***

KIMONO APRON

27. The pattern for the kimono, or bungalow, apron shown in Figs. 8 and 9 may be outlined directly on the material in a manner similar to the outlining of the long-sleeved apron, or a paper pattern may be formed so as to be preserved for future use.

28. Altering the Foundation Pattern.—As a foundation for the development of this pattern, use the standard kimono-waist pattern.

Decide on the sleeve length you desire and cut off the surplus length in the sleeve portion.

Slash the pattern on the shoulder crease that is formed in its development, extending this slash from the neck line to the lower edge of the sleeve and thus forming separate front- and back-pattern sections. The object in providing for shoulder seams is to lift

FIG. 8   FIG. 9

the front up at the under arms so that the apron will not drop down, as well as to keep the center back of the apron on a lengthwise thread of the material. Then, too, an apron cut with the seam on the shoulder is preferable to one without a seam, because it will not fall out toward the front and be in the wearer's way when she is working.

29. Drafting the Front.—Determine the right length for the front of the apron by measuring from the neck line at the shoulder seam down to the skirt length you desire.

Pin the front portion of the pattern to a piece of paper of sufficient length to accommodate the apron pattern, placing the upper portion of the pattern close to one end of the paper and the center front along a straight edge.

Outline the neck, shoulder, sleeve, and under-arm lines, and extend the under-arm line to form the skirt portion, as directed for the development of the long-sleeved apron. Draw the line at the lower edge after measuring down from the neck point of the shoulder line the length you wish the apron.

Form the pattern by cutting on the marked lines.

30. Drafting the Back.—Determine the correct length for the back of the apron by measuring from the neck line at the side down over the back of the figure to the skirt length you desire.

Pin the back portion of the pattern to a piece of paper of sufficient length to accommodate the apron pattern, placing the center back of the pattern with the neck line touching the edge of the paper and the waist line about $1\frac{1}{2}$ inches in from the edge so as to provide extra fulness.

Outline the neck, shoulder, sleeve, and under-arm lines, and extend the under-arm line for the skirt portion. Draw the line for the lower edge by measuring down from the side neck line of the pattern.

Form the back apron-pattern portion by cutting on the marked lines.

31. If you prefer to outline the apron directly on the material, follow, in general, the method suggested for forming the pattern, placing the center front on the lengthwise fold and the center back at the waist line $1\frac{1}{2}$ inches from the lengthwise fold. After outlining both sections, cut the material, making allowance for seams and hems.

FANCY APRONS

POINTED-PANEL APRON

32. Drafting the Apron Portion.—To draft the pattern for the pointed-panel apron shown in Fig. 10, draw on a sheet of paper 22 inches by 13 inches, one long edge of which is toward you, as shown in Fig. 11, a rectangle $ABCD$, each side of which is 20 inches and each end, 12 inches.

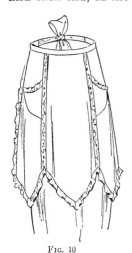

Fig. 10

Locate:

Point E on line AD one-half the width of the apron at the waist line, or 7 inches, above A.

Note.—This width was chosen since the width of this apron at the waist line is 14 inches.

Point F $1\frac{1}{4}$ inches to the left of A.

Draw:

Line FE, or the top edge of the apron by connecting points F and E with a heavy, slightly curved free-hand line, or place the square so that z is at E and the edge of the curve, between w and v, touches F.

Locate:

Point G on line FE $2\frac{1}{2}$ inches from F.

Note.—This width is chosen since the width of the middle panel at the waist line is 5 inches, or $2\frac{1}{2}$ inches on the draft.

Point H by measuring up from B on line BC, in order to make the width of this panel about 9 inches at the widest part.

Point H_2 by placing the square with the straight edge on G and H and marking H_2 5 inches to the right of H.

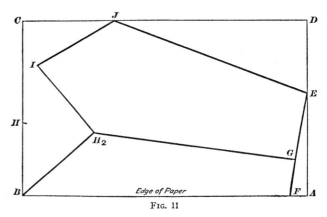

Fig. 11

Draw:

Line H_2G while the square is in position for locating H_2.

Line BH_2 by placing the square so that its corner is on H_2 and the straight edge of the long arm touches B.

Locate:

Point I by placing the square with the corner at H_2 and the long arm along H_2B and draw line H_2I while the square is in the same position, drawing a heavy 6-inch line along the straight edge of the short arm and lettering its termination I.

Point J on line CD $6\frac{1}{2}$ inches to the right of C.

Draw:

Line IJ by connecting J and I with a heavy diagonal line.

Complete the draft by connecting J and E with a heavy diagonal line.

33. Cutting the Drafted Pattern.—Form the pattern for this apron by cutting from F to E; from E to J; from J to I; from I to H_2; and from H_2 to B.

If you wish to form the apron of separate panels, cut the draft apart on line H_2G; otherwise, merely trace this line to be used as a guide in the placing of the trimming.

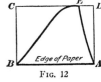

Fig. 12

34. Drafting the Pocket.—Draw and letter $ABCD$, a rectangle, each of whose sides is $5\frac{1}{2}$ inches and each of whose ends is 4 inches, as shown in Fig. 12.

Locate:

Point E on line CD 1 inch to the left of D.

Draw:

Curve AE by connecting A and E with a heavy, free-hand curved line, or by placing the square so that *hh* of the L. A. C. is at *E* and the edge of the curve, near *ff*, touches *A*.

Curve *BE* by connecting *E* and *B* with a heavy, free-hand curved line, or by placing the square so that *qq* is at *E* and the edge of the S. A. C., near *vv*, touches *B*.

35. Cutting the Pocket Pattern.—Form the pocket pattern by cutting the draft from *A* to *E* and from *E* to *B*. In connection with this pattern, it will be well to remember that line *EA* is the top of the pocket.

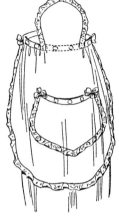

FIG. 13

VALENTINE APRON

36. Drafting the Apron Portion.—To draft the pattern for the valentine apron shown in Fig. 13, proceed as shown in Fig. 14, using a piece of paper 25 inches long and 12 inches wide. With one of the long edges of the paper toward you, measure in 6 inches from the right, and beginning at this point, draw a rectangle whose sides are each 18 inches and whose ends are each 11 inches, and letter the corners *A*, *B*, *C*, and *D*, as shown.

Locate:

Point *E* $3\frac{1}{2}$ inches below *D* on line *AD*.

Point *F* 6 inches to the right of *C* on line *CD*.

Point *G* midway between *B* and *C* on line *BC*.

Point G_2 1 inch to the right of *G*.

Point *H* $1\frac{1}{4}$ inches to the left of *A* on line *AB*.

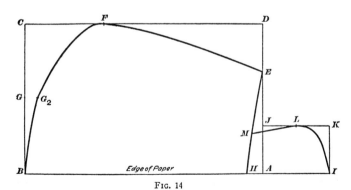

FIG. 14

Draw:

Curve *EH* by connecting *E* and *H* with a free-hand curve or by placing the square so that *z* of the L. A. C. is at *E* and the edge of this curve, near *v*, touches *H*.

Line *FE* by connecting *E* and *F*, turning the square so that *z* of the L. A. C. is still

at *E* and the edge of the curve, near *t*, touches *F*.

Curve FG_2 by turning the square around and placing it so that *i* of the S. A. C. is at *F* and the edge of the L. A. C., near *q*, touches G_2.

Curve G_2B by placing the square so that *ff* is at G_2 and the edge of the curve, near *cc*, touches point *B*.

37. Drafting the Bib.—On the portion of the paper reserved for the bib portion,

Locate:

Point *I* 5 inches to the right of *A* on the edge of the paper next to you.

Point *J* on line *AD* $3\frac{1}{2}$ inches above *A*.

Point *K* $3\frac{1}{2}$ inches above *I*.

Form rectangle *AJKI* by drawing a line from *J* to *K* and one from *K* to *I*.

Locate:

Point *L* on line *JK* midway between *J* and *K*.

Point *M* on line *HE* 3 inches above *H*.

Draw:

Line *ML* by connecting *M* and *L* with a diagonal line.

Curve *LI* by placing the square so that *j* of the L. A. C. is at *L* and the edge of the S. A. C., near *f*, touches *I*.

38. Cutting the Apron Pattern.—With the drafting completed, cut out the pattern for the valentine apron as follows: From *I* to *L*; from *L* to *M*; from *M* to *E*; from *E* to *F*; and from *F*, through G_2, to *B*.

39. Drafting the Pocket.—Draw rectangle *ABCD* on a sheet of paper of suitable size, with one long edge toward you, as shown in Fig. 15, making each of the sides $6\frac{1}{2}$ inches and each of the ends 5 inches.

Locate:

Point *E* $1\frac{1}{4}$ inches below *D* on line *AD*.

Point *F* midway between *C* and *D* on line *CD*.

Point *G* $\frac{1}{2}$ inch to the left of *A* on line *AB*.

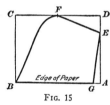

FIG. 15

Draw:

Line *GE* by connecting points *G* and *E* with a free-hand curve or by placing the square so that *z* is at *E* and the edge of the curve, near *x*, touches *G*.

Line *EF* by connecting points *E* and *F* with a diagonal line.

Curve *FB* by placing the square so that *qq* of the S. A. C. is at *F* and the edge of this curve, between *uu* and *vv*, touches *B*.

40. Cutting the Pocket Pattern.—Form the pattern by cutting from *G* to *E*; from *E* to *F*; and from *F* to *B*.

41. Drafting the Apron Portion.—To draft the pattern for the mother's apron illustrated in Fig. 16, draw first, on paper of suitable size, a rectangle $ABCD$, whose sides are each 36 inches and whose ends are each 18 inches, as shown in Fig. 17.

FIG. 16

Locate:

Point E 13 inches above A on line AD.

Point F $1\frac{1}{4}$ inches to the left of A on line AB.

Draw:

Line EF by connecting points E and F with a diagonal line.

NOTE.—The waist line thus drawn makes the apron wide enough at the waist line to permit the material to be gathered into the band when making the garment.

Locate:

Point G 18 inches to the right of C on line CD.

Point H 18 inches to the right of B.

Swing:

Arc BG and extend it to a point 5 inches beyond G, using point H as the center.

Connect:

The end of the arc and point E with a diagonal line.

Locate:

Point I 8 inches, or the ruffle width, to the right of B on line AB.

Point J $4\frac{1}{2}$ inches below E on line EF.

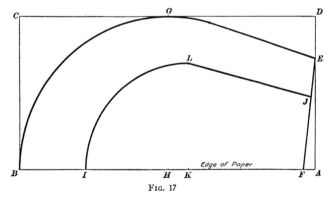

FIG. 17

Point K $12\frac{1}{2}$ inches to the right of I on line AB.

Point L $12\frac{1}{2}$ inches above K, placing the square, its short arm on line AB and its corner at K, so that the distance above K may be measured along the long arm.

Draw:

Curve IL by swinging an arc with K as the center.

Connect:

Points L and J with a diagonal line.

42. Cutting the Pattern.—To form the pattern for the apron, cut from F to E; from E to G; and from G to B.

43. Providing for the Ruffle.—The lower section of the apron pattern forms the ruffle pattern. To obtain this, cut from J, through L, to I.

To provide fulness in the ruffle, slash the pattern lengthwise and pin the sections to another piece of paper, separating them the amount necessary to give the fulness you wish. If you prefer, you may wait until you are cutting the apron material before you take care of the fulness. In this case, provide a slightly shaped ruffle section for the center front, and instead of placing the front edge of the drafted ruffle pattern on the fold when cutting the material, place it over selvages or straight cut edges so that they may be attached to the central ruffle portion.

44. Drafting the Pocket.—To draft the pocket for the mother's apron, proceed as shown in Fig. 18, using a sheet of paper of suitable size.

Draw rectangle $ABCD$, whose sides are each 6 inches and whose ends are each 12 inches.

Locate:

Point E $\frac{3}{4}$ inch to the right of B on line AB.

Point E_2 $2\frac{1}{2}$ inches to the right of B.

Point F 9 inches below C, placing the corner of the square at C and letting the straight edge of the long arm touch point E.

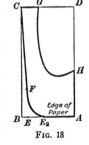

FIG. 18

Point G 2 inches to the right of C on line CD.

Point H 5 inches above A on line AD.

Draw:

Curve FE_2 by placing the square with e of the S. A. C. at F, and the end of the this curve touching E_2.

Line FC by extending the curve from F to C.

Curve GH by placing the square so that tt of the S. A. C. is at H and the edge of the L. A. C., near ii, touches G.

45. Cutting the Pocket Pattern.—Form the pattern by cutting from A to H; from H to G; from G to C; and from C, through F, to E_2.

ECONOMY APRON

46. Drafting the Apron Portion.—To draft a pattern for the economy apron, shown in Fig. 19, proceed as shown in Fig. 20. First draw on a sheet of paper of suitable size a rectangle $ABCD$, whose sides are each 27 inches and whose ends are each 18 inches.

Locate:

Point E 7 inches from D on line AD.

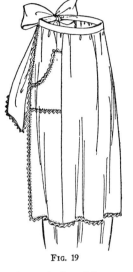

FIG. 19

NOTE.—As this apron is gathered into the band in making it, the gores must be reasonably wide at the top.

Point F $1\frac{1}{4}$ inches to the left of A on line AB.

Point G 2 inches to the right of C on line CD.

Draw:

The waist line, placing the square so that z of the L. A. C. is at E and the edge of this curve, between u and t, touches F.

Line GE for the outside edge of the side panel.

Locate:

Point H $6\frac{1}{2}$ inches from F on line FE.

NOTE.—For this apron, the width of the front gore at the waist line is 13 inches, or $6\frac{1}{2}$ inches on the draft.

Point I on line BC $10\frac{1}{2}$ inches from B, or one-half the width of the gore at the bottom.

Point J $\frac{3}{4}$ inch to the right of point I with the corner of the square at I and the long edge touching H.

Connect:

Points J and H with a diagonal line.

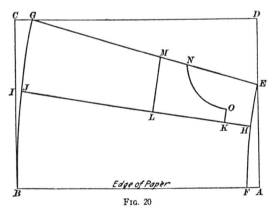

FIG. 20

Draw:

Curve GJ by placing the square so that the point midway between z and y is at G and the edge of the curve, near v, touches J.

Curve JB by sliding the square along until the point midway between z and y is at J and the edge of the curve touches line BC.

47. Drafting the Pocket.—Outline the pattern for the pocket directly on the apron pattern so as to simplify the work and insure accuracy.

Locate:

Point K 3 inches to the left of point H on line HJ.

Point L on line HJ 8 inches to the left of point K.

Point M by placing the square with its corner at point L and its short arm along line HJ, and drawing a line to line EG.

Point N 3 inches to the right of M on line EG.

Point O and draw line OK by placing the square with its corner at point K and its short arm along line HJ, and drawing a line $1\frac{1}{2}$ inches long.

Draw:

Curve NO by placing the square so that 5 on the F. C. is at N and the edge of the curve, near 2, touches O.

48. Tracing and Cutting Out Pattern.—Trace the pocket section to another piece of paper, tracing from K to L, from L to M, from M to N, from N to O, and from O to K.

Form the pattern parts of the apron by cutting from F to H, from H to J, and from J to B and then from H to E, from E to G, and from G to J.

———

SQUARE SEWING APRON

49. Drafting the Apron Portion.—For the development of the square sewing apron shown in Fig. 21, which consists of a middle panel, two side panels, a ruffle, and a pocket, provide a sheet of paper about 23 inches by 14 inches. Place one long edge of this toward you, and on it draw a rectangle whose sides are each 20 inches and whose ends are each 12 inches, and letter its corners A, B, C, and D, as shown in Fig. 22.

Locate:

Point E 8 inches above A on line AD, as the width of this apron at the waist line is 16 inches, that is, 8 inches on the draft.

FIG. 21

Point F $1\frac{1}{4}$ inches to the left of A on line AB.

Draw:

Line EF to form the top edge of the apron, placing the square so that z of the L. A. C. is at E and the edge of this curve, near v, touches F.

79

50. The side panels extend the full length of the apron, while the middle panel is cut off 6 inches from the bottom and a ruffle that connects with the side panels is set on. The width of each side panel at the waist line is $3\frac{1}{2}$ inches; therefore,

Locate:

Point G $3\frac{1}{2}$ inches from E on line EF.

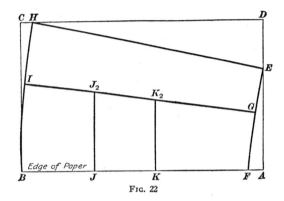

Fig. 22

For the outside corner of the lower part of the apron,

Locate:

Point H 1 inch to the right of C on line CD.

Draw:

The bottom edge of the apron, placing the square so that z of the L. A. C. is on H and the edge of this curve, near u, touches line BC.

Line HE by connecting points H and E with a diagonal line.

The side panels are $1\frac{1}{2}$ inches wider at the bottom than at the waist line; therefore,

Locate:

Point I by measuring down 5 inches from H on the curved line.

Draw:

Line IG by connecting I and G with a heavy diagonal line, thus forming the side-seam line of the pattern.

51. Drafting the Pocket.—The pocket pattern is outlined on the front section of the apron portion.

Locate:

Point J 6 inches to the right of B, since the ruffle is to be 6 inches wide.

Point J_2 at the intersection of a line drawn to GI perpendicular to line AB at J, thus forming line JJ_2.

Point K 5 inches to the right of J.

Point K_2 in the same manner as point J_2 was located.

NOTE.—The line KK_2 just drawn represents the top of the pocket and completes the drafting.

52. Cutting the Pattern.—Trace the pocket on another piece of paper as follows: From K to K_2; from K_2, on line GI, to J_2; and from J_2 to J.

Cut the draft from F, through G, to E; from E to H; and from H, through I, to B.

Cut the panels apart by cutting from I to G; and cut the ruffle part from the apron part by cutting from J to J_2.

53. Providing Fulness in Ruffle.—In order to provide fulness in the ruffle portion, pin the ruffle pattern to a longer piece of paper, placing the center front far enough from the end to provide the fulness you desire and then cutting from the end straight across to the ruffle pattern and around its upper, side and lower edges.

A pattern having fulness is not really necessary, however, as you may use the plain-ruffle pattern and place the center front of this a sufficient distance from a lengthwise fold to provide the fulness, following practically the same procedure as in forming a pattern.

———

CIRCULAR SEWING APRON

54. Foundation Pattern.—In preparing the pattern for the circular sewing apron shown in Fig. 23, use the circular-skirt pattern for a foundation, as in Fig. 24, which shows only that part of the circular-skirt pattern needed to illustrate how the apron pattern is developed.

55. Drafting the Apron Portion.—With the skirt pattern in front of you,

Locate:

Point A_2 by measuring out on the center-front line the length of apron desired, which, as a rule, is 22 inches.

Point B_2 midway between point A_2 and the waist line, or 11 inches to the right of A_2 on the center-front line.

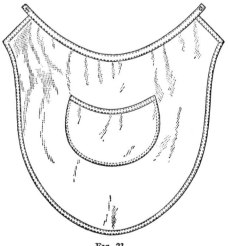

Fig. 23

Point C_2 with the short arm of the square on the center-front line of the pattern, and its corner at B_2, marking C_2 at the point where the straight edge of the long

arm touches the center side of the skirt
pattern.

Point D_2 by measuring from the waist line
$5\frac{1}{2}$ inches on the center-back line.

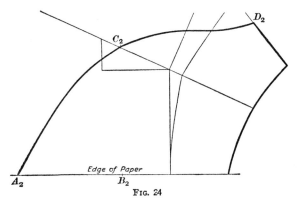

Fig. 24

Draw:
  Curve D_2C_2 by placing the square so that
  oo of the L. A. C. is at D_2 and the edge of
  the curve, near ee, is at C_2.
  Curve C_2A_2 by sliding the square along until
  jj is at C_2 and the edge of the curve, near
  aa, is at A_2.

56. Tracing and Cutting the Pattern.—In order
not to destroy the skirt pattern, trace the apron
pattern on a separate sheet of paper and then cut it
out, following the traced lines.

57. Drafting the Pocket.—Make the pocket pattern for this apron in much the same manner as the
one described for the valentine apron, but omit the
point on the lower edge.

CLOTHES-PIN APRON

58. Drafting the Apron Portion.—In preparation
for drafting a pattern for the clothes-pin apron shown
in Fig. 25, fold a sheet of paper
21 inches long and 24 inches wide
through the center, crosswise.
Then, with the folded edge toward
you, draw a rectangle $ABCD$, as
shown in Fig. 26, whose sides are
each 19 inches and whose ends are
each 11 inches.

Fig. 25

Locate:
  Point E $1\frac{1}{4}$ inches to the
  left of A on the fold.
  Point F $3\frac{1}{2}$ inches below
  D on the line AD.

  NOTE.—This position is suitable for a stand-
  ard-size apron for small and medium figures; if
  the waist measure is large, however, it is well to
  make the waist portion larger by locating point
  F from $\frac{1}{2}$ inch to 2 inches nearer point D, depending on the size of the waist.

  Point G $\frac{3}{4}$ inch to the right of C on line CD.

Draw:
  The waist line of the apron, using a slightly
  curved, free-hand line or placing the
  square so that z of the L. A. C. is at point
  F and the edge of the curve, near v,
  touches E.
  The bottom line as a slightly curved, free-
  hand line or connecting points G and B
  in the same manner as points F and E
  were connected; that is, with z at G and
  the edge of this curve, near u, at line
  BC.
  The side line by connecting points G and F
  with a diagonal line.

59. Drafting the Pocket.—The pocket of this
apron covers the apron with the exception of the
upper-side sections.

Locate:
  Point H 7 inches to the right of G on the
  line GF.

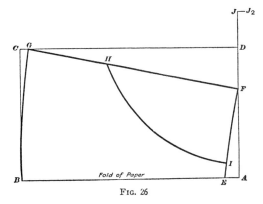

Fig. 26

  Point I $1\frac{1}{4}$ inches above E on the line EF.
  Point J by extending line AD 3 inches
  beyond point D.
  Point J_2 $\frac{5}{8}$ inch to the right of J for the point
  from which to swing the arc.
Swing:
  Arc HI with point J_2 as a center.

60. Cutting the Pattern.—Cut the draft from
E to F, from F to G, and from G to B.

Open out the paper and cut on the curved line
from H to I, and also on the fold, thus securing a
pattern for the pocket, as well as the apron.

CAPS AND SUNBONNETS

DUTCH BONNET

61. For the Dutch bonnet shown in Fig. 27, two
pattern parts must be drafted; one for the *crown*, or
the part of the cap that rests on the head; and the
other for the *vizor*, or *head-piece*, that is, the part of
the cap that turns back over the crown, or, in many

cases, projects from it and serves as a shield for the eyes.

62. Drafting the Crown.—The size of paper needed should be about 19 inches long and 11 inches wide.

FIG. 27

Draw rectangle *ABDC*, having sides each 17 inches and ends each $9\frac{1}{2}$ inches, following Fig. 28 as a guide.

Locate:

Point *E* with line *AB* next to you, marking point *E* $7\frac{1}{2}$ inches to the right of *D* on line *DC*.

Point *F* midway between *E* and *C* on line *CD*.

Point F_2 1 inch below *F*.

Point *G* $4\frac{1}{4}$ inches below *C* on line *AC*.

Point *H* by placing the short arm of the square along line *CD*, with its corner at point *E*, and measuring down the long arm $7\frac{1}{2}$ inches.

Point *I* $1\frac{1}{2}$ inches to the left of *A* on the bottom edge of the paper.

Swing:

Arc *BE* with point *H* as a center.

Draw:

Curve EF_2, placing the square so that *r* of the L. A. C. is at point *E* and the edge of the curve, near *t*, touches F_2.

Curve F_2G, placing *r* at F_2 and the edge of the curve, near *u*, at *G*.

Curve *GI* by placing *s* at *I* and the edge of the curve, near *v*, at *G*.

63. Cutting the Crown Pattern.—Form the pattern by cutting from *I* to *G*; from *G*, through F_2, to *E*; and from *E* to *B*.

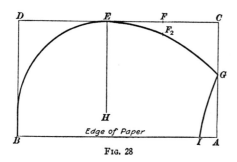

FIG. 28

64. Drafting the Vizor.—To draft the vizor for the Dutch bonnet, proceed in the manner shown in Fig. 29. The size of paper needed is about 10 inches wide and 22 inches long, or 10 inches by 11 inches when folded through the center, crosswise. Place the folded edge next to you, and draw rectangle *ABDC*, the sides of which are each $7\frac{1}{2}$ inches and the ends, each 10 inches.

Locate:

Point *E* $\frac{3}{4}$ inch to the left of *A* on the fold of the paper.

Point *F* $2\frac{1}{2}$ inches to the right of *B*, on the fold.

Point *G* $1\frac{1}{2}$ inches below *D* on line *BD*.

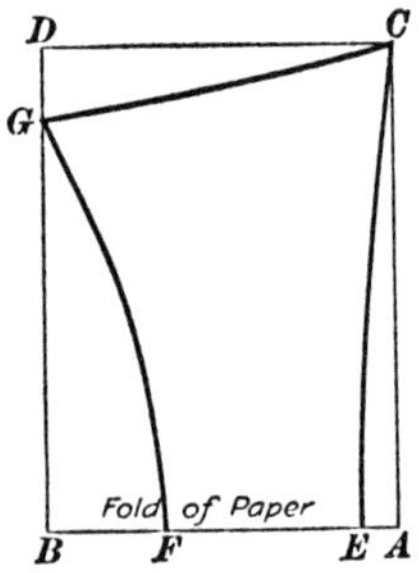

Draw:

Curve *EC* as a free-hand curve, or by placing the square so that *u* is at point *E* and the edge of the curve, near *z*, touches point *C*.

Curve *CG* as a free-hand curve, or by placing the square so that *z* is at *G* and the edge of the curve, near *v*, touches *C*.

Curve *GF* by placing the square so that *p* is at *G* and the edge of the curve, near *u*, touches *F*.

FIG. 29

65. Cutting the Vizor Pattern.—Form the pattern by cutting, with the paper still folded, from *E* to *C*; from *C* to *G*; and from *G* to *F*.

COMBINATION HOUSE CAP AND SUNBONNET

66. Drafting the Crown.—To draft the crown of the combination house cap and sunbonnet shown in Fig. 30, the size of paper necessary is 21 inches long and 12 inches wide.

Place one long edge of the paper next to you and use Fig. 31 as a guide.

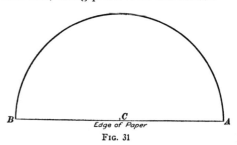

FIG. 30

Locate:

Point *A* 1 inch from the right edge of the paper on the bottom margin.

Point *B* $18\frac{1}{2}$ inches to the left of point *A* on the bottom edge of the paper.

Point *C* midway between the two points *A* and *B*.

Swing:

Arc *BA*, using point *C* as the center.

FIG. 31

67. Cutting the Crown Pattern.—In order to form the pattern for the crown, cut on the curved line from *A* to *B*.

68. Drafting the Vizors.—The size of paper needed is 6 inches wide and 16 inches long.

Fold this paper through the center, crosswise. Draw rectangle $ABCD$, with the folded edge next to you, as shown in Fig. 32, the sides being each $4\frac{1}{4}$ inches and the ends, each $7\frac{3}{4}$ inches.

Locate:
> Point E $\frac{3}{4}$ inch to the left of A on the fold.
> Point F $\frac{3}{4}$ inch to the right of C on the line CD.
> Point G $1\frac{1}{2}$ inches below D on line AD.

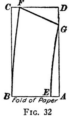
Fig. 32

Draw:
> Curve EG as a free-hand curved line, or by placing the square so that t of the L. A. C. is at E and the edge of the curve, near w, touches G.
> Curve BF with a line similar to EG by moving the square so that u of the L. A. C. is at B and the edge of the curve, near y, is at F.
> Line FG by connecting points F and G with a diagonal line.

69. Cutting the Vizor Pattern.—Form the pattern by cutting through both thicknesses of the paper from E to G; from G to F; and from F to B.

SWEEPING CAP

70. In order to draft a pattern for the sweeping cap shown in Fig. 33, which consists of a crown and two vizors, provide a piece of paper 21 inches long and 26 inches wide. As shown in Fig. 34, fold the paper through the center, crosswise, and with the folded edge of the paper toward you, draw as a guide for the pattern lines a rectangle $ABCD$, making the ends AD and BC each $11\frac{1}{2}$ inches and the sides AB and CD each $17\frac{1}{2}$ inches.

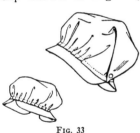
Fig. 33

71. Drafting the Crown of Cap.—With the fold of paper before you,

Locate:
> Point E 1 inch to the right of C on line CD.
Draw:
> The bottom line of the crown part by connecting points E and B with a heavy straight line.
Locate:
> Point F $4\frac{1}{2}$ inches to the right of E on line CD.
> Point G $3\frac{1}{2}$ inches to the left of A on the fold.

Connect:
> Points F and G with a light diagonal line.
Locate:
> Point H $11\frac{1}{2}$ inches to the left of A on the fold.
Swing:
> Arc FA for the top of the cap, using point H as a center.

72. Drafting the Vizors.—The pattern for the visors is drawn directly on the pattern for the crown.
Locate:
> Point I $7\frac{1}{2}$ inches to the right of F on the curved line FA.
> Point J $3\frac{1}{4}$ inches above A on curve IA.
> Point K $3\frac{1}{2}$ inches below F on the line FG.
Draw:
> Curve GJ by placing the square so that a of the S. A. C. is at point J and the edge of this curve, near f, is on G.

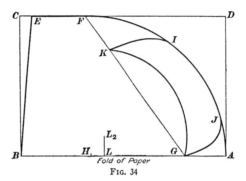
Fig. 34

> Curve KI by placing xx of the S. A. C. of the square on I and the edge of the curve, near tt, on K.
Locate:
> Point L $10\frac{3}{8}$ inches to the left of A on the fold.
> Point L_2 $1\frac{5}{8}$ inches above L on a line perpendicular to line AB.
Swing:
> Arc KG, using point L_2 as a center.

73. Forming the Pattern.—Trace the vizors, or projecting pieces, to the under piece of the paper, and form the vizor pattern by cutting on the traced lines.

Cut out the crown pattern by cutting on the curved line from A to F; from F to E; from E to B; and along the crease made in folding, from B to A.

TWO-PIECE SUNBONNET

74. The pattern for the two-piece sunbonnet shown in Fig. 35 consists of a crown and a head-piece of uniform width. The following instructions are porportioned for the average head-size. If you desire to make a larger or smaller pattern, merely alter the pattern drafted according to general instructions. For instance, if you wish to make the pattern smaller, trim it off from $\frac{1}{4}$ to 1 inch all around the edges. To make the pattern larger, add the extra size around all the pattern edges, making this allowance in cutting the material, if you desire.

FIG. 35

75. Drafting the Crown.—To draft the pattern for the crown, proceed as shown in Fig. 36.

On a sheet of paper of suitable size, draw rectangle $ABCD$, the sides of which are each $18\frac{1}{2}$ inches and the ends of which are each 9 inches.

Locate:
> Point E 1 inch to the right of C on the line CD.

Draw:
> The bottom line of the crown by connecting E and B with a heavy diagonal line.

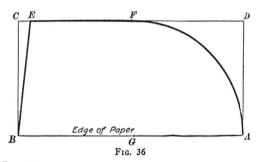
FIG. 36

Locate:
> Point F midway between D and C on line CD and make EF a heavy line.

Locate:
> Point G by measuring 9 inches to the left of A on line AB.

Swing:
> Arc FA, using point G as a center.

76. Cutting the Crown Pattern.—To form the pattern for the crown, cut from A to F; from F to E; and from E to B.

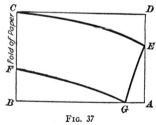
FIG. 37

77. Drafting the Head-Piece.—To draft the pattern for the head-piece of the sunbonnet, proceed as shown in Fig. 37.

With the fold of a sheet of paper of suitable size at the left, draw rectangle $ABCD$, the sides of which are each $10\frac{1}{2}$ inches and the ends, 7 inches.

Locate:
> Point E 3 inches below D on line AD.
> Point F $2\frac{1}{2}$ inches above B on line BC.
> Point G 2 inches to the left of A on line AB.

Draw:
> Curve EC by a free-hand curved line, or by placing the square so that t of the L. A. C. is at E and the edge of the curve, near s, is at C.
> Curve FG by a free-hand curve, or by placing w of the L. A. C. at G and the edge of the curve, near s, at F.
> Curve EG with a slightly curved line or by turning the square so that v is at E and the edge of the curve, near t, is at G.

78. Cutting the Head-Piece Pattern.—Form the pattern for the head-piece by cutting from F to G; from G to E; and from E to C.

CIRCULAR-RUFFLE SUNBONNET

79. The pattern for the circular-ruffle sunbonnet in Fig. 38 consists of three pieces; namely, a crown portion, a head-piece curved at the sides, and a ruffle portion. Develop these pattern pieces according to the following instructions, which are proportioned for average measurements. If you desire, you may change the size of this pattern according to the method suggested for changing the size of the two-piece sunbonnet pattern.

FIG. 38

80. Drafting the Crown.—To draft the pattern for the circular-ruffle sunbonnet crown proceed as shown in Fig. 39; using a sheet of paper of suitable size, draw rectangle $ABCD$, each of the sides of which is $20\frac{1}{2}$ inches and each of the ends, 10 inches.

Locate:
> Point E $1\frac{1}{2}$ inches to the right of C on line CD.
> Point F 5 inches to the left of D on line CD.
> Point F_2 2 inches below F, placing the long arm of the square along line CD and its corner at F.

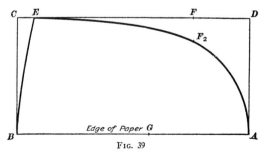
FIG. 39

Draw:
> Curve BE with a slightly curved free-hand line or by placing the square so that z is at E and the edge of the curve, near u, touches B.

Curve EF_2 with a free-hand curved line, or by placing the square so that the arrowhead of the L. A. C. is at E and the edge of the curve, near hh, touches F_2.

Locate:
Point G $8\frac{3}{4}$ inches to the left of A on line AB.

Draw:
Curve F_2A, which forms the top of the crown, by swinging an arc, using point G as a center.

81. Cutting the Crown Pattern.—Form the pattern for the crown by cutting from A, through F_2, to E, and from E to B.

82. Drafting the Head-Piece and Ruffle.—To draft the pattern for the head-piece and the ruffle of this sunbonnet, proceed as shown in Fig. 40.

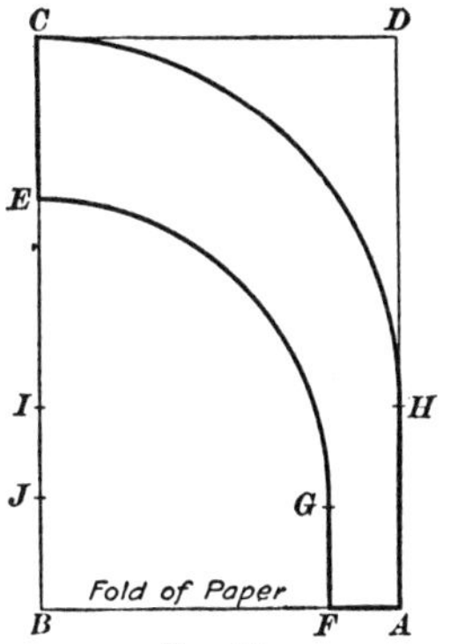

On a folded piece of paper draw rectangle $ABCD$, each side of which is 9 inches and each end, 14 inches.

Locate:
Point E the width of the ruffle at the back of the bonnet from C on line CB, in this case 4 inches.

Point F the width of the ruffle in front to the left of A on line AB, in this case $1\frac{3}{4}$ inches.

Point G $2\frac{1}{2}$ inches from point F, by placing the square so that its short arm is along line AB and its corner is at F.

Point H the width of the head-piece and ruffle in front, in this case 9 inches below D on line AD.

Point I the same distance below C as point H is below D.

Point J by measuring down $7\frac{1}{4}$ inches below E on line BC.

Swing:
Arc CH, using point I as a center.
Arc EG, which outlines the head-piece, using point J as a center.

83. Cutting the Pattern.—To form the *ruffle* part of the pattern, cut the draft from A, through H, to C; from C to E; from E, through G, to F; and from F to A. To form the *head-piece*, cut from E, through I and J, to B.

84. Providing Fulness in Ruffle Pattern.—In order to allow on the ruffle pattern for the flare of the sunbonnet ruffle, slash the ruffle pattern just made and separate the pieces a sufficient amount, as shown in Fig. 41. Beginning 3 inches from the wider end

FIG. 40

of the ruffle pattern, slash from the outside edge to within $\frac{1}{4}$ inch of the inside edge, or to a point just far enough from the inside edge to hold the pattern pieces together. Make three more slashes, each about 3 inches apart.

Pin the slashed ruffle pattern to a piece of paper that is from 3 to 6 inches larger than the pattern, separating all the pieces $\frac{1}{2}$ inch on the outer edge with the exception of the third slash, which should be separated 1 inch so as

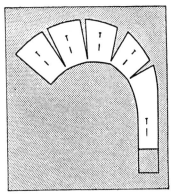

FIG. 41

to keep the shape of the pattern true. Extend the narrow end of the ruffle 2 inches, as shown, keeping it the same in width as that end of the ruffle pattern.

With the pattern thus spread and securely pinned, cut around its outside edge.

85. Providing Strings For the Sunbonnet.—Four strings of the same size are required for this sunbonnet. Make these of straight strips about $2\frac{3}{4}$ inches wide and 18 inches long, or cut the strips narrow, if you prefer.

SUN HAT

86. Two pieces, a crown and a brim portion, form the pattern for the sun hat shown in Fig. 42. This pattern, like those for the sunbonnets previously discussed, is proportioned according to average measurements and may be altered for smaller or larger sizes in the manner suggested for the sunbonnet patterns. The ruffle is formed simply of a straight piece of material of the desired width.

FIG. 42

Develop the pattern for the sun hat according to the instructions that follow.

87. Drafting the Crown.—To draft the pattern for the crown of the sun hat, proceed as shown in Fig. 43, using for it a sheet of paper that is 18 inches square.

Locate:
Point A 1 inch from the right edge of the paper and 5 inches from the lower edge.

Draw:
Rectangle $ABCD$, each of the sides of which is 16 inches and each end, $11\frac{1}{2}$ inches.

Locate:
Point E $2\frac{1}{4}$ inches to the right of C on line CD.

Draw:

> Curve *EB* for the bottom line of the crown, placing the square so that the arrowhead of the L. A. C. is at *E* and the edge of the curve, near *ff*, touches *B*.

Locate:

> Point *F* by extending line *BC* 4 inches below *B*.

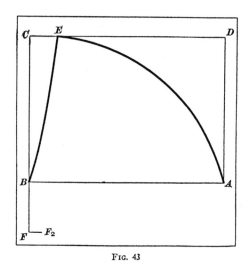

FIG. 43

Point *F₂* with the corner of the square at *F* and the arm along line *FB*, measuring 1 inch to the right of *F*.

Swing:

> Arc *EA* for the top line of the crown, using point *F₂* as the center.

88. Cutting the Crown Pattern.—Form the pattern by cutting the draft from *A* to *E*; from *E* to *B*; and from *B* to *A*.

89. Drafting the Head-Piece.—To draft the head-piece, or brim, for the sun hat, proceed as illustrated in Fig. 44, using a piece of paper 14 inches square.

Locate:

> Point *A* 1 inch from the right edge of the paper and 3 inches from the lower edge.

Draw:

> Rectangle *ABCD*, the sides of which are each $12\frac{3}{4}$ inches and the ends, 10 inches.

FIG. 44

Locate:

> Point *E* 3 inches below *C* on line *BC*.
> Point *F* $4\frac{1}{2}$ inches to the left of *A* on line *AB*.
> Point *G* by extending line *BC* down from *B* $1\frac{1}{4}$ inches.
> Point *H* $1\frac{1}{2}$ inches to the right of *G*.

Swing:

> Arc *EF*, using point *G* as a center.
> Arc *CA*, using point *H* as a center.

90. Cutting the Head-Piece Pattern.—Form the pattern for the brim of the sun hat by cutting along the curve from *A* to *C*; from *C* to *E*; along the curve from *E* to *F*; and from *F* to *A*.

REVIEW QUESTIONS

(1) Of what value is apron-pattern designing?

(2) (*a*) How do you consider that ideas or inspiration for apron-pattern development may be gained? (*b*) What feature is of decided importance in apron-pattern development?

(3) How would you work out a pattern for an unusual style of apron?

(4) How may fulness at the waist line of the plain foundation-waist pattern be removed so as to make it suitable for the one-piece, cover-all and the bodice aprons?

(5) What is the purpose of the dart in the long-sleeved apron?

(6) Tell briefly how the pattern for any flat apron-collar pattern may be developed.

(7) (*a*) What is the object of the shoulder seam in the kimono apron? (*b*) How should the length of the kimono-apron pattern be determined?

(8) How may fulness be provided in the ruffle for the mother's apron?

(9) How may variations in head-size be taken care of in sun-bonnet patterns?

(10) Select a design of a practical, unusual style of house apron and make a diagram illustrating the manner of developing the pattern for it. The design may be an original one or it may be a style that you have selected from a fashion publication.

CHAPTER VIII

PATTERNS FOR CHILDREN AND MISSES' GARMENTS

SIMPLICITY IN CHILDREN'S GARMENTS

1. To the person accustomed to drafting patterns for grown-ups, patterns for infants, children, and misses will present new principles only in so far as they are made according to smaller measurements.

The only measurements to consider for infants are those used in the drafting of the foundation slip and sleeve patterns, for all other infants' patterns may be developed with the use of these patterns. For children past the infant age and for misses, however, the patterns are drafted from measurements taken in the same way as those for grown-ups, except that they are taken a trifle looser, so as to produce patterns that will mean looser-fitting garments.

2. In the designing of garments for young persons, simplicity of pattern lines should be the prevailing thought; no pattern should be such as to call for cutting up material merely to sew it together again. Practically all mothers who make a study of children's clothes and their appropriateness hold to simple lines, and wise mothers appreciate this idea so much that they strive for almost severe simplicity in their children's garments. For years many designers have been endeavoring to produce simplicity in such garments and to make this thought the prevailing note, and manufacturers of children's garments are aiding them in this respect. In the best children's specialty shops, also, garments with straight, simple lines are almost invariably shown, the hand-work being the chief consideration.

Mothers, in contemplating patterns for children's garments, will do well to consider carefully the material that is to be used and the purpose of each garment, keeping in mind how necessary it is to have freedom for play and to provide for the growth of the child as well as to make garments that can be slipped on and off with ease. Likewise, they should decide whether the garment will appear as pleasing if cut in various shapes, whether they can spare the time to make all the joinings perfectly, and whether the finished product would be just as attractive as if simple, straight lines were employed. If, after reasoning the matter in this way, they see fit to design a garment in an elaborate fashion, it will be wholly permissible to form patterns accordingly.

3. In this chapter, infants' patterns are considered first. The drafting of such patterns is very simple, and, as in drafting patterns for women, the plain foundation waist, sleeve, and skirt form the basis for nearly all other patterns, so, in infants' patterns, the foundation-slip pattern is the one from which nearly all other patterns are derived.

Next in order come patterns for growing children. After a child has outgrown infant patterns and the body is filled out, making it compulsory to have more definite proportions in garments, measurements must be taken and the patterns drafted in much the same manner as those for adults. In connection with these patterns are explained the necessary changes, the difference between them and those for adults, as well as how to produce the required straight lines.

Following these patterns are considered patterns for misses.

INFANTS' PATTERNS

MEASUREMENTS

4. As has been mentioned, the only measurements required for patterns for infants are those used in drafting the foundation patterns. These measurements are:

	INCHES
Neck	$9\frac{1}{2}$
Bust	23
Center-back depth	$3\frac{5}{8}$
Armhole	$9\frac{1}{2}$
Inside sleeve length	$6\frac{3}{4}$ to 7
Wrist	$6\frac{1}{2}$
Dress length	26 to 27

The measurements given may be considered as standard for the infant of normal size—that is, one that weighs about 8 pounds at birth—and patterns drafted according to them will serve as guides for cutting out garments, as well as foundations from which other patterns may be developed.

For example, a larger pattern for a growing infant may be formed by pinning a foundation pattern to a sheet of paper and then adding $\frac{1}{8}$ to $\frac{1}{4}$ inch at the shoulder, the armhole, and the under arm. Later, as the neck, the width-of-chest, and the width-of-back measurements of a child increase, well-balanced patterns that will be suitable for use until the child is 2 or 3 years of age can be provided by adding to the center back and the center front. In addition, foundation patterns may be varied in many ways to suit the mode of the day and the build of the child.

FOUNDATION DRESS, OR SLIP, PATTERN

5. The most important pattern for infants is the little foundation dress, or slip, pattern used in develop-

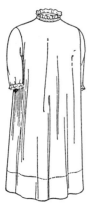

ing the style of the garment shown in Fig. 1, for it is with the aid of this foundation pattern that other slips or dresses are cut out and patterns for petticoats, kimonos, and similar garments are developed for the baby.

To draft this pattern, proceed according to Fig. 2, using a piece of paper 30 inches long and 18 inches wide.

6. Drawing the Back Foundation Lines.—Two foundation lines are required.

FIG. 1

Draw:

A vertical line along the long arm of the square, beginning the line 2 inches from the top of the paper and 3 inches from the right-hand edge, and making it 27 inches long.

A horizontal line with the square in the same position as for drawing the vertical foundation line, but drawing the line along the short arm a distance of 5 inches.

> NOTE.—This line is the back foundation neck-and-shoulder line.

7. Drawing the Back-Neck Curve.—Before changing the position of the square,

Locate:

Point A on the vertical line $\frac{5}{8}$ inch below the intersection of the foundation lines.

Point B $3\frac{3}{8}$ inches below point A.

Point C $1\frac{3}{4}$ inches to the left of the intersection of the foundation lines. Then,

Connect:

Points C and A by placing the square with qq at C and the edge of the S. A. C., near ss, touching A.

8. Drawing the Bust Line and Locating the Under-Arm Point.—According to the customary order in drafting, the bust line is the next to be drawn.

Locate:

Point D by placing the square with its corner at B and its short arm on line AB and drawing an $11\frac{1}{2}$-inch line from B along the long arm, marking D at its termination.

88

Point E midway between B and D on line BD.

9. Drawing the Back-Shoulder Line and Armhole Curve.—It will be necessary first to locate two points.

Locate:

Point F $2\frac{3}{4}$ inches to the left of C on the foundation neck-and-shoulder line.

Point G $\frac{5}{8}$ inch directly below F.

Draw:

Line CG, a diagonal line from C to G.

Curve GE by placing the square with the arrowhead of the S. A. C. at E and the edge of the curve, near vv, touching G.

10. Drawing the Front Foundation Lines.—A point is located at which the foundation lines intersect.

Locate:

Point H with the corner of the square at D and its short arm on line BD, drawing a $4\frac{3}{4}$-inch vertical line along the long arm and lettering its termination H.

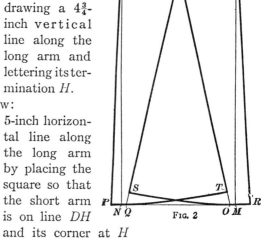

Draw:

A 5-inch horizontal line along the long arm by placing the square so that the short arm is on line DH and its corner at H

> NOTE.—This line is the front foundation neck-and-shoulder line.

FIG. 2

11. Drawing the Front-Neck Curve.—First,

Locate:

Point I $1\frac{3}{4}$ inches below H.

Point J $1\frac{3}{4}$ inches to the right of H on the front foundation neck-and-shoulder line.

Draw:

Curve JI by placing the square with h at I and the edge of the curve, near k, touching J.

12. Drawing the Front-Shoulder Line and Armhole Curve.—Two points must first be located.

Locate:

Point K $2\frac{3}{4}$ inches to the right of J on the foundation shoulder line.

Point L $\frac{5}{8}$ inch directly below K.

Draw:

Line *JL* by connecting points *J* and *L* with a diagonal line.

Curve *LE* by placing the square so that *ss* of the S. A. C. is at *E* and the edge of the L. A. C., near *nn*, touches *L*.

13. Drawing the Foundation Skirt Lines.

Locate:

Point *M* at the lower end of the vertical foundation line drawn in beginning the draft.

> NOTE.—In this case, the pattern is drafted 27 inches long, but a longer distance may be used, if desired.

Point *N* by measuring below point *D* a distance equal to that from *M* to *B*.

Connect:

Points *M* and *N* with a straight line.

14. Adding Width to the Front Section.—To provide fulness at the bottom,

Locate:

Point *O* 11 inches to the right of *N*.

Point *P* 1 inch to the left of *N* on the bottom line.

Connect:

Points *O* and *E* with a diagonal line.

Locate:

Point *T* by measuring up $1\frac{1}{4}$ inches from *O* on line *OE*.

Draw:

Line *ET* by making heavy the line between points *E* and *T*.

Line *PI* by connecting points *P* and *I* with a heavy diagonal line.

15. Adding Width to the Back Section.—The back section also has width added at the bottom.

Locate:

Point *Q* 11 inches to the left of *M*.

Point *R* $1\frac{1}{2}$ inches to the right of *M*.

Connect:

Points *Q* and *E* with a diagonal line.

Locate:

Point *S* $1\frac{1}{4}$ inches from *Q* on line *QE*.

> NOTE.—Points *T* and *S* are located in order to prevent sagging on the sides.

Draw:

Line *RA* by connecting points *A* and *R* with a diagonal line.

Line *ES* by making heavy the line between points *E* and *S*.

16. Drawing the Bottom Lines.—With the bottom lines drawn, the draft is completed.

Connect:

Points *R* and *M* with a horizontal line.

Points *P* and *N* with a horizontal line.

Draw:

Curve *TN* using a slightly curved free-hand line or by placing the square with the arrowhead of the L. A. C. at *T* and the edge of the curve, near *ff*, at *N*.

Curve *SM* by a free-hand curve or by placing the square with the end of the L. A. C. at *S*, and the edge of the curve, near *u*, at *M*.

17. Cutting the Draft Apart.—Paste underneath the draft a piece of paper large enough to accommodate the space between lines *EQ* and *EO*, pasting this paper on the front portion with one of its edges 1 inch to the left of line *EQ*. Trace on lines *ET* and *QT*.

Cut out the draft for the *back* part of the slip by cutting from *R* to *A*; from *A* to *C*; from *C* to *G*; from *G* to *E*; from *E* to *S*; and from *S* to *R*, being careful not to cut the paper underneath.

Form the pattern for the *front* portion by cutting from *P* to *Q*; on the traced lines from *Q* to *T* and from *T* to *E*; then from *E* to *L*; from *L* to *J*; from *J* to *I*; and from *I* to *P*.

18. Making a Yoke Pattern for an Infant's Slip. Determine how deep the yoke is to be and mark the pattern accordingly; then either fold the pattern back or cut it off on the marked line.

In cutting out a garment with a pattern so prepared, cut the yoke portion and the skirt portion separately, allowing fulness in the skirt portion if desired. Usually, one and one-half to two straight widths of material are required for a yoke dress.

19. Making a Panel Front for an Infant's Slip. Mark the yoke depth on the pattern and then measure the width desired for the panel at the bottom of the yoke and the bottom of the skirt. As a rule, a panel is 5 inches wide at the top and 7 inches wide at the bottom, or $2\frac{1}{2}$ inches and $3\frac{1}{2}$ inches, respectively, on the draft.

In cutting out such a slip, the yoke and the panel are cut in one and the sides have a slight amount of fulness added.

———

SLEEVE FOR FOUNDATION SLIP

20. For use with the foundation-slip pattern, a plain one-piece sleeve, such as the one shown in Fig. 3, is needed. The drafting of this sleeve is very simple and the pattern is easily made.

For this draft, procure a sheet of paper 10 inches long and 12 inches wide, and fold it crosswise through the center with the folded edge toward you.

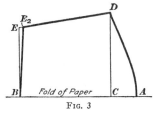

FIG. 3

21. Locating Construction Points.—All the construction points can be located in succession.

Locate:

Point A by measuring 1 inch from the right edge of the paper on the fold.

Point B by placing the square with its corner at A and its long arm on the fold, and measuring 8 inches to the left of A on the long arm.

Point C $1\frac{3}{4}$ inches to the left of A on the fold.

Point D with the corner of the square at C and the short arm on the fold, and drawing a $5\frac{1}{2}$-inch line along the long arm.

Point E by placing the square with its corner at B and its short arm on the fold, and drawing a $4\frac{1}{2}$-inch line along the long arm.

Connect:

Points E and D with a light diagonal line.

Locate:

Point E_2 $\frac{1}{4}$ inch to the right of E on line ED.

22. Drawing the Pattern Lines.—Now you may outline the pattern.

Draw:

Curve AD by placing the square so that ss of the S. A. C. is at D and the edge of the curve, near ww, touches A.

Line DE_2 by making heavy the diagonal line connecting points D and E_2.

Curve BE_2 by a free-hand curve between points B and E_2, or by placing the square so that z is at E_2 and the edge of the curve, near x, touches B.

23. Cutting the Draft Apart.—With the lines for the foundation-slip sleeve pattern drawn, form the pattern by cutting, through both thicknesses of the paper, from A to D; from D to E_2; and from E_2 to B.

FIG. 4

INFANTS' PETTICOAT PATTERN

24. To develop a pattern for an infants' petticoat that will lap and button over the shoulders, like the one shown in Fig. 4, the foundation-slip pattern is used, as shown in Fig. 5. No changes are made in the drafted pattern other than marking the neck line of the petticoat, and this in no way injures the pattern pieces.

25. Developing the Front-Pattern Section.—Pin the front of the foundation-slip pattern to a sheet of paper of suitable size, placing it so that the center-

front line is exactly along one straight edge of the paper. Then, as in view (a),

Locate:

Point A_2 on the center-front line $\frac{1}{2}$ inch above the bust line.

Point B_2 $1\frac{1}{4}$ inches to the left of the armhole curve on the shoulder line.

Draw:

The front-neck curve with a free-hand curved line or by placing the square with $1D$ of the R. F. C. at B_2 and the edge of this curve, near $3F$, at A_2.

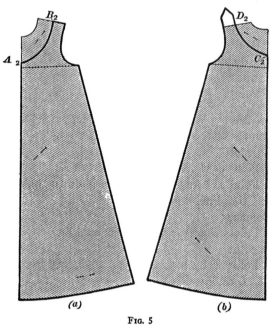

FIG. 5

26. Cutting the Front Section.—Trace curve A_2B_2; then cut along the foundation-slip pattern lines, except the shoulder line from B_2 to the neck curve and the neck curve itself. Remove the foundation-slip pattern and cut on the traced neck curve.

27. Developing the Back-Pattern Section.—Pin the back of the foundation-slip pattern to a sheet of paper, placing it so that the center-back line is exactly parallel with the straight edge of the paper. Then, as in view (b),

Locate:

Point C_2 $1\frac{1}{4}$ inches above the bust line on the center-back line.

Point D_2 $1\frac{1}{4}$ inches to the right of the armhole on the shoulder line.

Draw:

The back-neck curve with a free-hand curved line, or by placing the square so that $1D$ of the R. F. C. is at C_2 and the edge of this curve, near $3F$, touches D_2.

Provide the shoulder extension by measuring up 1 inch from D_2 and 1 inch from the armhole and drawing lines to connect these points, as shown. Make the end of the tab round or pointed, as desired.

28. Cutting the Back Pattern Apart.—Trace on the new pattern lines made for the back of the petticoat and follow the foundation-slip pattern lines in tracing the remainder of the pattern.

Remove the foundation-slip pattern and cut on the traced lines.

INFANTS' KIMONO PATTERN

29. For an infants' kimono, one style of which is shown in Fig. 6, a pattern drafted in the manner shown

FIG. 6

in Fig. 7 is required. Such a pattern is very useful, for, in addition to being used for cutting out kimonos it may be employed in developing slips, dresses, coats, nightgowns, and other infants' garments. This pattern is developed in much the same manner as a kimono pattern for a grown-up, with the exception that only the front part of the foundation-slip pattern is needed.

30. Placing Foundation-Slip Pattern on Paper.—The size of paper necessary is 56 inches long and 14 inches wide. Fold the paper through the center crosswise and place it with the fold away from you. Pin the front part of the foundation-slip pattern, placing it so that the intersection of the neck curve and the center-front line is exactly on the left edge of the paper and the intersection of the neck curve and the shoulder line is exactly on the fold. This will bring the bottom of the slip pattern 2 inches to the right of the left edge of the paper, as shown.

31. Drawing the Neck Curves.—Points A_2 and B_2 must be located for the neck curves.

Locate:

Point A_2 $\frac{5}{8}$ inch from the fold on the left edge of the paper.

Point B_2 $2\frac{1}{2}$ inches below I on the edge of the paper.

Draw:

The back-neck curve by placing the square so that J is at the intersection of the neck and shoulder lines and the edge of the curve, near h, is at A_2.

The front-neck curve by connecting B_2 and the intersection of the neck and shoulder lines with a curved line, placing the square with r at the intersection of these lines and the edge of the curve, near t, touching B_2.

NOTE.—If a V-neck is not desired for the kimono, point B_2 may be omitted and the original neck line used.

32. Drafting the Sleeve.—Several construction points can be located in succession.

Locate:

Point C_2 by placing the square with its short arm on the fold and adjusting it so that the 5-inch mark of the long arm touches the under arm of the slip pattern.

Point D_2 by drawing a vertical line from point C_2 to the fold along the long arm, lettering the intersection of this line and the fold, D_2.

Point E_2 the length of the sleeve desired to the right of point D_2 on the fold.

Point F_2 with the square placed so that the short arm is on line C_2D_2 and its corner is at C_2, drawing a horizontal line to the right along the long arm and making it $\frac{1}{2}$ inch shorter than line D_2E_2.

Point G_2 on line C_2F_2, 2 inches to the right of C_2.

Point F_3 on a curve connecting E_2 and F_2 and extended $\frac{1}{2}$ inch. Use either a free-hand slightly curved line or place the square so that u is at E_2 and the edge of the curve, near x, touches F_2.

Draw:

Line E_2F_3 by making heavy the curve just drawn.

Line F_3G_2 by connecting F_3 and G_2 with a diagonal line.

The curved underarm line with a free-hand curve or by placing the square so that h is at G_2 and the edge of the curve at k touches the under-arm line of the slip where it will.

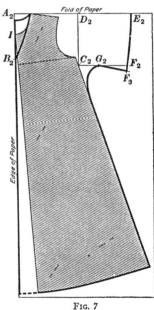

FIG. 7

33. Forming the Pattern.—Trace the back-neck curve from A_2 to the fold of the paper.

Extend the bottom line to the left edge of the paper, which is really the center-front line of the kimono pattern. Cut through both thicknesses of paper, from E_2 to F_3; from F_3, through G_2 and on the new under arm, as well as along the under arm of the pattern, to the bottom; and then along the bottom to the center front. This completes the cutting out of the sleeve and the lower portion of the infants' kimono pattern.

Open out the paper, still keeping the foundation-slip pattern attached, and trace the front-neck line, through only one thickness of the paper, from B_2 or I to the intersection of the neck and shoulder lines.

Remove the foundation pattern and cut out the front- and the back-neck curve of the kimono pattern.

NIGHTINGALE, OR SACQUE, PATTERN

34. Among the garments for infants, the nightingale, or sacque, one style of which is shown in Fig. 8, is necessary. A pattern for such a garment is drafted in the manner shown in Fig. 9.

FIG. 8

The size of paper necessary is 25 inches long and 12 inches wide.

35. Drawing the Foundation Lines.—Fold the paper crosswise through the center and then, with the folded edge away from you, draw rectangle $ABCD$, each of whose sides is 11 inches and each of whose ends is 12 inches, and allowing the folded edge of the paper to form one side of the rectangle.

36. Determining the Sleeve Curve.—To form the pattern for the sleeve,

Locate:
    Point E $7\frac{1}{2}$ inches below D on line AD.
    Point F with the square placed so that the corner is at E and the straight edge of the long arm touches C, placing point F $1\frac{1}{4}$ inches from E.
    Point G with the square in the same position as for locating F, drawing a line $4\frac{1}{2}$ inches from point F along the long arm and lettering its termination G.
    Point H $1\frac{1}{2}$ inches to the right of G on line FG.

Draw:
    Curve HD by placing the square so that g is at H and the edge, near o, touches D.

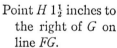

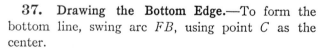

FIG. 9

37. Drawing the Bottom Edge.—To form the bottom line, swing arc FB, using point C as the center.

38. Drawing the Front-Neck Curve.—For a rather snug-fitting neck,

Locate:
    Point I $1\frac{3}{4}$ inches below C on line BC.
    Point J $1\frac{3}{4}$ inches to the right of C on the fold.

Draw:
    Curve IJ by placing the square so that k is at J and the edge of the curve, near h, touches I.

    NOTE.—If a low neck is desired, as is shown by the dotted line, locate point L 2 inches below I on line BC, and then connect L and J by placing the square so that j is at L and the edge of the curve, near o, touches J.

39. Drawing the Back-Neck Curve.—For the back-neck curve,

Locate:
    Point K $\frac{5}{8}$ inch below C on line BC.

Draw:
    Curve JK by placing the square so that j is at J and the edge of the curve, near h, touches K.

40. Cutting the Draft Apart.—Cut through both thicknesses of paper from B to F; from F to G; on the curved line from D to H; and from B to L or to I.

Then trace the back-neck curve from K to J, open out the paper, and cut the front-neck curve from J to I or from J to L, as the case may be, and the back-neck curve by cutting on the traced line.

41. Making a Small-Size Pattern.—For a new baby that is rather small, you will find that by using three-fourths of each of the measures given above you will obtain a good-fitting draft made in the same proportion. The curves for the neck and sleeves will have to be changed as follows:

Alter:
    The front-neck curve IJ by placing the square with k at J and the edge of the curve, near i, touching I.
    The back-neck curve KJ by placing the square with i at J and the edge of the curve, near h, touching K.
    The low-neck curve JL by placing the square with j at L and the edge of the curve, near m, touching point J.
    The sleeve curve HD by placing h at point H with m touching point D. Or, if the sleeve seems too long, you may locate point D_2 1 inch to the left of D on line CD and connect points D_2 and H for the sleeve curve.

INFANTS' CAP PATTERN

42. An effective infants' cap, similar to the one shown in Fig. 10, can be developed with the aid of head-piece and crown patterns drafted in the manner illustrated in Figs. 11 and 12.

43. Drafting the Head-Piece.—The size of paper necessary is 16 inches long and 7 inches wide. With the paper folded through the center crosswise, place it in front of you so that the folded edge is to the right.

Draw rectangle $ABCD$ 1 inch above the lower edge of the paper, and use the fold as one end. Make the sides each $7\frac{1}{4}$ inches and the ends each $5\frac{1}{4}$ inches.

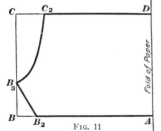

Locate:

Point B_2 1 inch to the right of B on line AB.

Point B_3 $1\frac{1}{2}$ inches above B on line BC.

Point C_2 $1\frac{1}{2}$ inches to the right of C on line CD.

Draw:

Line B_2B_3 by connecting B_2 and B_3 with a diagonal line.

Curve B_3C_2 by placing the square so that i is at B_3 and the edge of the curve, near m, touches C_2.

Fig. 10

44. Cutting the Draft Apart.—Form the pattern for the head-piece by cutting the draft apart, through both thicknesses of paper, from D to C_2; from C_2 to B_3; from B_3 to B_2, and from B_2 to A.

45. Drafting the Crown.—The size of paper needed should be $4\frac{1}{2}$ inches square.

Fold through the center and place it so that the fold is toward you, as shown in Fig. 12.

Using the fold as one side, draw a rectangle, each of whose sides is $2\frac{3}{4}$ inches and each of whose ends is $1\frac{3}{8}$ inches, and letter the corners A, B, C, and D.

Fig. 11

Locate:

Point A_2 midway between A and B on the fold.

Swing:

Arc BA by using A_2 as a center and making the arc touch line CD.

46. Cutting the Draft Apart.—Form the pattern by cutting through both thicknesses of the paper on the arc from A to B.

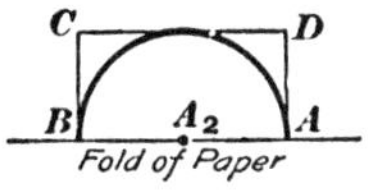

Fig. 12

47. Making a Large-Size Pattern.—In order to make a bonnet for a larger child, the only change necessary in drafting is to change the size of the rectangle for the head-piece. This should be $8\frac{1}{4}$ inches long and $5\frac{3}{4}$ inches wide.

INFANTS' COAT

48. Sometimes it is rather difficult to handle a baby because its dresses, coats, and slips are so long and full. Hence, a coat with a yoke is sometimes desirable because the bulk at the neck is eliminated and yet there is sufficient fulness around the bottom to keep the child warm.

49. Drafting the Yoke and Sleeve Portions.—The foundation-slip pattern can be used to advantage in developing the yoke and sleeve sections on such a coat, for the yoke is similar to the upper part of the slip, and the sleeves are, in reality, the same as the one-piece foundation sleeve. Outline the yoke by measuring down 4 inches from the neck at the center back and $4\frac{1}{4}$ inches from the neck at the center front.

An allowance of $\frac{1}{4}$ inch outside the seam allowance should be made on all edges of the sleeve and yoke for freedom.

50. Cutting the Skirt Portion.—For the skirt portion, no pattern is required. Simply cut the material so that it will be from 40 to 48 inches wide and about 32 inches long when finished.

51. Drafting the Cuff Pattern.—To make a cuff pattern for an infants' coat sleeve, proceed in the manner shown in Fig. 13, using a piece of paper 8 inches long and 4 inches wide.

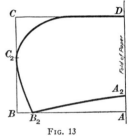

Fig. 13

Fold the paper through the center, crosswise, and place it in front of you so that the folded edge is to the right. Draw rectangle $ABCD$ $\frac{1}{2}$ inch above the lower edge of the paper, making the sides each $3\frac{1}{2}$ inches and the ends each 3 inches.

Locate:

Point A_2 $\frac{1}{2}$ inch above A on the fold.

Point B_2 $\frac{1}{2}$ inch to the right of B on line AB.

Point C_2 $1\frac{1}{4}$ inches below point C on the line BC.

Draw:

The outer edge of the cuff by placing the square with rr at C_2 and the edge of the square, near pp, touching line CD where it will; then with rr still at point C_2, moving the square so that the edge, near tt, touches B_2 and drawing a curved line to connect C_2 and B_2.

The lower edge of the cuff by placing the square so that ff is at A_2 and the edge of the curve, near ee, touches B_2.

52. Cutting the Cuff Draft Apart.—Form the cuff pattern by cutting, through both thicknesses of the paper, from D to C_2; from C_2 to B_2; and from B_2 to A_2.

53. Providing a Cape.—With a coat of this kind, a short circular cape with a flat collar is usually worn; for, besides adding warmth over the shoulders, it gives a more pleasing appearance to the entire garment. If such a cape is desired, the pattern for it as well as for the collar should be made as explained in Arts. **54** to **60,** inclusive.

INFANTS' SHORT CAPE

54. A kimono pattern should be used as a foundation for the short cape and collar pattern to be used with an infant's coat. Also, a sheet of paper is necessary, the required size being 28 inches long and 14 inches wide.

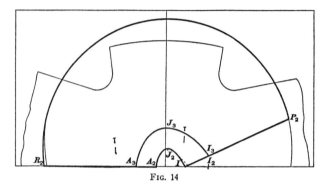

Fig. 14

55. Placing Kimono Pattern on Paper.—Fold the sheet of paper in the center crosswise, and crease. Open out the paper, place the pattern on it with the center back on one of the long edges and the shoulder crease of the pattern on the crease of the paper. Pin the pattern securely and place it in front of you with the front section at the right, as shown in Fig. 14.

56. Outlining the Collar Pattern.—The collar pattern should be drafted first.

Locate:

Point A_2 as in the kimono draft, Art. **31.**

Point A_3 2 inches to the left of point A_2 on the neck curve.

Point J_2 2 inches from the neck curve on the crease.

Point I_2 $2\frac{1}{4}$ inches to the right of point I on the edge of the paper.

Point I_3 1 inch above point I_2.

Connect:

The center-front point I and point I_3 with a diagonal line.

Points I_3 and J_3 by placing the square with 5 of the F. C. at I_3, and the edge of the curve, near 3, touching J_3.

Points J_3 and A_3 by placing the square with uu at A_3 and the edge of the curve, near xx, touching J_3.

NOTE.—If you desire, you may change the shape of the collar by rounding the corner at I_3.

57. Lowering the Front-Neck Curve.—Lower the front-neck curve $\frac{1}{4}$ inch at the center front, point I, as shown by the dotted line.

NOTE.—This is necessary in order to give freedom at the neck in front and to prevent the coat or cape from appearing drawn around the neck.

94

58. Drawing the Bottom Line.—This is the last pattern line to be drawn.

Locate:

Point J_2 on the neck line $\frac{1}{2}$ inch in front of the shoulder crease.

Using point J_2 as a center, and with a 12-inch radius, swing an arc from the center-front line to the center-back line. A longer radius should be used if a longer cape is desired.

Locate:

Point R_2 on the center-back line $\frac{1}{2}$ inch below the lower edge of the arc and draw a freehand curve connecting point R_2 with the arc.

Point P_2 by drawing a diagonal line from point I through point I_3, extending it the length of the cape.

59. Cutting the Cape Draft Apart.—Trace the neck line, A_2 through J_2 to I, and along the dotted line in front; then along the new front line to P_2, and along the arc from P_2 to the center back at R_2.

Remove the kimono pattern and cut along the traced lines.

60. Cutting the Collar Draft Apart.—Trace the back-neck and the dotted front-neck curves, line A_2A_3, from I_3, toward I, to the dotted line, and the curve from A_3, through J_3, to I_3.

Remove the kimono pattern and cut the draft on the traced lines.

INFANTS' LONG CAPE

61. Some mothers find that a long cape is more satisfactory than a coat because it can be more easily put on and yet keeps the child just as comfortable as a coat. Sometimes a close-fitting round hood is attached, making an over-garment that is always ready for wear.

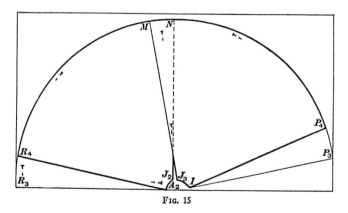

Fig. 15

The kimono pattern is used for this draft and the flat draft is drawn in the same way as the short cape given in connection with the long coat. For the long cape, however, this method of drafting gives so much fulness at the lower edge that it is necessary to alter the pattern, as shown in Fig. 15, the dart on the shoulder giving the cape a more fitted appearance, which is not at all undesirable.

The size of paper needed is 52 inches long and 30 inches wide.

62. Preliminary Drafting.—Pin the kimono pattern on the paper in exactly the way that it was pinned for the short cape shown in Fig. 14, and follow the same procedure for drawing the neck, center-back, and center-front lines and locating point J_2.

63. Drawing the Bottom Line.—Swing an arc having a radius of 25 inches, using point J_2 as a center. This arc P_3R_3 should have its radius made $\frac{1}{2}$ inch longer at the center front and center back.

64. Cutting the Draft Apart.—Trace the neck line and remove the pattern. Cut on the traced line at the neck and along the arc from P_3 to R_3.

65. Removing the Fulness.—Fold the pattern in half with the center-front and center-back lines together. Crease on this fold and cut the pattern apart on the crease. Pin the sections of the pattern on another piece of paper with the center back along one of the long edges, separating them about 1 inch at the neck and allowing the lower edges to overlap about 5 inches.

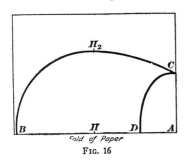

Fig. 16

66. Drawing the New Center-Front and Center-Back Lines.—To remove more fulness,

Locate:
Point P_4 5 inches above P_3 on the arc.
Point R_4 5 inches above R_3 on the arc.
Draw:
Line IP_4 by connecting points I and P_4 to form the center-front line.
Line A_2R_4 for the center-back line.

67. Cutting the Draft Apart.—Cut on line IP_4, around the arc P_4R_4, along the back line from R_4 to A_2, from A_2 to J_2; then cut the dart and the remainder of the neck curve from J_3 to I.

68. Drafting a Hood Pattern.—When a hood is desired on the cape just drafted, provide a sheet of paper 20 inches long and 14 inches wide. Fold the paper through the center crosswise and place it with the folded edge next to you, as shown in Fig. 16.

Locate:
Point A on the edge of the fold.
Point B $13\frac{3}{4}$ inches to the left of point A.
Point C 5 inches above point A.
Point D 3 inches to the left of point A.

Draw:
Curve CD by placing the midway point between tt and ww on point D and the edge of the curve near the arrowhead touching point C.
Locate:
Point H 7 inches to the left of point A.
Point H_2 by placing the square with one arm on line AH, its corner at H, and marking the point 7 inches above H.
Draw:
Curve BC, using H as a center to describe arc BH_2, and drawing a free-hand curve between H_2 and C, or, if you desire to use the square, placing the midway point between r and s on H_2.

69. Cutting the Pattern.—To form the pattern, cut from D to C and from C, through H_2, to B.

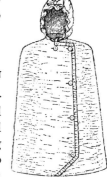

Fig. 17

CHILD'S SLEEPING-BAG PATTERN

70. An excellent style of sleeping bag for an infant is illustrated in Fig. 17. It consists of a pointed shirred hood, or cap, and a bag that buttons at the left side. To develop such a covering for a baby, it is necessary to have a pattern for the bag, as well as one for the hood, or cap.

The size of paper necessary is 30 inches long and 20 inches wide.

Provide for the front lap by placing one long edge of the paper next to you, measuring up 5 inches at each end, drawing a line to connect these two points, and then folding the paper under on this line.

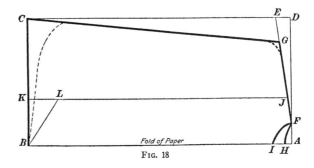

Fig. 18

Place the paper with the fold toward you, draw rectangle $ABCD$, using the fold to form one side of it and making each of its sides 27 inches and each of its ends $12\frac{1}{2}$ inches, as shown in Fig. 18.

71. Drawing the Shoulder Line.—The first line to be drawn is the shoulder line.

Locate:
Point E $1\frac{1}{2}$ inches to the left of D on line CD.

Point F 2 inches above A on line AD.
Connect:
Points E and F with a diagonal line.
Locate:
Point G $2\frac{1}{2}$ inches below E on line EF.
Draw:
Line FG by making heavy the diagonal line between these two points.
Line CG by connecting C and G with a heavy diagonal line.

NOTE.—If a round shoulder is desired, round off the corner at G, as shown by the dotted lines.

72. Drawing the Neck Curves.—Two more points must be located for the neck curves.
Locate:
Point H $\frac{3}{4}$ inch to the left of A on the fold.
Point I 2 inches to the left of A on the fold.
Draw:
The back-neck curve, using a free-hand curve or placing the square so that qq is at H and the edge of the curve, near oo, is at F.
The front-neck curve, using a free-hand curve or placing the square so that l is at I and the edge, near i, is at F.

73. Drawing the Outer Edges of the Lap.
Locate:
Point J $2\frac{1}{2}$ inches above F on line EF.
Point K $4\frac{1}{2}$ inches above B on line BC.
Connect:
Points J and K with a straight line.
Locate:
Point L 3 inches to the right of K on line JK.
Connect:
Points B and L with a diagonal line.

NOTE.—Lines BL and JFI and the edge of the paper LJ then form the lap. But if the lap is desired straight across the top, as in Fig. 17, instead of curving around the neck, the straight effect may be secured by drawing a line from I to line LJ, parallel to the edge of the paper.

74. Tracing and Cutting the Back Section.—Use a piece of paper as large as the space occupied by the rectangle. Place this paper underneath the drafted pattern with one of its long edges exactly along the fold. Pin it securely in place, so that it will not slip when tracing. Trace along the back-neck curve from H to F; from F to G; if a curved shoulder is desired, trace the curved dotted line; then from G to C; and from C to B.
Remove the traced piece and cut on the traced lines.

75. Tracing and Cutting the Front Section Apart.
Trace on the front-neck curve from I to F; from F to J; and from L to B.
Open out the paper and cut on the traced lines BL, IF, and FJ; then on the pattern lines from I to F;

from F, through J, to G, cutting on the dotted curved line if a curved shoulder is desired; from G to C, and from C, through K, to B. This draft when folded represents the left side, and when unfolded, the right, or extended, side.

NOTE.—If it is desired to have the lower corners of the sleeping bag rounded, the light dotted line may be followed.

76. Drafting the Hood Pattern.—The size of paper should be 21 inches long and 13 inches wide. Fold this paper through the center, crosswise, and place it so that the folded edge is next to you, as shown in Fig. 19. Then draw rectangle $ABCD$ about 1 inch from the right edge of the paper on the fold, making each end 11 inches and each side 9 inches.
Locate:
Point E $3\frac{3}{4}$ inches to the right of C on line CD.
Point F $1\frac{1}{2}$ inches below D on the line AD.
Draw:
Line EF by connecting E and F with a diagonal line.
Locate:
Point G $1\frac{1}{4}$ inches to the left of A on line AB.

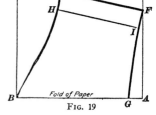
FIG. 19

Draw:
Curve FG with a free-hand curve or by placing the square with ff at F and the edge of the curve, near bb, at G.
Curve EB by placing the square with pp at E and the edge of the curve, near hh, at B.

77. Indicating the Turn-Over Portion.—To determine the turn-over,
Locate:
Point H $1\frac{1}{2}$ inches below E on the line EB.
Point I $1\frac{1}{2}$ inches below F on the line FG.
Connect:
Points H and I with a diagonal line.

78. Cutting the Draft Apart.—Form the pattern for the hood, or cap, by cutting through both thicknesses of the paper from G to F; from F to E; and from E to B. Trace on line HI.

PATTERNS FOR OTHER SLEEPING GARMENTS

79. Although patterns for Teddy Bear sleeping garments, as well as other sleeping garments having leg portions containing shaped feet, can be drafted, the work is tedious and consumes considerable time. Instead of drafting patterns, it is recommended that tissue-paper patterns be used in their development. In selecting a tissue-paper pattern for a sleeping garment, a size that corresponds to the age of the child is generally satisfactory. Sometimes it is advisable to reshape the tissue-paper pattern with the aid of a plain foundation-waist pattern drafted according to the measurements of the child for whom the garment is to be made; but, as a rule, a good-fitting sleeping garment can be procured without making any pattern alterations.

PATTERNS FOR GROWING CHILDREN

MEASUREMENTS AND DRAFTING PROCEDURE

80. As has already been mentioned, children's patterns are developed in practically the same manner as those for adults; that is, foundation patterns are used for obtaining the pattern lines and patterns are slashed and adjusted to give the fulness and effect that fashion and comfort require. Although measurements of children do not control the proportion of the pattern, practically the same plan of drafting adults' patterns with the square is followed in drafting patterns for little folks. The measurements and a few other exceptions should therefore be carefully noted, so that no difficulty will be experienced in developing patterns for growing children.

81. **Taking Children's Measurements.**—In preparing patterns for children, it is well to bear in mind that they should never be drafted so that garments made with their aid will fit absolutely tight, for such garments will not serve for any length of time nor be pleasing in effect. Measurements for children should be taken a trifle looser than for adults. It is really surprising how small a child will prove to be when measured; therefore, if the tape line is placed as close as it would be for an adult, from $\frac{1}{4}$ to 1 inch should be added to each measurement.

82. The measurements needed for drafting patterns for children are: the neck, the bust, the length-of-back, the center-back depth, the width-of-back, the front, the chest, the armhole, and the front-skirt length from the waist line down. The waist measurement should be as large as the bust, and it can be determined from the bust measurement. The hip measurement need not be taken, as it will be practically the same as the bust and waist measurements.

For a skirt pattern, a hip measurement 1 inch larger than the bust measurement should be supplied. This will give sufficient width through the hips in drafting to permit of the proper flare for either a plain or a circular skirt. In taking skirt lengths of children, the back length is very frequently shorter than the front. This is due more to the way in which children stand than to actual measurements. Therefore, it is advisable to take only a side measurement, measuring from the waist line to the bend of the knee, and then to make the back measurement $\frac{1}{4}$ inch shorter than the front or the side. This makes a better hanging skirt.

83. For convenience in drafting, Table II, the accompanying table of average measurements of children, has been prepared. It will furnish measurements for practice drafts and will serve as a check in the drafting of patterns for different children. Of course, you understand that since growing children vary greatly in size for a given age, this table cannot be used as an infallible guide in taking measurements.

TABLE II

AVERAGE PROPORTION OF CHILDREN'S MEASUREMENTS

Age	Neck	Breast	Front	Chest	Width of Back	Len'th of Back	Cen'r Back Dep.	Arm-hole	Waist	Inside Sleeve Finish
4	$11\frac{1}{4}$	$23\frac{1}{2}$	15	$10\frac{1}{4}$	10	$10\frac{1}{2}$	5	11	$22\frac{1}{2}$	10
6	$11\frac{1}{2}$	$25\frac{1}{2}$	$15\frac{1}{2}$	$10\frac{3}{4}$	$10\frac{1}{2}$	11	$5\frac{1}{4}$	$11\frac{1}{2}$	24	$11\frac{1}{2}$
8	$11\frac{3}{4}$	$26\frac{1}{2}$	16	$11\frac{1}{4}$	11	$11\frac{1}{2}$	$5\frac{1}{2}$	12	$25\frac{1}{2}$	13
10	12	28	17	$11\frac{3}{4}$	$11\frac{1}{2}$	$12\frac{1}{4}$	6	13	$26\frac{1}{2}$	14
12	$12\frac{1}{4}$	$29\frac{1}{2}$	18	$12\frac{1}{4}$	12	13	$6\frac{1}{4}$	$13\frac{1}{2}$	26	$15\frac{1}{4}$
14	$12\frac{1}{2}$	$31\frac{1}{2}$	19	$12\frac{3}{4}$	$12\frac{1}{2}$	$13\frac{3}{4}$	$6\frac{1}{2}$	14	25	$16\frac{1}{2}$
16	$12\frac{3}{4}$	$33\frac{1}{2}$	20	$13\frac{1}{2}$	13	$14\frac{3}{4}$	$6\frac{3}{4}$	$14\frac{3}{4}$	$25\frac{1}{2}$	17

CHILD'S FOUNDATION-WAIST PATTERN

84. In drafting a foundation-waist pattern for a child of 4 years or more, the same principles are followed as in drafting for adults, including the same additions to bust, chest, front-length, and width-of-back measures. A few changes, however, are necessary in locating some of the points. For example, *D* is omitted from the center-back line and the back-shoulder curve is straightened somewhat.

To make the child's draft, follow directions for locating construction points as in the adult founda-

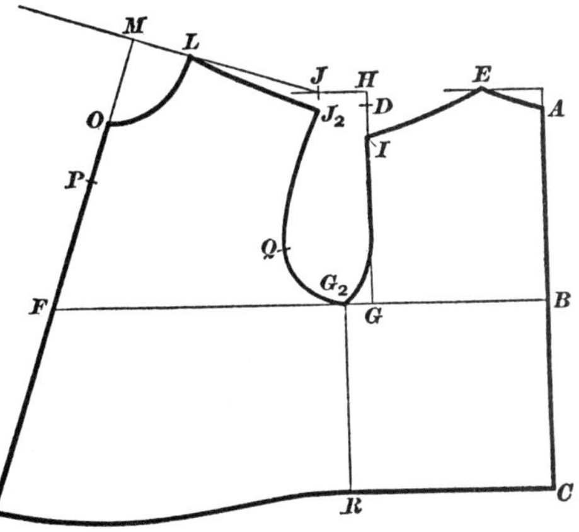

FIG. 20

tion-waist draft, Chapter II, with the exception of the points that follow.

85. **Straightening the Back-Armhole Curve.**—In order to shorten the back-shoulder line, it is necessary to straighten the back-armhole curve.

Locate:

Point G_2 one-sixth of one-half the armhole measure to the left of *G*.

Point I one-eighth of the armhole measure, minus $\frac{1}{4}$ inch below H.

Draw:

The back armhole by placing the square in the same position as for the adult draft, but adjusting it so that the curve will touch G_2 and I; usually, vv or a point near it will be at G_2.

86. Drawing the Foundation Front-Shoulder Line.

A foundation line must be drawn before the true shoulder curve can be obtained.

Locate:

Point D one-third of line HI below H.

Point J one-eighth of the armhole measure, plus $\frac{1}{2}$ inch, to the left of H.

Draw:

The foundation front-shoulder line by placing the square with its corner at D and the straight edge of the long arm at J, drawing a 6- or 7-inch line to the left of J.

87. Drawing the Front-Shoulder Curve.—This curve is drawn as in the adult draft.

Locate:

Point L the length of the back-shoulder line, minus $\frac{1}{4}$ inch, to the left of J on the foundation front-shoulder line.

Point J_2 $\frac{1}{2}$ inch below J.

Draw:

Curve LJ_2 as in Art. **25**, Chapter II.

88. Drawing the Front Armhole.—To obtain the front-armhole curve,

Locate:

Point P $1\frac{1}{2}$ inches below O.

Point Q one-half the width-of-front measure from P, using the square in the same way as in the adult draft.

Draw:

Curve J_2G_2 by adjusting the square so that ll or kk is at J_2 or above it and letting the edge of the curve touch Q and G_2, as in making an adult draft.

89. Drawing the Under-Arm and Waist Lines.

Under-arm curves do not have to be considered in drafting a child's foundation-waist pattern, because children's waists do not have to fit close at the sides.

Draw:

The under-arm line, therefore, as a straight line, as in Art. **32**, Chapter II.

Locate:

Point R as in the adult draft, Art. **33**, Chapter II.

Draw:

The waist line by placing the square with n at R and the edge of the curve, near u, at N.

98

90. Cutting the Draft Apart.—The pattern is cut out in the same manner as a foundation-waist pattern for an adult.

———

91. The pattern for a child's underwaist is a development of the child's plain foundation waist. Pin the front and the back sections of the waist on a piece of paper about 27 inches long and 16 inches wide. Fig. 21 shows clearly that the center-front is on the straight edge of the paper and next to you, and that the shoulder lines meet.

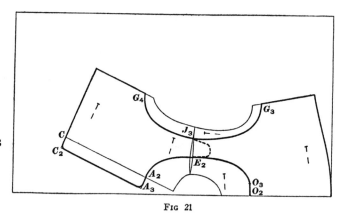

FIG 21

92. Drafting the Front Section.—To form the pattern for the front section,

Locate:

Point G_3 $\frac{3}{4}$ inch to the right of the armhole curve on the under-arm line of the front section.

Point J_3 1 inch below the armhole edge on the shoulder line.

Draw:

Curve G_3J_3 by placing a on G_3, with the edge of the curve, near g, touching J_3, or by drawing a free-hand curve connecting these points.

Locate:

Point O_2 $2\frac{1}{2}$ inches to the right of the neck curve on the center-front line.

Point O_3 by placing the corner of the square at O_2 with the long arm on the center-front line and marking O_3 $\frac{3}{4}$ inch above O_2.

Point E_2 $1\frac{1}{2}$ inches below J_3.

Connect:

Points O_3 and E_2, using a free-hand curve or by placing the square with the midway mark, between xx and yy, on O_3 and the edge of the curve, near tt, touching E_2.

Points O_2 and O_3 with a straight line.

93. Drafting the Back Section.—To draft a pattern for the back section,

Locate:

Point G_4 on the under-arm line $\frac{3}{4}$ inch to the left of the armhole curve.

Draw:

Line J_3G_4 by placing the square with the midway point, between the arrowhead and yy, on G_4 and the edge, near tt, at J_3.

Locate:

Point A_2 on the center-back line $2\frac{1}{2}$ inches to the left of the neck curve.

Point A_3 by placing the corner of the square at A_2 and the long arm along the center-back line, and measuring toward the edge of the paper 1 inch.

Point C_2 by measuring 1 inch from C of the child's foundation-waist draft in the same way that A_3 was located.

Connect:

Points A_3 and C_2 with a straight line.

Points C_2 and C with a straight line.

Points A_3 and A_2 with a straight line.

Points E_2 and A_2 by placing a on point A_2 and the edge, near f, touching point E_2.

Round the corners slightly at A_3 and C_2 and complete the shoulder strap by extending the lines G_4J_3 and A_2E_2 the desired length. The end of the strap may be rounded as shown in Fig. 20.

94. Cutting the Pattern.—To cut the *back* draft apart, trace from A_2, through E_2, around the strap to J_3, and along the curve J_3G_4. Trace the under-arm line and bottom line, through point C, to C_2.

To cut the *front* draft apart, unpin the front section and move it to the space above so as to supply paper for the shoulder strap. Trace along the curved line from O_2, through O_3, to E_2. Follow the shoulder line to J_3 and then along the curve J_3G_3. Trace the under-arm, bottom and center-front lines.

Remove both waist-pattern sections and cut along the traced lines and the lines A_2A_3, A_3C_2, and C_2C.

ONE-PIECE DRAWERS

95. After a youngster has passed the age of wearing diapers, possibly the most suitable drawers to be worn are those cut with the aid of the one-piece pattern shown in Fig. 22. A garment cut from this pattern, when opened out appears as in Fig. 23, a, b, c, and d representing the side-seam lines. In making the garment, a and c are joined, also, b and d.

Provide a sheet of paper 25 inches long and 12 inches wide.

96. Locating Construction Points.—Fold the paper crosswise through the center and place the folded edge next to you, drawing rectangle $ABCD$ by using the fold as one end of the rectangle and measur-

ing off $11\frac{1}{2}$ inches. This is line AB. Make the sides of the rectangle $10\frac{1}{2}$ inches.

Locate:

Point E 5 inches to the left of A on the fold.

Point F $4\frac{1}{4}$ inches above A on line AD.

Point G 4 inches to the left of D on line CD.

Point C_2 $1\frac{1}{4}$ inches below C on line BC.

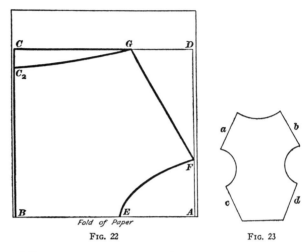

Fold of Paper

Fig. 22   Fig. 23

97. Drawing Pattern Lines.—Now, all pattern lines can be drawn.

Draw:

Curve C_2G by placing the square with ff at C_2 and the edge of the curve, near bb, at G.

Line FG, a diagonal line between points F and G.

Curve EF by placing the square with the midway point, between qq and rr, at E and the edge of the curve, near jj, at F.

98. Cutting the Draft Apart.—Cut through both thicknesses of the paper from E to F; F to G; G to C; C to B. Open out the paper and cut from C_2 to G. Line C_2G forms the front waist line, CG, the back waist line, and EF, the opening for the leg.

PATTERN FOR PLAIN DRAWERS

99. Drawers for a child of 3 years or more may be developed from a pattern drafted in the manner shown in Fig.

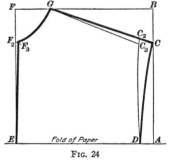

Fold of Paper

Fig. 24

24, on a paper about 30 inches long and 15 inches wide. The only measurements needed are those of the waist and the side.

100. Locating Construction Points.—Several construction points can be located in succession.

Locate:

Point *A* by folding the paper crosswise through the center, and with the fold next to you, marking *A* about 2 inches from the right edge on the fold.

Point *B* with the corner of the square at *A* and its short arm on the fold, drawing along the long arm a line equal in length to one-half the waist measure, and lettering its termination *B*.

Point *C* on line *AB* 3 inches below *B*.

Point *D* $1\frac{1}{4}$ inches to the left of *A* on the fold.

Point *E* the side length to the left of *D* on the fold.

Point *F* by placing the corner of the square at *E* and its short arm on the fold, drawing along the long arm a line the same length as line *AB* and lettering its termination *F*.

Connect:

Points *F* and *B* with a straight line, so as to form a rectangle.

Locate:

Point *G* one-fourth of the side measure from point *F* on line *BF*.

Point F_2 one-fourth of line *FE* from *F* on line *FE*.

101. Drawing Pattern Lines.—All the pattern lines can be drawn in succession.

Draw:

Line *GC* as a diagonal line between points *C* and *G*.

Locate:

Point C_2 $1\frac{1}{4}$ inches to the left of *C* on line *CG*.

> NOTE.—This makes the front portion shorter than the back, which is necessary for a well-fitting garment.

Connect:

Points *C* and *D* with a free-hand curve or by placing the square with *ff* at point *C* and the edge of the curve, near *bb*, at point *D*.

Points C_2 and *D* in the same way as *C* and *D* were connected.

Locate:

Point C_3 $\frac{1}{2}$ inch below point C_2 on the curve C_2D.

Connect:

Points C_3 and *G* with a diagonal line.

> NOTE.—This is done to take out some of the fulness in the front.

Points *G* and F_2 with a free-hand curve or by placing the square with *D* of the R. F. C. at *G* and the edge of the curve, near 3*F*, at F_2.

Locate:

Point F_3 $\frac{1}{4}$ inch to the right of F_2 on curve GF_2.

Draw:

Line F_3E as a diagonal line between points F_3 and *E*.

102. Cutting the Draft Apart.—Cut, with the paper folded, from *D* to *C*; from *C*, through C_2, to *G*; from *G* to F_3; and from F_3 to *E*. Open out the paper and cut from *D* to C_3 and from C_3 to *G*.

CHILD'S ONE-PIECE SLEEVE PATTERN

103. A one-piece sleeve pattern is often very desirable and a convenience when making garments for children, as it requires less time to construct it than a two-piece sleeve. Detailed instruction for making a draft for such a pattern is not given, but the method to be followed is the same as that given for the adults' plain foundation sleeve, Arts. 43 to 49, inclusive, Chapter II. Of course, you will find it necessary to straighten the curves somewhat in accordance with the straighter lines of a child, but the experience you have gained in drafting will enable you to do this successfully.

CHILD'S TWO-PIECE SLEEVE PATTERN

104. Changes from Adult's Pattern.—To draft a child's two-piece sleeve pattern, Fig. 25, proceed in

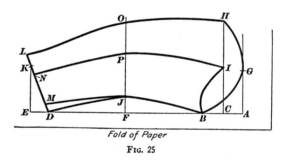

Fold of Paper

FIG. 25

the same manner as in drafting a two-piece sleeve pattern for an adult. But

Locate:

Point *J* 1 inch above *F* if the inside sleeve length is less than 14 inches.

Draw:

Curve *LH* by placing the square with *n* at *L* and the edge of the curve, near *w*, at *H*.

Curves *NP*, *MJ*, and *DJ* by placing the square with *ee* at *P* and *J*, respectively, and the edge of the square, near *b*, touching *N*, *M*, and *D*, respectively.

105. Cutting the Draft Apart.—Cut the draft apart in the same manner as a two-piece sleeve draft for an adult would be cut.

106. A child's kimono-waist pattern is always a convenience when making little girls' dresses because of the ease with which the kimono style of dress is constructed. The drafting of the pattern is not at all difficult, particularly if you have mastered the adult's draft, for it is made in much the same manner.

107. Changes in the Adult's Pattern.—A few changes, however, will have to be made in the directions for the adult's draft, which are as follows:

In pinning the child's foundation-waist pattern on the paper, place the shoulder points only $\frac{1}{2}$ inch apart.

Since points U and V are omitted in the child's foundation draft, place the under-arm lines together at point R and pin the front and the back together at this point; then make the fold as directed for the adult pattern.

Locate:
> Point A_2 $\frac{1}{2}$ inch below point T.
> Point B_2 on the original waist line on point R, or $\frac{1}{2}$ inch to the left of point R.
> Point D_2 $\frac{1}{2}$ inch below point B_2.

Draw:
> Line G_3H_2 one-half the hand measure plus $\frac{3}{4}$ inch.
> The under-arm curve by placing k so that it touches line E_2H_2.

108. Cutting Draft Apart.—Cut the draft apart as directed for the adult pattern.

---

109. French Dresses.—In the development of French dresses, the plain-waist pattern is simply extended to provide for the length desired in the body portion. A slightly flaring under-arm line is added to both the front and the back, similar to the under-arm lines of an infant's slip; that is, 1 inch of fulness is added to the bottom of the waist portion of both the front- and the back-pattern pieces, and this fulness is tapered to nothing at the armhole. The skirt of a French dress is usually two or three times as full as the lower portion of the body of the dress, being cut straight of the material and gathered or plaited at its upper edge, where it joins the waist portion.

110. Empire Dresses.—Materials have much to do with the development of patterns for children, especially in the case of Empire dresses. The waist portion of an Empire dress is shaped from the child's plain-waist and plain-sleeve patterns, and the skirt represents from one and one-half to four straight widths of material, the number of widths depending on the width of the material that is used, as well as on the size of the child and the prevailing styles. The skirt should almost invariably be twice as wide

as the waist measurement; for instance, if the waist measurement is 24 inches, the skirt measurement should be twice 24, or 48 inches. Often it is more, but seldom is it less. The material for children's dresses is usually a plaid, a check, or a flouncing, any of these materials making it necessary to have a skirt that is cut on the straight of the material.

FIG. 26

---

111. Although aprons are cut in many instances without the aid of drafted patterns, there is one style of apron, namely, the Mother Goose apron, Figs. 26 and 28, for which it is convenient to have a pattern.

The size of paper needed is about 32 inches long and 16 inches wide.

112. Locating First Construction Points.—With the long edge of the paper next to you,

Locate:
> Point A by measuring in 15 inches from the right on the lengthwise edge, as in Fig. 27.
> Point B one-half the bust measure from A by placing the corner of the square at point A and the short arm on the lengthwise edge.

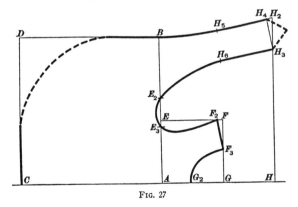

FIG. 27

> Point C the desired length of the apron to the left of A on the edge.

> NOTE.—For a 3-year-old size, the length is made $12\frac{1}{2}$ inches, and, as a rule, 1 inch is added for each additional year.

> Point D by placing the square so that its corner is at C and the short arm is on the lengthwise edge, and drawing a line

along the long arm, making it the same in length as line AB, that is, one-half the bust measure.

Connect:

Points D and B with a straight line.

113. Locating Construction Points for the Bib Section.—Time can be saved by locating all the construction points for the bib before drawing any lines.

Locate:

Point E one-half the chest measure, plus $\frac{1}{4}$ inch, above A on line AB.

Point E_2 2 inches above E.

Point E_3 $\frac{1}{2}$ inch below E.

Point F by placing the square with the corner at E and the short arm on line AB and measuring from E one-half the armhole measure.

Point G by drawing a vertical line from F to the fold of the paper, placing the corner of the square at F and the short arm on line EF, and lettering the end of this line G.

Point F_2 $\frac{1}{2}$ inch to the left of F on line FE.

Point F_3 $2\frac{1}{2}$ inches or the width that the strap is to be, below F.

Point G_2 one-fourth the neck measure, plus $\frac{1}{2}$ inch, to the left of G on the fold.

114. Drawing the Bib Portion.—To draw the lines that form the bib,

Connect:

Points F_2 and F_3 with a diagonal line.

Points G_2 and F_3 with a free-hand curve or by placing the square with a at G_2 and the edge of the curve, near e, at F_3.

Points E_3 and F_2 with a curved line by placing the square with i at E_3 and the edge of the curve, near o, at F_2.

Points E_3 and E_2 by placing the square with j at E_3 and the edge of the curve, near g, at E_2.

115. Drafting the Shoulder Strap of the Apron.

Locate:

Point H the length-of-back measure to the right of A on the lengthwise edge.

Point H_2 by drawing a vertical line from point H one-half the bust measure, plus $1\frac{1}{2}$ inches.

Draw:

Curve BH_2, a curved free-hand line or by placing the square with gg at B and the edge of the curve, near bb, at H_2.

Locate:

Point H_3 $2\frac{5}{8}$ inches below H_2 on line HH_2.

Point H_4 $\frac{1}{2}$ inch to the left of H_2 on line BH_2.

Point H_5 $4\frac{1}{2}$ inches to the left of H_4 on line BH_2.

Point H_6 with the square placed with its corner at H_5 and the straight edge of the short arm touching B, and marking H_6 $2\frac{1}{2}$ inches below H_5.

Draw:

Line H_4H_3 by connecting points H_4 and H_3.

Line H_3H_6 by connecting points H_3 and H_6 with a diagonal line.

Curve E_2H_6 by connecting E_2 and H_6 with a free-hand curve or by placing the square with pp at E_2 and the edge of the curve, near ii, at H_6.

NOTE.—If a sharp point is formed at H_6, the lines may be blended together with a slight curve. The end of the shoulder strap may be made pointed, as shown by the dotted lines, or it may be rounded, as desired.

116. Determining the Bottom of the Apron. Locate a point about 5 inches to the left of B on line BD and another point the same distance from C on line CD; then connect these points as shown by the dotted curve, which may be drawn free-hand.

FIG. 28

117. Cutting the Draft Apart. Cut from G_2 to F_3; from F_3 to F_2; from F_2 to E_3, around the curved line to E_2, and through H_6 to H_3; around the pointed end to H_4; and then from H_4, through H_5 and B and around the curved dotted line, to C.

118. Drafting the Circular Pocket.—For the pocket pattern shown in Fig. 28, three points must be located, one under the arm about $6\frac{1}{2}$ inches from the center-front line and about 3 inches from the bust line, and the other two placed on the center-front line, one $5\frac{1}{2}$ inches and the other $9\frac{1}{2}$ inches to the left of point A.

Connect the point under the arm with each of the points on the center-front line with free-hand curves. Trace the pocket pattern to a separate piece of paper and cut out on the traced lines.

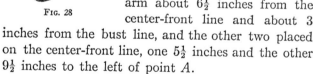

MISSES' PATTERNS

119. Patterns for misses and small women are drafted in practically the same manner as patterns for fully developed women; in fact, the difference lies chiefly in the style of the garment, which, for misses, almost invariably has straight lines instead of fitted lines.

The individual measurements of a young girl are so proportioned one to another that they will usually give the desired simple, straight lines. The measurements, however, should be taken a little looser than those for an adult would be, so that garments developed from the patterns will have the necessary freedom.

The waist and bust lines of garments for a young girl should never be prominently featured, and the under arm should be made straight; that is, it should not be shaped from the waist line to the armhole. The additional fulness caused by the omission of the under-arm lines should be retained at the waist line to produce the straight-line effect.

In skirt drafting, darts also are omitted, in order to permit the skirt to hang almost straight; that is, the foundation plain skirt is used without darts. When Fashion decrees that skirts be full at the lower edge, a circular-skirt pattern may be used satisfactorily if, in drafting, 1 inch is added to the waist-line measurement, as well as to the hip line.

REVIEW QUESTIONS

(1) What should be the prevailing thought in designing garments for young people?

(2) What pattern is the most important of all infants' patterns?

(3) What pattern is used in developing an infant's kimono pattern?

(4) (a) What must be taken into consideration in taking the measurements of growing children? (b) What patterns are required in developing a sleeping bag?

(5) Why does the back length of children's dresses appear shorter than the front?

(6) Why are the curved under-arm lines omitted on a child's plain-waist pattern?

(7) Select a picture of a dress for a child from 3 to 6 years old, and decide what lines are pleasing to you and how you would prepare a pattern for the dress.

(8) Select a picture of a school dress for a miss. Describe its attractive features, and tell how you would develop a pattern for it.

CHAPTER IX

PATTERNS FOR COATS AND CAPES

THE PATTERN IN RELATION TO THE GARMENT

1. When you have reached the point in pattern drafting when the making of coat patterns is to be done, the drafting of the pattern itself should give little trouble, particularly as the only real difference between the developing of dress and coat patterns is in the allowance that must be made for ease in the coat.

By this time, you have sufficient knowledge of patterns, their proportions, and their major lines to be able to handle them perfectly. So it will be possible for you to give first attention to the style of the pattern to be drafted. In the first place, it should always be of conservative design for it is useless to put skilful workmanship where it will be only temporary. Then, in the drafting, correct lines must be obtained if sleeves, collar, pockets, and facings are to be finished to the point of perfection required in tailored garments.

After drafting a pattern according to the instructions given here, it will be advisable, by means of muslin and flat designing, to prepare a model that conforms perfectly to the line and style of coat desired. Then this model, which should have all fitted seams accurately marked, may be used as a guide in cutting the material, thus saving time and producing a perfect coat or cape with good workmanship.

If good taste is exercised in the style chosen and the material selected and care is used in the drafting of an accurate pattern, the result will be a garment of which you will be proud and on which you will be glad to put your best work. ———

FOUNDATION BOX COAT WITH NOTCH COLLAR

———

DRAFTING THE COAT PROPER

2. Box coat is the term that is generally applied to a severely plain-finished coat that hangs straight from the shoulders. Modifications of the box coat are to be seen almost every season.

To produce the straight box effect from the bust line down, so necessary in a regulation box coat and at the same time provide sufficient fulness across the front, it is necessary, in drafting a box-coat pattern, to provide between the lapel and the armhole a dart that extends from the shoulder to the bust line.

3. Measurements.—In Fig. 1 is illustrated in reduced size the method of drafting a foundation

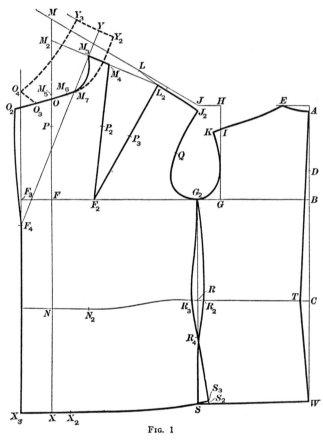

Fig. 1

pattern for a box coat to be made according to the following model measurements:

	INCHES
Neck	13
Bust	38
Front	21½
Chest	14
Width of back	13½
Length of back	15
Center-back depth	7
Armhole	15
Waist	25
Hip	38
Dart	8

4. Additions to Measurements.—The size of paper should be 36 inches wide and 12 inches longer than the coat is to be.

To allow for freedom and to make the coat large enough to be worn over a dress, add 2 inches to the bust line or 4 inches to the bust measure, as in the plain waist, 2 inches to the front length, $1\frac{1}{4}$ inches to one-half the chest measure, $\frac{1}{2}$ inch to one-half the width-of-back measure, and 3 inches to one-half the hip measure.

5. Following Previous Directions.—The procedure in drafting this pattern is much the same as that for drafting the plain foundation-waist pattern.

Locate:

Points A, B, C, D, E, F, G, G_2, H, I, J, J_2, and K according to the same methods as those given in drafting the plain foundation-waist pattern, Chapter II, Arts. **16** to **24**, inclusive.

Locating these points will take care of foundation lines BF, GH, and JH, also the foundation center-back and back-neck lines, and pattern lines AT, AE, EK and KG_2.

6. Drawing the Front Foundation Shoulder Line. Use the same method as is used in the plain foundation waist, for the front foundation shoulder line, Art. **23**, Chapter II, only draw the line longer, about 16 or 18 inches.

Locate:

Point L by using the same method given for locating L in the plain foundation waist, Art. **24**.

7. Drawing the Upper Part of the Center-Front Line.—The drawing of the upper part of the center-front line is done at the same time as the determining of point M.

Locate:

Point M by placing the square with its corner at F, its short arm on the bust line, and drawing a vertical line along the long arm to connect with the foundation shoulder line just drawn. Mark the intersection point M.

8. Drawing the Front-Shoulder Curve.—Use the same method to connect L and J_2 as was used in the plain foundation waist, Art. **25**.

Locate:

Point L_2 one-third of the front-shoulder curve to the right of point L, and make heavy the portion of the curve between L_2 and J_2.

Note.—The distance from L to L_2 is the length of the shoulder line that is later represented by M_3M_4.

9. Determining the Shoulder Dart and Completing the Shoulder Line.—The dart at the shoulder is needed to bring the rest of the pattern lines into correct proportion as well as to insure a good fitting garment.

Locate:

Point F_2 one-fourth of line FG from point F on the bust line.

Point M_2 one-half the length of line FF_2 below point M.

Connect:

Points M_2 and L_2 with a diagonal line.

Locate:

Point M_3 one-fourth the neck measure to the right of point M_2 on line M_2L_2.

Point M_4 the same distance to the right of point M_3 as point L_2 is to the right of point L on the shoulder curve.

Note.—The distance from M_4 to L_2 represents the top of the dart and the line M_3M_4 is the transferred shoulder line.

Draw:

The sides of the dart by connecting points F_2 and L_2, and points F_2 and M_4, with diagonal lines.

10. Drawing the Neck Curve at the Center Front.—Several points must first be located.

Locate:

Point M_5 one-third the neck measure below point M_2 on the upper center-front line.

Point M_6 $1\frac{1}{4}$ inches to the right of point M_5, placing the square with its corner at point M_5 and its short arm on the center-front line.

Connect:

Points M_6 and M_3 by placing the arrow-head of the S. A. C. at point M_6 and the edge of the curve, near vv, at point M_3, and following the curve with a heavy line.

Locate:

Point O $\frac{3}{8}$ inch below point M_5 on the center-front line.

11. Drawing the Front-Armhole Curve.—First, locate several points as follows:

Locate:

Point P $2\frac{1}{2}$ inches below point M_5 on the center-front line.

Point P_2 by placing the square with its short arm on the center-front line and its corner at point P. The intersection of the long arm of the square and the line M_4F_2 is point P_2.

Point P_3 by measuring the distance from P to P_2, and then placing the square with the straight edge on points B and P_2, and adjusting it until the measured distance from P to P_2 is on line L_2F_2. Placing the square in this position saves time in the next operation, the locating of Q.

Example.—Suppose the distance from P to P_2 is $4\frac{1}{8}$ inches. With the straight edge of the square on points B and P_2, adjust the square until the $4\frac{1}{8}$-inch mark on the scale is on line L_2F_2. This is point P_3.

Point Q with the square in the position for locating point P_3, measuring from the corner of the square to the right a distance equal to one-half the chest measure plus $1\frac{1}{4}$ inches.

Draw:

The armhole curve as directed in the plain foundation-waist draft, remembering to adjust the square so that the lines of the front and back portions of the armhole blend together well and appear as one continuous curve.

12. Extending the Center-Front Line.—Place the square with its corner at F and its short arm on the bust line. Draw a line along the long arm to the bottom of the paper or a length suitable for the coat.

13. Locating Construction Points for the Front Waist Line.—Two points must be located.

Locate:

Point N below point M_2, the front length minus one-sixth the neck measure, plus 2 inches.

NOTE.—Follow the directions in Art. **28,** Chapter II, for locating point N of the plain foundation waist, but use a 2-inch instead of a 1-inch addition.

Point N_2 with the corner of the square at point N and its short arm on the center-front line, and drawing a 3-inch line along the long arm, lettering its termination N_2.

14. Drawing the Back Waist Line and Foundation Under-Arm Line.—These lines are drawn at right angles.

Draw:

The back waist line as for the plain foundation waist, Art. **33,** Chapter II.

The foundation under-arm line as in the plain foundation-waist draft, Art. **32,** Chapter II.

Locate:

Point R at the intersection of the under-arm line and the back waist line.

Point S the dart length plus $\frac{1}{4}$ inch below point R.

15. Extending the Center-Back Line and Drawing the Bottom Line of the Back Section.

Locate:

Point W the dart length below C.

Connect:

Points T and W, thus completing the center-back line.

Points W and S with a horizontal line.

16. Drawing the Under-Arm Curves to the Waist Line.—Not all of the under-arm curves can be drawn now.

Locate:

Point R_2 $\frac{1}{2}$ inch to the right of R on the back waist line.

Point R_3 $\frac{1}{2}$ inch to the left of R on the extension of the back waist line.

Draw:

The back under-arm curve to the waist line by placing ff on R_2 and the edge of the curve, near bb, at G_2.

The front under-arm curve to the waist line by placing mm at point R_3 and allowing the edge, near hh, to touch the under-arm line, where it will.

17. Completing the Front Waist Line.—Draw N_2R_3 by placing the square with m at R_3 and the edge of the curve, near t, at N_2.

18. Drawing the Back Under-Arm Line Below the Waist Line.—This line contains a curved section.

Locate:

Point R_4 by placing the square with kk at R_2 and the edge of the curve at hh touching the foundation under-arm line where it will, marking the intersection R_4.

Draw:

Curve R_2R_4 by making heavy the curve just drawn.

Line R_4S by making heavy the foundation under-arm line between R_4 and S.

19. Locating Construction Points for the Front Section Below the Waist Line.—Several construction points are necessary.

Locate:

Point X the dart length plus $\frac{1}{4}$ inch below point N.

Point X_2 $1\frac{1}{2}$ inches to the right of point X by placing the square with its corner at X and one arm on the center-front line.

Connect:

Points X and X_2 with a horizontal line.

Locate:

Point S_2 by measuring from S to W on the back section, placing the square with the point on the scale indicating this measurement at point X with the straight edge of the square on point S, and marking point S_2 to the right of point X a distance equal to one-half the hip measure, plus 3 inches for fulness.

NOTE.—It is necessary to measure the distance between S and W in order to subtract it from one-half the hip measure and determine how much remains, or how long to make line XS_2. The same principle applies as in measuring the waist line of the tight-waist draft, Art. **12,** Chapter V.

Point S_3 by placing the square with its corner at point R_3 and the straight edge on S_2, and marking point S_3 the dart length plus $\frac{1}{4}$ inch below R_3.

20. Drawing the Front Under-Arm Curve Below the Waist Line.—This curve is in two parts.

Draw:

Curve R_3R_4 by placing n at point R_3 and the edge of the curve at q touching the foundation under-arm line at R_4.

Line R_4S_3 by placing the arrowhead of the L. A. C. at R_4 and the edge of the curve, near cc, at S_3, and connecting the two points.

21. Completing the Bottom Line of the Front Section.—So far, line XX_2 is the only section of the bottom line drawn.

Draw:

Line X_2S_3 by placing z at X_2 and the edge of the curve, near t, touching S_3 and connecting the two points.

22. Drawing the Lap for the Front Section.

Locate:

Point F_3 by extending the bust line $2\frac{1}{2}$ inches to the left of point F, as a lap of $2\frac{1}{2}$ inches is generally sufficient.

Point X_3 by extending the bottom line $2\frac{1}{2}$ inches to the left of the center front.

Extend:

The waist line by adding $2\frac{1}{2}$ inches to the waist line at the center front.

Connect:

These three points with a vertical line and extend it almost to the shoulder.

———

23. In connection with the drafting of all coat collars, the terms break line, turn-over, and stand portion must be understood.

The *break line* is that line at which the collar turns, or rolls over, thus separating the turn-over and stand portions.

The *turn-over* is the portion of the collar that turns back and becomes a part of the outer surface of the coat.

The *stand portion* is the extension below the break line, the part of a collar that is covered by the turn-over. It is very essential in order that the collar itself will fit snug at the neck.

24. Outlining the Lapel.—The lapel should be outlined next.

Locate:

Point F_4 2 inches below F_3 on the vertical line drawn as directed in Art. **22**.

NOTE.—Point F_4 indicates the depth of the turn-back of the lapel.

Draw:

The break line by connecting points F_4 and M_3 with a diagonal line.

The top of the lapel by placing w at M_6 and the edge of the curve, near v, at point O and extending this line $\frac{1}{2}$ inch beyond the lap line.

Locate:

Point O_2 as the termination of the $\frac{1}{2}$-inch extension.

Draw:

The outside line by placing ff at point O_2 and the edge of the curve, near aa, at point F_4 and drawing O_2F_4.

25. Drafting the Stand Portion of the Collar.

Locate:

Point Y by extending the line F_4M_3 one-sixth the neck measure.

Point Y_2 $1\frac{1}{4}$ inches to the right of Y by placing the square with its corner at Y and its short arm along YF_4.

Connect:

Points Y and Y_2 with a dotted line.

Locate:

Point M_7 at the intersection of YF_4 and the neck curve of the coat.

Draw:

The neck curve of the collar by placing xx at M_7 and the edge of the curve, near tt, at Y_2, using a dotted line.

26. Drafting the Turn-Over Portion of the Collar.

Locate:

Point O_3 $1\frac{3}{4}$ inches to the right of point O_2 on line O_2O.

Point O_4 $1\frac{1}{4}$ inches above line O_2O on the foundation line that indicates the lap for the front.

Connect:

Points O_3 and O_4 with a dotted diagonal line.

27. Drawing the Center-Back Line of Collar. Place ee at point Y and the edge of the square, near dd, at Y_2, and draw a dotted line to the left of Y to point ff, marking its termination Y_3.

28. Drawing the Outside Curve.—Place ii at O_4 and the edge of the curve, near ee, at Y_3 and draw O_4Y_3, making this a dotted line.

29. Cutting the Collar Draft Apart.—Place a sheet of paper under the collar section and trace as follows: From O_3, through O, M_6, and M_7, to Y_2; from Y_2, through Y, to Y_3; from Y_3 to O_4; and from O_4 to O_3. Trace also the line where the collar is to turn, M_7M_3Y.

Remove the traced paper and cut out the collar pattern by cutting on the outside traced lines, but not on line M_7Y, which indicates the turn-over.

30. Cutting the Coat Draft Apart.—Paste one edge of a strip of paper under the front section along the part extending from point R_4 at the under arm to the bottom of the coat and then trace line R_4S_3. This paper is needed, because the front and back of the pattern overlap at the bottom under-arm curves. Cut out the pattern for the back of the box coat as follows: From W, through T, to A; from A, through E and I, to K; from K to G_2; from G_2, through R_2 and R_4, to S, being careful not to cut the paper pasted underneath; and from S to W.

Cut out the pattern for the front, as follows: On the traced line of the piece of paper pasted to the drafting paper from S_3 to R_4; then on the draft from R_4, through R_3, to G_2; from G_2, through Q, to J_2; from J_2, through L_2 and M_4, to M_3; from M_3, through M_7, M_6, O, and O_3, to O_2; from O_2, through F_4, to X_3; and from X_3, through X, X_2, and S, to S_3. Cut the dart out, cutting from L_2 to F_2 and from M_4 to F_2.

VARYING THE BOX-COAT PATTERN

31. To lengthen a draft of this kind so as to provide for a longer box-coat pattern, it is simply necessary to extend the lines below the hip measurement and connect them at the bottom. But, to insure accuracy, it is always necessary to draft the pattern to the hip measurements first, as in the draft just described.

For a shorter box-coat pattern, the procedure is the same, except, after drafting as just explained, the lines below the waist may be shortened and then connected.

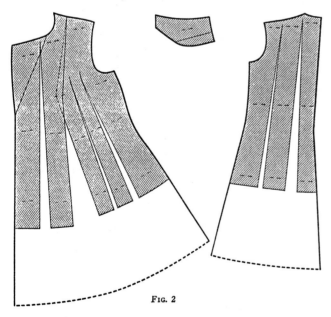

FIG. 2

In Fig. 2 are illustrated ways in which a box-coat pattern may be slashed and separated in order to produce a pattern for a coat that is to be full at the lower edge, as well as the manner in which the pattern may be lengthened.

108

SHAWL COLLAR

32. In the directions for drafting a foundation box-coat pattern, the only collar considered is the notch collar. As other collars, namely, the shawl collar, the sailor collar, and the large round collar, are often required for women's coats, the drafting of patterns for such collars is taken up here.

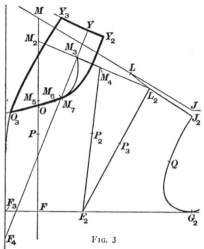

FIG. 3

33. The **shawl collar**, the drafting of which is illustrated in Fig. 3, differs chiefly from the notch collar in that its edge is without a notch; that is, the lapel and the collar are in one.

To draft a pattern for a shawl collar, it is necessary to utilize the box-coat draft, as in drafting a pattern for a notch collar. Therefore, proceed at first as in drafting the notch collar, but omit points O_2 and O_4, and do not locate Y_3 and O_3 as before, for these points determine the outside line, which is to be changed.

34. Drawing the Outer Edge.—To make the changes that distinguish the shawl collar from the notch collar,

Locate:

Point Y_3 $2\frac{1}{4}$ inches to the left of point Y on the center-back line of the collar.

Draw:

The curve from M_6 to the lap line, or outer edge of the box-coat pattern, in the same way as in drafting the notch collar.

Locate:

Point O_3 on the curve just drawn, marking O_3 $\frac{3}{8}$ inch to the right of the lap line.

Connect:

Points Y_3 and O_3 by placing the square with t at O_3 and the edge of the curve, near x, at point Y_3.

Point O_3 with the lap line by placing the square with t at point O_3 and a point midway between r and s touching the lap line, or outside edge, and drawing a line downwards to the left.

35. Cutting the Draft Apart.—Place a piece of paper under the collar part of the draft and trace as follows: From Y_2, through Y, to Y_3; from Y_3 to O_3; and from O_3, through O, M_6, and M_7, to Y_2.

To indicate the line on which the collar turns over, or the break line, trace the straight line from M_7, through M_3, to Y.

To form the pattern for the shawl collar, remove the traced paper from underneath the box-coat draft and cut on the outside traced lines.

———

SAILOR COLLAR AND LARGE, ROUND COLLAR

36. Very often fashions demand that a large collar in the shape of a sailor collar or in cape or shawl effect, with the corners rounded or square, be used. Such patterns, depending on the style of garment with which they are to be used, may be drafted on the plain foundation-waist pattern, the tight-fitting foundation pattern, or the box-coat foundation pattern. Because of the width of such a pattern, it is necessary to have a seam at the shoulder to prevent the collar from rolling up or appearing clumsy around the neck. This fact should therefore be kept in mind in preparing such patterns, the drafting of which on a box-coat pattern is illustrated in Fig. 4.

37. Drafting the Sailor Collar.—To draft a pattern for a sailor collar on a foundation box-coat draft, proceed in the same manner as for a notch collar, omitting points O_3 and O_4. Then,

Locate:

　Point M_8 to the left of M_3 the desired width of the collar at the shoulder, placing the square so that a straight edge is on line M_2M_3.

　　NOTE.—Generally $5\frac{1}{2}$ inches is a satisfactory width at the shoulder.

　Point M_9 at the intersection of lines M_3M_4 and Y_2M_7.

Draw:

　Curve M_3M_8 by placing the square with mm at M_3 and the edge of the curve, near hh, at M_8. This curve will be part of the shoulder seam.

　Curve M_8O_2, the outer edge of the front part of the collar, by placing the square with gg at M_8 and the edge of the curve, near dd, at O_2.

Extend:

　Line YY_2 with the straight edge of the long arm of the square on line YY_2 and draw a 6- or an 8-inch dotted line to the left of Y.

Locate:

　Point Y_3 on line YY_2 the desired depth of the collar to the left of Y.

　　NOTE.—Generally 6 inches is a good depth.

Draw:

　The lower edge of the collar by placing the

square, L. S. up, so that its corner is at Y_3 and the short arm is on line Y_3Y_2, and drawing an 8- or a 9-inch dotted line along the long arm.

Locate:

　Point Y_4 on the line just drawn from Y_3 one-half the width-of-back measure from Y_3.

Draw:

　Line Y_4Y_5 with the corner of the square at Y_4 and one of the arms on line Y_3Y_4, drawing a 3- or a 4-inch dotted line to the right of Y_4.

Locate:

　Point Y_5 on the line drawn to the right of point Y_4 as far from M_3 as M_8 is from M_3.

Draw:

　Curve M_3Y_5 by placing the square with m at M_3 and the edge of the curve, near r, at Y_5.

38. Cutting Out Sailor-Collar Pattern.—Trace the *back section* of the collar on a piece of paper slipped underneath the pattern. Trace from Y_2 to Y_3; from Y_3 to Y_4; from Y_4 to Y_5; from Y_5 to M_3; from M_3, to M_9; and from M_9 to Y_2.

Indicate the turn-over of the back collar portion by tracing from M_3 to Y.

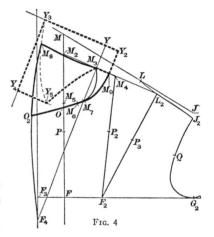

FIG. 4

To form the pattern of the *side-front* section, slip a piece of paper underneath and trace from O_2, through O, M_6, and M_7, to M_9; from M_9, on the straight line to M_3; on the curved line from M_3 to M_8; and from M_8 to O_2.

To indicate where the collar turns over, trace on the straight line M_7M_3.

Cut the outer traced lines of both back and side-front sections on the separate sheets of paper.

39. Cutting the Collar Draft Apart.—Cut on the outer traced lines.

　NOTE.—When cutting out the pattern for the front body portion of the coat, keep in mind the fact that the neck line extends from O_2, through M_7, on the curve, to M_3. The neck line of the collar extends from O_2 to M_7 and from M_7 to M_9. The neck line of the back collar portion extends from Y_2 to M_9.

40. Joining the Collar to the Coat.—In making the collar, join the edge of the back collar portion that begins at M_9 and extends through M_3 to Y_5, to the edge of the front collar portion that begins at M_9

and extends through M_3 to M_8. Line Y_2Y_3 corresponds to the center back.

41. Drafting a Large, Round Collar.—If a large, round collar is desired, mark the back part of the collar with a slightly curving line from Y_5 to Y_3, as indicated by the light dotted line in Fig. 4, and trace the collar in the manner described for the sailor collar, omitting the section outside the dotted line from Y_5 to Y_4 to Y_3.

FOUNDATION COAT SLEEVE

42. For a coat sleeve, there is required a pattern different from any sleeve pattern heretofore considered, because a coat sleeve must be straight in line, comfortably large, moderately loose at the hand, and yet should fit without a wrinkle at the armhole of the coat. In a coat sleeve, also, it is always desirable to have the inside sleeve line come far enough to the inside to permit a crease to be pressed in the upper part of the coat sleeve, this crease taking the same position as the inside sleeve line in dresses and blouses. A sleeve having these characteristics will hang straight from the shoulder at the armhole, and will also have

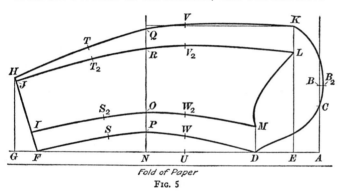

Fig. 5

the true mannish "set," which is always sought in any tailored suit.

43. The manner in which a suitable foundation coat-sleeve pattern may be drafted is shown in reduced size in Fig. 5. The measurements that govern the drafting of all other sleeves apply in this case; that is, the arm hole, the inside sleeve length, and the hand measure. The draft here illustrated is developed from the following model measurements:

	Inches
Armhole	15
Inside sleeve length	17
Hand	8

As in the case of other foundation drafts, the directions and rules for drafting this sleeve pattern may be applied in drafting similar patterns to different measurements.

44. Locating Construction Points for the Upper-Sleeve Portion.—Fold through the center, with the

folded edge next to you, a sheet of paper 27 inches square.

Locate:

Point A by placing the square with the long arm 1 inch above the fold of the paper, and parallel to it, and the short arm 1 inch from the right edge of the paper, and parallel to it, drawing a line the full length of each arm and marking point A at the place where these two lines meet.

Point B on the vertical foundation line one-third the armhole measure above point A.

Point B_2 $\frac{1}{4}$ inch to the right of B.

Point C $1\frac{1}{2}$ inches below B on line AB.

Point D on the horizontal foundation line, one-third the armhole measure to the left of point A.

Point E one-half the distance between points A and D, plus $\frac{1}{2}$ inch, to the right of point D.

Point K by placing the square with its corner at point E and its short arm on the horizontal foundation line, drawing along the long arm a vertical line equal in length to one-half the armhole measure, plus 2 inches, and lettering the termination of this line K.

Point L one-half the armhole measure above point E on line EK.

Point M 2 inches above point D by placing the corner of the square at point D with one arm on the line AD and measuring 2 inches from D.

45. Drawing the Top Curve.—As in all sleeves there are two top curves.

Draw:

Curve B_2K by placing the square with 5 of the F. C. at point B_2 and the edge of the curve, near 3, at point K.

Curve CD by placing the square with $2E$ of the R. F. C. at point C and the edge of this curve, near $4G$, at point D.

Curve B_2C with $2E$ of the R. F. C. at point C and moving the square until the curve touches B_2.

46. Drawing the Under Curve.—Connect points M and L, placing the square with b of the S. A. C. at point M and the edge of the curve, near g, at L.

47. Drawing the Wrist Section.—To determine the wrist section,

Locate:

Point F the inside-length measurement to the left of D.

Point G $1\frac{3}{4}$ inches to the left of F.

Point H by placing the square with its corner at point G and the straight edge of the short arm on line AG, and drawing a vertical line the length of one-half the hand measure, plus $1\frac{1}{2}$ inches.

Connect:

Points H and F with a diagonal line.

Locate:

Point I $1\frac{1}{2}$ inches above F on line HF.

Point J one-half the hand measure above I.

48. Determining the Elbow Lines.—To determine the elbow line,

Locate:

Point N midway between points D and F on line AG.

Draw:

The elbow line by placing the square so that a straight edge is on line AG and its corner at point N and drawing a vertical line the full width of the folded paper.

49. Locating Construction Points for the Lengthwise Pattern Lines.—All of these points are located on the elbow line.

Locate:

Point O on the elbow line 3 inches above point N.

Point P midway between points N and O.

Point Q by placing the square with the short arm on line EK and its corner at K, drawing a light line to the left of K to connect with the elbow line, and marking Q $\frac{1}{4}$ inch below the intersection of these lines.

Point R $1\frac{1}{2}$ inches below point Q on the elbow line.

50. Drawing the Lengthwise Pattern Lines.

Draw:

Curve PD by placing the square with t at P and the edge of the curve, near x, at D.

Curve OM in the same way as PD was drawn.

Curve RL by placing t on point R and the edge of the curve, near z, at L.

Curve QK in the same way as RL was drawn.

Curves FP, IO, JR, and HQ by placing the square with ff on points P, O, R, and Q, in turn, and the edge of the curve, near aa, at F, I, J, and H, in turn.

51. Providing Ease at the Elbow.—So that the seams will not pull apart because of the bending of the arm, slight fulness is allowed at the elbow.

Locate:

Point S to the right of F on line FP the length of one-third the inside sleeve measure.

Point S_2 on line IO the same distance to the right of I as S is from F.

Point T_2 to the right of J on line JR one-third the inside measure plus $\frac{1}{2}$ inch.

Point T on line HQ the same distance to the right of H as T_2 is from J.

Point U 3 inches to the right of point N on the horizontal foundation line, AG.

Points V, V_2, W and W_2 with a straight edge of the square on the foundation line and its corner at point U, drawing short vertical lines, $\frac{1}{2}$ or 1 inch long, to intersect each of the lines QK, RL, PD, and OM, lettering the intersecting points of these lines as follows: V on line QK; V_2 on line RL; W on line PD; and W_2 on line OM.

NOTE.—In order to have a sleeve of this kind "set" properly at the elbow, it is necessary to stretch the front upper section carefully and to hold the front edge of the under arm a trifle full; also, it is necessary to gather in a little fulness above and below the elbow line at the back.

52. Cutting the Draft Apart.—Trace the *under portion* of the sleeve as follows: From M to L; from L, through V_2, R, and T_2, to J; from J to I; and from I, through S_2, O, and W_2, to M. Also, mark points W_2, V_2, T_2, and S_2, and trace the elbow line from O to R. Next, unfold the paper and form the pattern for the under portion of the sleeve by cutting the outside tracings on the paper that was underneath.

The pattern for the *upper section* of the sleeve may then be cut out as follows: From D, through C and B_2, to K; from K, through V, Q, and T, to H; from H, through J and I, to F; and from F, through S, P, and W, to D. Trace the elbow line and mark points W, V, T, and S.

NOTE.—The top curve of this pattern will test out larger than the armhole measure used. This, however, is necessary in the making of coat sleeves, because the top must be gathered with short, close stitches and the fulness drawn up and shrunken out to insure a perfect-fitting sleeve.

SEMIFITTING COAT

DRAFTING THE COAT

53. The lines of a tight-fitting or semifitting coat follow closely the lines of the human figure, and, in order to produce such lines, the drafting principles employed in developing a pattern for a tight-fitting foundation waist must be employed. Therefore, before taking up the drafting of a semifitting coat, as shown in Fig. 6, it will be well to review the drafting of the tight-fitting foundation waist, Fig. 1, Chap. V, for in the discussion of that pattern is explained fully the proportion of the waist line, as well as the manner in which the darts must be arranged in order to take out the fulness at the waist and to give the tight-fitting or the semifitting garment.

54. **Additions to Measurements.**—Since the great difference between the semifitting coat draft and the tight-fitting waist draft is that more ease is necessary, some additions must be made to the original measurements. The following additions are quite satisfactory: 2 inches to the bust measure, or 1 inch to the bust line, $\frac{1}{4}$ inch to one-half the width-of-back measure, $\frac{1}{2}$ inch

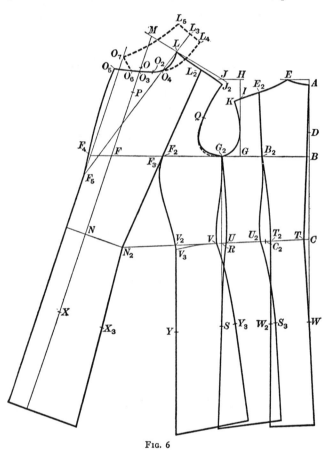

FIG. 6

to one-half the chest measure, 1 inch to the front-length measure, $2\frac{1}{2}$ inches to one-half the waist measure and 1 inch to one-half the hip measure.

55. **Size of Paper.**—Provide a sheet of paper 36 inches wide and 10 inches longer than the coat length, measuring from the tip of the shoulder to the length desired for the coat.

56. **Copying Points and Lines of the Tight-Waist Draft.**—All points and lines should be drawn and located as described for the tight-waist draft except that the above additions should be used.

57. **Drawing the Center-Front and Waist Lines.**
Locate:
Point M one-sixth the neck measure plus $\frac{3}{4}$ inch to the left of point L.

Draw:
The center-front line from M, through F, as in Art. **27**, Chapter II.
Locate:
Point N as in Art. **28**, Chapter II, but allowing for the additions to measurements given in Art. **54.**
Draw:
The front waist line as in Art. **4**, Chapter V.
Locate:
Points O, P, and Q as in Art. **28**, Chapter II.

58. **Drawing the Armhole Curves.**—The armhole curves may be drawn next.
Draw:
The back armhole curve the same as in drafting a pattern for a waist.
The front-armhole line in the same way as in drafting a pattern for a waist and then adjust the square in order to draw the dotted line shown in Fig. 6, placing the square with pp on the curve J_2G_2 and the edge of the curve, near ss or tt, touching the bust line near G_2.

NOTE.—The purpose of this additional curvature is to give a little more freedom at the armpit, a very important point to consider in this type of coat.

59. **Drawing the Front-Neck Curve of Coat.**
Locate:
Point O_2 by placing the square with its corner at O and its short arm along the center-front line and measuring $1\frac{1}{4}$ inches to the right of O on the long arm.
Draw:
The front-neck curve by placing the square with the arrowhead of the S. A. C. at O_2 and the edge of the curve resting on L.
Locate:
Point O_3 $\frac{3}{8}$ inch below O on the center-front line.

60. **Drawing the Side-Front Line of Coat.**
Locate:
Point L_2 one-half of the distance between L and J_2, plus $\frac{1}{4}$ inch, to the right of L.

NOTE.—The position of point L_2 is governed by prevailing fashions. Sometimes the side-front and the side-back seams come at the center point of the shoulder, and sometimes they are as much as $1\frac{1}{2}$ inches below the midway point, measuring from L.

Point N_2 to the right of N on the front waist line one-third of the bust line from F to G_2, plus $\frac{1}{4}$ inch.

NOTE.—In order to give a straight line to the front and sufficient freedom to allow the coat to hang straight from the bust line down, points N_3 and X_2 are omitted from the draft. Therefore, in determining the waist and the hip lines, measure from N and X.

Connect:

Points L_2 and N_2 with a diagonal line.

Locate:

Points F_2 and F_3 as in drafting the tight-fitting waist pattern, Art. 5, Chapter V.

61. Locating Construction Points for the Darts. In locating the following points and lines, proceed as in drafting the tight-fitting waist pattern.

Draw:

The under-arm line from G_2 down.

The foundation waist line from C to N_2.

Locate:

Point C_2 midway between points R and C.

Points U and V each $\frac{1}{2}$ inch from R.

Point T $\frac{1}{2}$ inch to the left of C.

Point U_2 $\frac{1}{2}$ inch to the left of C_2.

Point T_2 $\frac{1}{2}$ inch to the right of C_2.

Point E_2 one-half of the distance between K and E, plus $\frac{1}{4}$ inch, to the left of point E.

62. Drawing the Darts and Center-Back Line. Draw lines E_2B_2, T_2B_2, and U_2B_2, as well as the under-arm curves G_2U and G_2V and the center-back line, following the directions given for drawing these lines in the tight-fitting waist draft.

63. Drawing the Front and Waist-Line Curves of the Front Under-Arm Section Above the Waist Line.

Locate:

Point V_2 following the directions given in making the tight-fitting waist draft.

Point V_3 from F_3 the distance from N_2 to F_3, minus $\frac{3}{8}$ inch. In measuring this distance, follow the directions given in making the tight-fitting waist draft.

Draw:

Curve V_3V in the usual manner.

Curve V_3F_3 by placing the square with n of the L. A. C. at V_3 and the edge of the curve, near t, at F_3.

The short curve from F_2 to line F_3V_3 as in drafting the tight-fitting waist pattern.

64. Drafting Below the Waist Line.—Measure the hip sections as for the tight-fitting waist pattern and extend the lines the desired length of the coat, as in the drafting the princesse-slip pattern.

65. Drafting the Lap for the Front.—For a lap of 2 inches,

Extend:

The waist line, the bust line and the bottom line 2 inches to the left of the center-front line.

Locate:

Point F_4 at the termination of the 2-inch extension of the bust line.

Connect:

The ends of these three extended lines with a straight line, drawing it almost to the shoulder line.

————

DRAFTING THE LAPEL AND COLLAR

66. Drawing the Break Line.—The first line of the lapel to be drawn is the break line.

Locate:

Point F_5 2 inches below F_4 to indicate the depth of the turned-back lapel, or the lower extremity of the break line.

Connect:

Points F_5 and L with a diagonal line.

Locate:

Point L_3 by extending line F_5L one-sixth of the neck measure above point L.

67. Drafting the Stand Portion of the Collar.

Locate:

Point L_4 $1\frac{1}{4}$ inches to the right of L_3 by placing the square with its corner at L_3 and the short arm along line L_3F_5.

Connect:

Points L_3 and L_4 by drawing a dotted line between these two points.

Locate:

Point O_4 at the intersection of line F_5L_3 and the neck curve.

Draw:

The bottom line of the stand portion of the collar by placing the square with xx at O_4 and the edge of the curve, near tt, at L_4.

68. Drawing the Top and Outside of the Lapel. The top of the lapel is drawn during the locating of point O_5.

Locate:

Point O_5 by placing the square with u at O_2 and the edge of the curve, near v, at point O_3, extending the line $\frac{1}{2}$ inch beyond the lap line of the draft.

Draw:

The outside line by placing the square with ff at O_5 and the edge of the curve, near aa, at F_5 and drawing curve O_5F_5.

69. Providing the Notch.—To obtain the line that completes the notch,

Locate:

Point O_6 $1\frac{3}{4}$ inches to the right of O_5 on line O_5O_3.

Point O_7 $1\frac{1}{4}$ inches above line O_5O_3 on the line that indicates the lap for the front.

Connect:

Point O_7 and O_6 with a dotted diagonal line.

70. Drawing the Center-Back Line of the Collar. Place the square with *ee* at L_3 and the edge of the curve, near *dd*, at L_4 and draw a curved line to the left of L_3 to a point between *ff* and *gg*.

Locate:

Point L_5 $1\frac{1}{2}$ inches, or the collar width, to the left of L_3 on an extension of line L_4L_3, using the straight edge of the square in measuring the distance.

71. Drawing the Outer Edge of the Collar.—For this edge a curve is necessary so that the turned-over edge will fit closely around the back of the neck.

Connect:

Points L_5 and O_7 with a curved line, placing the square with *ii* at O_7 and the edge of the curve, near *ff*, on L_5.

also, after cutting to point L, it is necessary to cut on the front-neck curve, through O_4, O_2, O_3, and O_6 to O_5; from O_5 to F_5; and from this point on the lap line to the bottom line.

CIRCULAR CAPE

74. Nature of Capes.—A cape is a loose, sleeveless garment that hangs from the neck and shoulders. It may be straight or circular in line and may be developed with or without a pattern. The straight cape is usually gathered into a collar at the neck, or it may be gathered on a small yoke, which a large collar conceals. In any case, straight pieces of material that are as wide at the top as at the bottom are used in the construction of the straight cape.

The circular cape is easily developed with a pattern

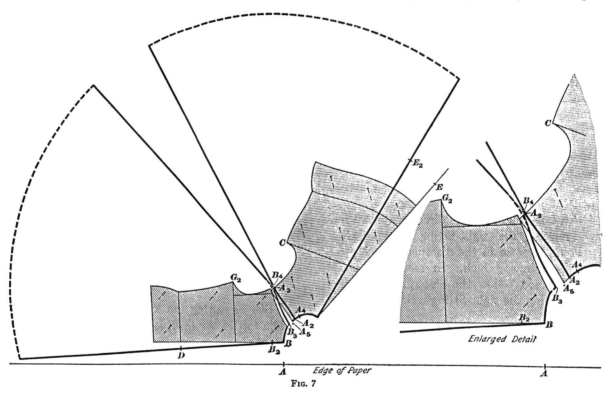

Fig. 7

72. Cutting the Collar Draft Apart.—Place a piece of paper under the collar portion of the draft, pin it in place securely, and trace as follows: From O_6, through O_3, O_2, and O_4 to L_4; from L_4, through L_3, to L_5; from L_5 to O_7; and from O_7 to O_6. To indicate where the collar is to turn over, trace the diagonal line from O_4, through L, to L_3.

Remove the traced paper and cut out the collar pattern, cutting on the outside traced lines, but not on the line O_4L_3, which simply indicates where the collar will turn over.

73. Cutting the Coat Draft Apart.—The pattern for the coat proper is cut out in the same manner as the pattern for the tight-fitting waist, except that the dotted curved line of the front armhole is followed;

such as the one shown in Fig. 7. This garment has as its foundation the plain foundation waist on which several construction points and lines are located. The most important of these construction points is the pivot, or foundation, point.

75. Pinning the Foundation-Waist Back in Position.—On a piece of paper equal in width to the length that the cape is to be and of a length that is one and three-fourth times the cape length,

Locate:

Point A with one long edge of the paper toward you, as shown, marking A the length of the cape, plus about 2 inches, from the left edge of the paper.

Point B 3 inches above A.

Pin:

The back part of the pattern to the paper, placing it so that the neck curve at the center back is at B and the center-back edge of the pattern is parallel with the edge of the paper.

76. Pinning Foundation-Waist Front in Position.

Locate:

Point B_2 one-eighth of the neck measure to the left of B.

Point C one-fourth the bust measure from G_2, placing the square with its corner at point G_2 of the back section of the foundation draft and the straight edge of the long arm on B_2.

Pin:

The front of the foundation pattern with G_2 at point C of the cape draft, letting the front and the back shoulder lines of the pattern pieces touch where they will, as shown, but do not allow the pattern pieces to overlap.

Note.—Remember that G_2 is the intersection of the bust and armhole line on both the front and the back of the foundation-waist pattern.

In a cape that is to fit close to the shoulder, the line that extends from the neck to the tip of the shoulder directly over the arm is the line in the cape that gives the square shoulder, which is characteristic of military capes. It should, therefore, extend in a graceful, easy manner from the neck to the tip of the shoulder and be a little farther toward the front than a similar line in a blouse or a coat. Since the combined shoulder and side seam of the cape should come on top of the shoulder, it is necessary to raise the back part of the waist pattern and lower the front part.

77. Drawing the New Shoulder Lines.—With the pattern placed, you are ready to draw new shoulder lines.

Locate:

Point B_3 $\frac{1}{2}$ inch to the right of point E of the foundation-waist pattern.

Point B_4 $\frac{1}{2}$ inch to the right of the intersection of the back-shoulder and armhole line, as shown in the enlarged detail.

Connect:

Points B_3 and B_4 by placing the square with nn at B_3 and the edge of the curve, near ii, at B_4.

Locate:

Point A_2 $\frac{1}{2}$ inch to the right of the intersection of the shoulder line and the front-neck curve.

Point A_3 $\frac{1}{2}$ inch to the right of the intersection of the shoulder line and the armhole.

Connect:

Points A_2 and A_3 by placing the square with n at A_2 and the edge of the curve, near s, at A_3.

78. Drawing the Side Line of the Back Section.

Locate:

Point A_4 $\frac{3}{4}$ inch to the right of A_2 on the front-neck curve.

Draw:

The side line from B_4 the full length of the square, by placing the square with its corner at A_4 and the straight edge of the long arm at B_4, slipping the square up until a line of the desired length is drawn.

Note.—So that the pattern will fit perfectly at the shoulder, blend the lines a trifle, as shown by the dotted line near B_4.

79. Drawing the Center-Back Line.—For the flare at the center back, locate point D by measuring down 1 inch from the waist line and draw a line from the neck curve, through D, the length desired.

80. Drawing the Side Line of the Front Section.

Locate:

Point A_5 $\frac{5}{8}$ inch to the right of B_3.

Draw:

The side line from A_3 the full length of the square, by placing the corner of the square at A_5 and the straight edge of the long arm on A_3.

81. Drawing the Center-Front Line.—A new center-front line must be drawn.

Locate:

Point E by measuring the side-dart length from the waist line at the center front of the pattern, marking E this distance below the waist line on the extended center-front line.

Point E_2 by placing the square with its corner at E and the long arm on the extended center-front line and measuring out one-eighth of the hip measure on the short arm.

Note.—Point E_2 must be located in this manner in order to permit a new center-front line to be drawn. This new line is necessary because of the drop of the front-neck curve at the shoulder and the fulness allowed for at the left of point C.

Connect the neck curve at the center front and point E_2 with a diagonal line, continuing this line the length desired.

82. Determining the Length of the Cape.—The *back length*, which is any length desired, is the basis for determining the side and the front lengths.

For the *side length*, measure from the tip of the shoulder, or points A_3 and B_4, the same distance as the back length minus 1 inch.

For the *front length*, measure 1 or 2 inches longer than the back length, according to the size of the bust.

83. Drawing the Bottom Line.—Connect the ends of the center back, the center front and the side lines with dotted curved lines.

84. Reducing the Width of the Cape.—The foundation-cape pattern is rather wide, measuring about 5 yards at the lower edge, but you may easily reduce the width if you wish. To do this, take 6 or 8 inches from both front and back sections at the side-seam lines, blending the new side lines into the original outline at the shoulder or B_4. If still more width needs to be removed, lay folds in the center of the pattern sections, tapering them to nothing in the upper portion of the cape pattern.

85. Cutting the Draft Apart.—Trace the front- and the back-neck curve, the waist lines, the new shoulder line on the front part, the section of the back-shoulder line that appears on the front part, and the new center-front line. Remove the foundation-waist pattern.

For the *front pattern* cut the traced line from A_2, through A_3, and the side line to the lower edge of the draft, the new center front, the lower edge of the draft, and the traced neck curve.

For the *back pattern*, cut the traced back-neck curve from B to B_3, from B_3 along the new back-shoulder line and around the dotted line near B_4, on the side line, on the lower edge of the draft, and on the center-back line.

Note.—If, in cutting out a garment with the aid of this pattern, a seam is desired at the center back and only a dart at the shoulder, the two side lines should be placed together.

CAPE COLLARS

STAND COLLAR

86. Capes were brought into prominence by their use as a covering for army uniforms. They not only served as a protection to the soldiers, but lent dignity to their costumes. For such capes, a **military,** or **stand,** collar was always used. Therefore, in connection with the development of the foundation cape here considered, the method of drafting a military, or stand, collar is taken up. A pattern for such a collar may be drafted in the manner shown in Fig. 8, the size of paper necessary being 17 inches long and $3\frac{1}{2}$ inches wide.

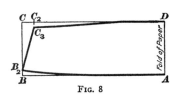

Fig. 8

87. Locating Construction Points.—Fold the paper crosswise through the center, and, with the fold to the right of you, draw on it, $\frac{1}{2}$ inch above the lower edge, a rectangle, each of whose sides is equal to one-half the neck measure, plus $\frac{1}{2}$ inch, and each of whose ends is equal to the desired width of the stand, usually $2\frac{1}{2}$ inches. Letter the corners of the rectangle A, B, C, and D.

Locate:

Point B_2 $\frac{1}{4}$ inches above B on line BC.

Point C_2 $\frac{1}{2}$ inch to the right of C on line CD.

Point C_3 $\frac{1}{4}$ inch below C_2.

88. Drawing the Pattern Lines.—With the foundation points located,

Draw:

The upper neck line by connecting C_3 and line CD with a curved line, placing the square with *ff* at C_3 and the edge of the curve, near *dd*, touching line CD.

The center-front line by connecting C_3 and B_2 with a diagonal line.

The lower neck line by connecting B_2 and the line AB with a curved line, placing the square with *ff* at B_2 and the edge of the curve, at *dd*, touching line AB.

89. Cutting the Draft Apart.—To form the military collar pattern, cut, through both thicknesses of the paper, from D to C_3; from C_3 to B_2; and from B_2 to A.

TURN-OVER CAPE COLLAR

90. Very often on a tailored cape a small **turn-over collar** that may be used with the stand collar is desired. A pattern for such a collar may be drafted in the manner shown in Fig. 9, the size of paper necessary being 8 inches wide and 20 inches long.

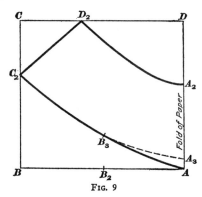

Fig. 9

91. Locating Construction Points.—With the paper folded crosswise through the center and placed so that the fold is to the right, draw, $\frac{1}{2}$ inch above the lower edge of the paper, a rectangle, each of whose sides is equal to one-half the neck measure, plus $1\frac{1}{2}$ inches, and each of whose ends is the desired width of the collar, plus 3 inches.

Example.—As 4 inches is a good width for such a collar, the ends of the rectangle are, in this case, 7 inches.

Letter the corners A, B, C, and D, as shown.

Locate:

Point A_2 the width of the collar above A on the fold.

Point C_2 $2\frac{1}{2}$ inches below C on line CB.

Point D_2 one-half the neck measurement, minus $1\frac{1}{2}$ inches, to the left of D on line CD.

Point B_2 midway between A and B on line AB.

Point B_3 $1\frac{1}{2}$ inches above B_2.

92. Drawing the Pattern Lines.—The pattern lines may now be drawn.

Draw:

Curve A_2D_2 by placing the square so that qq is at A_2 and the edge of the curve, near kk, touches D_2.

Line C_2D_2 by connecting C_2 and D_2 with a diagonal line.

Curve C_2A by placing the square so that hh is at C_2 and the edge of the curve, near

ee, is at B_3; then sliding the square along until hh is at B_3 and the edge of the curve, near ff, is at A, continuing the curve to A.

93. Providing for a Rounded Edge.—If a collar that has a round line at its lower edge is preferred to one that is slightly pointed, locate a point, as A_3, $\frac{1}{2}$ inch above A and connect points A_3 and B_3 in the manner directed for connecting points A and B_3.

94. Cutting Turn-Over Collar Draft Apart.—To form the turn-over cape collar pattern, cut, through both thicknesses of paper, from A_2 to D_2; from D_2 to C_2; and from C_2, through B_3, to A, or A_3 if a rounded edge is desired.

NOTE.—When using the turn-over section as suggested in Arts. 26 to 29, join the line A_2D_2 to line C_3D of the stand collar.

REVIEW QUESTIONS

(1) What is a box coat?

(2) What does the portion of the box-coat draft between M_4F_2 and F_2L_2 represent?

(3) Describe the procedure in locating point Q in the box-coat draft.

(4) What is: (a) The break line of a collar? (b) The turn-over portion? (c) The stand portion?

(5) How may length and fulness be provided in a box-coat pattern?

(6) What changes are made in the measurements during the drafting of a semifitting coat?

(7) What is a cape?

(8) How may the width of the foundation-cape pattern be reduced?

CHAPTER X

PATTERNS FOR MEN AND BOYS' GARMENTS

HOME SEWING FOR MEN AND BOYS

1. In this chapter, the drafting of patterns to be utilized in the development of garments for men and boys is discussed. In order that the method of procedure in drafting such patterns may be thoroughly understood, the measurements, as well as the manner in which they should be taken, first receive consideration, and then the actual drafting of the patterns is discussed in detail.

2. Although not every woman may be called on to make garments for men or boys, there is a decided advantage in knowing how such patterns are drafted, even if no immediate use is to be made of them, for a knowledge of the lines suitable for garments intended for men and boys serves to give a clearer insight into the value of lines for all manner of garments. Thus it assists in the development of greater originality and permits of greater latitude of expression in designing.

Occasionally you will hear of some woman who has built up a very successful business by making one or two types of such garments. For instance, she may make nothing more than shirts, yet her shirts are always in demand, because of their perfect fit, their wearing qualities, and the pleasant "feel" of the materials in them. The home woman, too, will find the information in this chapter of great service, for there are few homes where husband, brother, or father does not prefer his shirts made-to-order. And there is an advantage not only in being able to have a better shirt for the money put into it, but also in its satisfying the needs and whims of its wearer. A drafted shirt can take care of any physical peculiarities, such as unusually long arms or large neck measure or fulness or extra material; also, it gives the man an opportunity to have a pocket just where he wants it or to have any other change in style to which the ready-made shirt of a certain season does not attempt to cater.

A knowledge of the drafting of boys' patterns, also, is of value to many women. Perhaps the making of entirely new garments of this kind may not be a part of many women's programs, but the utilization of old materials in make-overs or "hand-me-downs" is likely to be a necessary consideration in the majority of households. In fact, many a thrifty woman there is who converts old materials into new garments for smaller proportions, by studying the proper ways and means and applying these to the materials at hand.

TAKING MEASUREMENTS

3. Before considering the drafting of patterns for men and boys' garments, it is necessary to understand how the measurements should be taken, for the accuracy of the drafts will depend on the accuracy of the measurements from which they are made. Fourteen measurements are required for drafting the various foundation patterns here considered. They are: (1) the neck, (2) the breast, (3) the width of back, (4) the center-back depth, (5) the armhole, (6) the shoulder yoke, (7) the sleeve length, (8) the hand, (9) the waist, (10) the front length, (11) the back length, (12) the outside length, (13) the inside length, and (14) the knee.

4. In taking the measurements required for the development of patterns to be used in the construction of garments for men and boys, it is necessary to observe the same precautions as in taking measurements for drafting patterns for women. In other words, the tape measure must be correctly placed and each measurement taken accurately.

5. The **neck measure** is taken by measuring around the base of the neck, where the neck band or the collar of a shirt will come.

6. The **breast measure** is taken in the same position as the bust measurement for a woman; that is, around the body, over the vest if an adult, close under the arms, and across the shoulder blades in the back. In taking this measure, the tape line should be kept snug, but not tight.

7. The **width-of-back measure** is taken across the back from armhole to armhole and about 5 inches below the prominent bone at the back of the neck.

8. The **center-back-depth measure** is taken the same as the center-back depth for a woman; that is, after the tape is in place around the breast, the measurement is made from the prominent bone at the back of the neck down to the top of the tape.

9. The **armhole measure** is taken by placing the tape line around under the arm, bringing it close to the body, and then up around the arm to the shoulder point.

10. The **shoulder-yoke measure** merely indicates the depth of the yoke from the center back down on the body of the shirt. The depth of yoke for the average man is $2\frac{1}{2}$ inches. For large men, it is $2\frac{3}{4}$ to 3 inches, and for boys it is generally $1\frac{1}{2}$ inches.

11. The **sleeve-length measure** is determined by placing the tape line at the middle of the back at the

Fig. 1

neck, as indicated in Fig. 1, continuing down over the shoulder and elbow to the wrist, and then subtracting one-half the width-of-back measure from this measure. This measurement is taken in this way in order to have the shoulder yoke of a length that corresponds properly with the width of the back.

12. The **hand measure** is taken by measuring around the hand at the fullest part, including the thumb.

13. The **waist measure** is taken by measuring all around the body at the waist line over the trousers, or pants.

14. The **front-length measure** is taken by measuring from the prominent bone at the back of the neck and around the base to the front, continuing straight down as far below the waist line as it is desired to have the length of the garments. A shirt, for example, may extend from 10 to 15 inches below the waist line, depending on the height of the person and the length of shirt desired.

15. The **back-length measure** is taken by measuring from the prominent bone at the back of the neck to a point as far below the waist line as the front-length measure was taken.

16. The **outside-length measure** is taken by measuring from the waist line down over the hip to the length desired, or to the knee in case of a young boy.

17. The **inside-length measure** is taken by measuring from close up in the crotch to the knee, to the heel of the shoe, or down to a point that indicates the desired length.

18. The **knee measure** is taken by measuring around the knee and then adding to this an amount sufficient to make the trousers, or pants, the width desired at that point.

———

DRAFTING PATTERNS FOR MAN'S SHIRT

19. Measurements.—The method of drafting a pattern for a man's shirt, in coat style, is illustrated in Fig. 2. Such a pattern is decidedly useful, for in addition to developing shirts with its aid, many other garments, such as nightshirts, robes, pajama coats, etc., may be developed.

The same principles are followed in drafting a boy's blouse pattern as are used for a man's shirt pattern. Make the shirt of a size to conform to the measurements of the boy and in cutting make only sufficient allowance below the waist line to provide for the blouse and a casing through which an elastic may be run.

As will be observed from the model measurements given for drafting the pattern shown in the illustration, only eight measurements are required for drafting a shirt pattern; namely,

	INCHES
Neck	14
Breast	36
Center-back depth	9
Width of back	$14\frac{1}{2}$
Shoulder yoke	$2\frac{1}{2}$
Front length, finished	32
Back length, finished	34
Sleeve length	34

20. The drafting of the patterns for the collar and the neck band are not considered in connection with this draft, because directions for drafting these patterns are given in Arts. **87** to **93** inclusive, Chapter II.

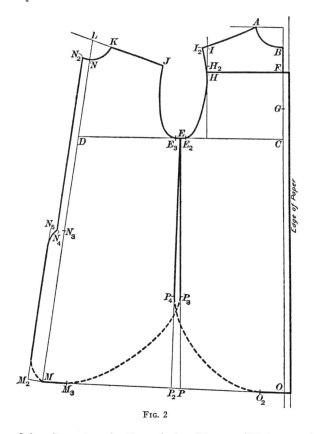

Fig. 2

21. Drawing the Foundation Lines.—With one of the long edges of a 36 in. by 50 in. piece of paper to the right, place the square with the long arm 1 inch from the right edge of the paper and parallel to it and the short arm 5 inches from the top and parallel to it.

Draw a light line the full length of the long arm and another line along the short arm, making this about 4 or 5 inches long.

22. Drawing the Back-Neck Curve.—As in the plain foundation-waist pattern, the back-neck curve is the first to be drawn.

Locate:

Point A by measuring out on the short line one-fifth of the neck measure from the point where the foundation lines meet.

Point B by measuring down on the long line one-seventh of the neck measure from the point where the foundation lines meet.

Draw:

Curve AB by placing the square with the arrowhead of the S. A. C. at A and the edge of the curve, near vv, at B, following the curve with a heavy line.

23. Drawing the Breast Line.—This line corresponds to the bust line of a waist pattern.

Locate:

Point C the center-back-depth measure below B.

Point D by placing the square with its corner at C and its short-arm on line BC, drawing a light line along the long arm, making it one-half the breast measure, plus 3 inches, and lettering its terminations D.

Note.—If the back measure is unusually wide, 4 or 5 inches must be added to one-half the breast measurement when drawing line CD.

24. Locating Construction Points on the Breast Line.—Certain points are to be located on the breast line.

Locate:

Point E midway between points C and D.
Point E_2 $\frac{1}{2}$ inch to the right of E.
Point E_3 $\frac{1}{2}$ inch to the left of E.

25. Determining the Back Yoke.—A man's shirt always has a back yoke.

Locate:

Point F the shoulder-yoke measurement below B.

Note.—This is usually $2\frac{1}{4}$ inches.

Point H with the corner of the square at F and the short arm along line FB, drawing a line along the long arm, making it one-half the width-of-back measurement, plus $\frac{1}{2}$ inch.

26. Drawing the Back Foundation Armhole Line.—Place the square with the short arm on the breast line and the long arm touching point H and draw a light

line along the long arm, making it about 10 inches in length.

Locate:

Point H_2 $\frac{1}{2}$ inch above H on the back foundation armhole line.

27. Drawing the Back-Shoulder Line.—This line contains a slight curve.

Locate:

Point I the shoulder-yoke measurement above H, on the back foundation armhole line.

Point I_2 by placing the square with u at A and the edge of the curve, near x, at I, drawing a line to connect these points, and extending it $\frac{1}{2}$ inch beyond I for its termination I_2.

28. Drawing the Back-Armhole Line.—Place the square with tt at I_2 and the edge of the curve, at vv, on the line below H, and follow the curve. Then turn the square so that i is at E_2 and the edge of the L. A. C. touches the upper curve and complete the armhole.

Note.—If a point is formed in joining these curves, blend the lines with a slight free-hand curve.

29. Drawing the Front-Shoulder Line.—Two points must first be located.

Locate:

Point G one-third of the center-back-depth measurement above C on the long foundation line.

Point J by placing the square with its corner at H_2 and the long arm on line IH_2, and measuring to the left on the short arm one-eighth of the breast measurement.

Draw:

The foundation front-shoulder line by placing the corner of the square at G and allowing the straight edge of the long arm to touch J, drawing a line 9 or 10 inches to the left of J.

Locate:

Point K by measuring along the front-shoulder line the same distance as the back shoulder minus $\frac{1}{4}$ inch.

30. Drawing the Front-Armhole Curve.—Place the square with rr at E_3 and the edge of the curve, near jj, at J, and draw curve JE_3.

31. Drawing the Foundation Center-Front Line.
Locate:

Point L on the front-shoulder line one-seventh of the neck measurement to the left of K.

Point M by extending the center-front line from L, through D, the center-front length, plus one-seventh of the neck measure, and lettering its termination *M*.

Point *N* one-seventh of the neck measurement below *L* on the line just drawn.

32. Drawing the Front-Neck Curve.—Connect points *N* and *K* by placing the square with the arrowhead of the S. A. C. at *N* and the edge of the curve, near *ww*, at *K*.

33. Providing for the Lap.—A lap is always found on such a shirt.

Locate:

Point N_2 by extending the front-neck curve $\frac{3}{4}$ inch beyond *N*, lettering its termination N_2.

Point N_3 on line *LM* by adding 2 inches to the entire front length and marking N_3 one-half of this sum below *N*.

Point N_4 $\frac{3}{4}$ inch to the left of N_3.

Point N_5 $\frac{3}{4}$ inch to the left of N_4.

Connect:

Points N_2 and N_4 with a diagonal line, thus forming the upper center-front line of the pattern.

Locate:

Point M_2 $1\frac{1}{2}$ inches to the left of *M*.

Connect:

Points M_2 and *M*, as well as M_2 and N_5, with straight lines.

NOTE.—The line N_5M_2 is an extension of the center-front line, forming a lap for the shirt, which is in the style of a coat shirt.

Draw:

A curved line from N_4 to line N_5M_2 by placing the square with the arrowhead of the S. A. C. at N_4 and the edge of the curve, near *xx*, on line N_5M_2.

A curved dotted line from line M_2N_5 to *M*, using a free-hand curve.

NOTE.—In work shirts and soft negligée shirts, this extension at the center front is sometimes omitted and the front plait made to extend the entire length of the shirt front.

34. Extending the Back and Bottom Foundation Lines.—One construction point must first be located.

Locate: .

Point *O* the entire back length below *B*.

Connect:

Points *M* and *O* with a straight line, extending it beyond *O* to the edge of the paper.

Locate:

Point M_3 on line *MO* $2\frac{1}{2}$ inches to the right of *M*.

Point O_2 $2\frac{1}{2}$ inches to the left of *O*.

35. Drawing the Front Under-Arm Lines.

Draw:

The front under-arm line by placing the square with its corner at *E* and the short

arm on the breast line, and drawing a line along the long arm from *E* to the bottom line.

Locate:

Point *P* at the intersection of this under-arm line and the bottom line.

Point P_2 1 inch to the left of *P* on line *OM*.

Draw:

The back under-arm line by connecting points P_2 and *E* with a diagonal line.

36. Drawing the Bottom Curves.—Two curves are drawn to shape the sides and lower edges of the skirt-pattern pieces.

Locate:

Point P_3 9 inches above *P* on line *PE*.

Point P_4 9 inches above P_2 on line P_2E.

Connect:

Points M_3 and P_3 and points P_4 and O_2 with free-hand curves, as shown.

37. Completing the Back Section of the Shirt. Continue the line *HF* from *F* to the edge of the paper.

NOTE.—This is the line that joins the yoke to form the back of the shirt.

38. Cutting the Yoke Pattern.—To form the yoke pattern, cut from *B* to *A*; from *A*, through *I*, to I_2; from I_2 to *H*; from *H* to *F*; and from *F* to *B*.

39. Tracing and Cutting the Back Section. Before cutting out the back-pattern pieces, sew or paste underneath the draft a piece of paper large enough to accommodate the extension of the front section and trace line EP_3; also, trace from P_3 along the dotted line for a few inches.

Then, cut from *H* to *E*; from *E* to P_4, taking care to lift the draft to avoid cutting the paper underneath; and then from P_4, through O_2 and *O*, to the edge of the paper; also, cut from the edge of the paper to point *F*.

40. Cutting Out the Front Section.—Cut from *E* to *J*; from *J* to *K*; from *K* to N_2; from N_2 to N_4; from N_4 around the curves to *M*; from *M* to M_3; from M_3 around the long, dotted, curved line to the traced portion; and then on the traced lines to point *E*.

MAN'S SHIRT SLEEVE

41. A sleeve pattern for a man's shirt is drafted in much the same manner as the sleeve pattern for a mannish shirtwaist, as shown in Fig. 3. Only three measurements are to be used for drafting this sleeve pattern, the following being model measurements:

INCHES

Armhole (obtained by measuring the armhole of the shirt draft) 19
Sleeve length (center back of neck to hand) 34
Hand 9

In drafting a sleeve according to these measurements, a piece of paper about 33 inches long and 24 inches wide is required. Before beginning to draft, fold the paper lengthwise through the center.

42. Drawing the Armhole Curves.—Two curves, the upper and the lower, must be drawn, but before this is possible several points must be determined.

Locate:

Point *A* with the fold next to you, measuring in 6 inches from the right edge of the paper, as shown.

Point *B* by placing the square U. S. up with its corner at *A* and the short arm on the fold, drawing a line along the long arm, making it equal to one-half of the armhole measurement, minus $\frac{1}{2}$ inch, and lettering its termination *B*.

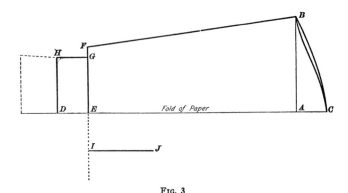

FIG. 3

Point *C* one-third of the length of line *AB* to the right of *A* on the fold.

Draw:

The upper curve by placing the square with *hh* at *C* and the edge of the curve, near *cc*, at *B*.

The lower curve by placing the square with *m* at *B* and the edge of the curve, near *t*, at *C*.

43. Drafting the Lower Sleeve Section.—Outlining the lower sleeve section includes the locating of several points.

Locate:

Point *D* the sleeve length, minus one-half the length of the yoke, or the distance between points *H* and *F*, Fig. 2, to the left of *C*, Fig. 3.

Point *E* the width of the cuff desired to the right of *D*.

NOTE.—A good width for the cuff is 3 inches.

Point *F* by placing the square, U. S. up, with the corner at *E* and the short arm on the fold, drawing a line along the long arm, making it equal to one-half the hand measure, plus $1\frac{3}{4}$ inches.

Point *G* one-half the hand measure, plus $\frac{3}{4}$ inch, above *E*.

44. Drawing the Seam and Cuff Lines.—The drawing of the under-arm seam line will complete the upper section of the sleeve draft.

Connect:

Points *F* and *B* with a diagonal line.

Locate:

Point *H* by drawing a line from *D* parallel with line *EF*, making this line equal in length to one-half the hand measure, plus $\frac{3}{4}$ inch, and lettering its termination *H*.

Connect:

Points *H* and *G* with a straight line.

NOTE.—The corners of the cuff may be rounded, if desired, as shown by the dotted line.

45. Drawing the Cuff Opening.—To obtain the opening in the lower-sleeve section,

Locate:

Point *I* by tracing the bottom sleeve line from *E* to *F*, opening the draft and measuring down from *E* on the traced line a distance equal to two-thirds of one-half the cuff measure, and marking point *I*.

Point *J* to the right of *I*, by drawing a line parallel to the creased line formed by the fold, making it equal in length to one-half the cuff measure, plus 1 inch, and lettering its termination *J*.

46. Drafting the French Cuff.—If a French, or soft, cuff is desired, it will be necessary simply to add a turn-back portion to the plain cuff, as shown by the dotted lines.

Locate:

A point to the left of *D* a distance equal to the length of line *DE*, plus $\frac{1}{2}$ inch.

Draw:

A line from this point parallel to line *DH*, making it $\frac{1}{4}$ inch longer than line *DH*.

NOTE—Line *DH* forms the fold when the cuff is turned back in position.

Connect:

The termination of this line and point *H* with a diagonal line.

47. Cutting the Draft Apart.—To cut out the *cuff pattern*, fold the paper again and cut from *E* to *G*; from *G* to *H*; and from *H* to *D*. If a *French cuff* is desired, cut around the dotted lines instead of on line *DH*.

For the *sleeve pattern*, cut, through both thicknesses of the paper, from *C* to *B* on the upper curved line; from *B* to *F*, and from *F* to *G*. Then open the paper and cut on the lower curve, from *C* to *B*.

For the *cuff openings*, slash the line from point *I* to point *J*.

48. In order to make a shirt appear complete, it is advisable to apply a pocket, especially if it is a negligée or a work shirt. The method of drafting a shirt-pocket pattern having the lap and the lower edge pointed is shown in Fig. 4.

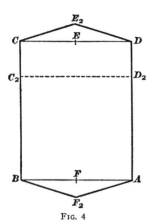

Fig. 4

The size of paper necessary is 10 inches long and 7 inches wide.

49. Drawing the Foundation Rectangle A B C D. Locate:

Point A with one of the short edges of the paper next to you, measuring in 1 inch from the right edge and up 2 inches from the lower edge and marking A at this point.

Draw:

Rectangle $ABCD$, each end of which is 5 inches and each side, 6 inches.

50. Drafting the Turn-Over of the Lap.—The lap has a turn-over section, which is drawn as follows:

Locate:

Points C_2 and D_2 $1\frac{1}{2}$ inches below C and D, respectively.

Connect:

Points C_2 and D_2 with a dotted line.

51. Drafting the Pointed Sections.—Two points must be located for each pointed section.

Locate:

Point E midway between points C and D.
Point F midway between points A and B.
Point E_2 $\frac{3}{4}$ inch above E.
Point F_2 $\frac{3}{4}$ inch below F.

Connect:

Points E_2 and C and E_2 and D with diagonal lines.
Points F_2 and A and F_2 and B with diagonal lines.

52. Cutting the Draft Apart.—Cut from A to F_2 to B; from B, through C_2, to C; from C to E_2 to D; and from D, through D_2, to A.

Note.—It will not be necessary to cut off the pocket lap of the pattern unless the material from which the shirt is to be made has a right and a wrong side, as the pocket and lap will be cut in one piece and the lap simply turned down on the pocket along the dotted line C_2D_2. If material with a right and a wrong side is to be used, however, cut the pattern apart on line C_2D_2, and, in cutting out the material, make a seam allowance on both the top and the bottom of the lap portion, as well as the top of the pocket. (Allowance is made in the draft for the finish on all other edges.)

53. The drafting of patterns to be used in the developing of men's trousers is not considered in connection with the drafting of patterns for men's garments. It is more economical of time to use a suitable tissue-paper pattern to get the general outline for such garments.

BOYS' TROUSERS

54. The making of boys' trousers, both of the heavy type and of the wash-suit variety, often falls to the lot of the woman who sews, and as good results depend on the patterns used in cutting out such garments a knowledge of drafting suitable patterns for boys' trousers will not come amiss.

The measurements required for drafting such a pattern are the waist, the outside leg length, the inside leg length, and the knee. In taking the measurements, care should be exercised not to have the waist measure tight, bearing in mind that the finished draft should measure a trifle larger than the waist measurement. Especially is this necessary in the case of heavy trousers in order to provide for the heavy band and lining that are required. Less allowance, however, is necessary when using the pattern for wash suits.

55. In Fig. 5 is shown the way in which a pattern for boys' trousers may be drafted for boys from 5 to 9 years old. The measurements, which in this case, are model measurements for a boy 5 years of age, are as follows:

	Inches
Waist	26
Outside leg length	15
Inside leg length	8
Knee	$12\frac{1}{2}$

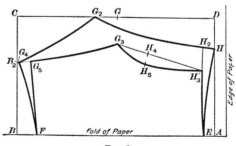

Fig. 5

The size of paper necessary is 35 inches long and 26 inches wide. This should be folded in half crosswise with the fold placed next to you.

56. Drawing Rectangle ABCD.—To draw the foundation rectangle,

Locate:

Point A 1 inch from the right-hand edge and on the fold.

Point B the outside leg length, plus $2\frac{3}{4}$ inches, from A.

Point C one-third the waist measure, plus $1\frac{1}{2}$ inches, from B.

Point D as far from C as B is from A.

Connect:

Points A, B, C, and D with straight lines to form the rectangle $ABCD$.

57. Drafting the Back Section.—As will be noted, the back section is larger than the front.

Locate:

Point E 1 inch to the left of A on the fold.

Point F the outside length to the left of E.

Point B_2 one-half the knee measurement above B on line BC.

Point G the inside leg length, plus 1 inch, to the right of C on line CD.

Point G_2 2 inches to the left of G on line CD.

Draw:

Curve B_2G_2 by placing the square with t at G_2 and the edge of the curve, near x, at B_2, and connecting B_2 and G_2.

Locate:

Point G_4 the inside leg measure to the left of G_2 on line B_2G_2.

Point H one-fourth the waist measure, plus 1 inch, above A on line AD.

Draw:

Curve G_4F by placing the square so that t is at G_4 and the edge of the curve, near w, is at F.

Curve HE, the back waist line, by placing the square with ff at H and the edge of the curve, near bb, at point E.

Curve HG_2 by placing the square with hh at G_2 and the edge of the curve, near bb, at H.

58. Drafting the Front Section.—To outline the front, or smaller, section,

Locate:

Point G_3 by placing the square with its corner at G and the short arm on line CD, and measuring $2\frac{1}{4}$ inches on the long arm.

Draw:

Curve B_2G_3 by placing the square with t on G_3 and the edge of the curve, near y, at B_2.

Locate:

Point G_5 on curve B_2G_3 the inside leg measure to the left of G_3.

Point H_2 1 inch to the left of H on the curve HG_2.

Draw:

Curve H_2E by placing the square with ff at H_2 and the edge of the curve, near bb, at E.

Locate:

Point H_3 2 inches below point H_2 on line H_2E, making the front waist line H_3E.

Connect:

Points H_3 and G_3 with a diagonal line.

Locate:

Point H_4 5 inches to the left of H_3 on line H_3G_3.

Point H_5 1 inch below H_4, placing the square with its corner at H_4 and one of its arms on line G_3H_3.

Draw:

Curve G_3H_5 by placing the square with ww at G_3 and the edge of the square, near uu, at H_5.

Curve H_5H_3 by placing the square with gg at H_5 and the edge of the curve, near dd, at H_3.

Line G_5F, a straight line between points G_5 and F.

59. Tracing and Cutting the Draft Apart.—Before the draft thus made is cut apart to form the pattern, trace the front part of the pattern from E to H_3; from H_3, through H_5, to G_3; from G_3 to G_5; and from G_5 to F.

With the tracing completed, open out the paper and slash it on the fold.

Then cut out the *back pattern* section by cutting from E to H; from H, through H_2, to G_2; from G_2 to G_4; and from G_4 to F. For the *front pattern* section, cut on the traced lines of the other piece of paper.

KNICKERBOCKERS

60. After a pattern for a pair of boys' trousers has been developed, it is a simple matter to produce a

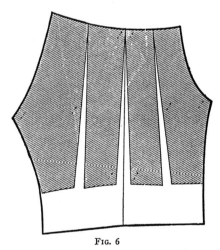

FIG. 6

pattern for a pair of knickerbockers. All that has to be done is to slash the pattern for the trousers, separate the pieces to allow for fulness, and then make an extension below the knee length for the parts that blouse, as is shown in Fig. 6.

To develop the knickerbocker pattern, pin the upper edge of the front and back pattern pieces to a sheet of paper, bringing them together at the waist line and separating them 1½ inches at the bottom.

Then measure the lower edge of the back pattern piece, and locate a point in its center.

Locate a point on the waist line of the back portion, placing it the same distance from the side line as the point on the lower edge of the pattern is from the side line.

Mark points on the front-pattern piece in the same way, and then draw on each pattern piece a vertical line to connect the point at the bottom line with that at the waist line.

With these lines drawn, slash along the lines to the waist line, separating the pattern pieces 1 inch at the lower edge and allowing them to meet at the waist line, as shown. Pin them securely to the paper.

Extend the inside leg lines 4 inches to allow for the blouse at the knee, and draw the side line from the waist line between the slashed portions, as shown, extending it 4 inches below the original pattern.

Draw new bottom lines to connect these lines, as shown.

With these lines drawn, form the knickerbocker pattern by cutting around the ouside of the original pattern, and on the new lines drawn for the extension, the inside leg portion, and the bottom. The pattern is usually cut on the center-side line, forming two pieces, one for the front and the other for the back.

REVIEW QUESTIONS

(1) How many measurements are required in drafting patterns for men and boys' garments?

(2) Describe the method of taking: (*a*) The sleeve measure; (*b*) The knee measure; (*c*) The width-of-back measure.

(3) How is the turn-back portion of the French cuff provided for in drafting?

(4) How may a pattern for knickerbockers for a boy of 5 years be made?

CHAPTER XI

DESIGNING WITH FOUNDATION PATTERNS

VALUE OF KNOWLEDGE OF PATTERN DESIGNING

1. Early Pattern Development.—As every woman who sews realizes, patterns are simple, interesting, and necessary articles. The word *simple* is not indiscriminately used in referring to patterns, for they are truly simple when they are thoroughly analyzed and the lines they give are perfectly understood. Our grandmothers were not blessed with the inventions and methods of the present day when it came to the making of dress patterns. They had to secure the measurements of the individual for whom a dress was to be made, without a tape line or a rule, by pinning a piece of paper, usually newspaper, or a worn sheet over the body, and then carefully, yes, even tediously and most laboriously, to cut out a plain waist, a skirt, and a sleeve pattern. With the aid of such patterns, though, they were enabled to cut out material that could be basted and fitted to make acceptable garments.

When once made, such patterns were preserved and used indefinitely for all the blouses, dresses, skirts, coats, and other garments that were required. However, not all the garments made over these patterns were plain; instead, many were tucked and plaited and befrilled and beruffled in various ways, great ingenuity in their use being exercised, as any fashion book of even 40 years back will prove. A fact that holds true even to this day, namely, that a true plain-foundation pattern of a waist, a skirt, and a sleeve may be so used as to cut out any woman's garment that carries in its lines the outlines of the human figure, was discovered during the early use of patterns.

2. Advantages of Pattern Designing.—Designing is perhaps the most interesting part of Pattern Drafting, for here is shown the application of fashion to the foundation draft. In the case of a plain waist, skirt, and sleeve, an unlimited variety of garments may be made by altering the standard draft. In this way, a woman need not be restricted to the development of a design exactly as it is, but can combine ideas from several designs or apply original features to advantage.

Very frequently the silhouette of the body part of a design suits exactly, but possibly the sleeve is not desirable, the collar is unsatisfactory, or the skirt has more plaits than are wanted. In such cases, provided you have a correct understanding of foundation patterns and the relation of their lines to those of the individual, you will be able to use a sleeve of one design and a collar of another, or vice versa; also, you may proceed with assurance in taking out a plait that is not desirable or in adding a plait or necessary fulness if the skirt is too plain.

The exercise of a little thought and ingenuity will enable you to get very satisfactory results from the use of patterns. When you remember that the purpose of a pattern is merely to serve as a guide in cutting out material for a garment, and that the details—fitting, finishing, and trimming—are left almost entirely to a person's own inclination and preference, you will be able to use patterns for what they are intended and then work out of them satisfactorily fitting, neatly finished, and attractively trimmed garments.

3. Style Possibilities of Tissue-Paper Patterns. In connection with a study of pattern drafting and flat designing, you will do well to keep in mind the value of special tissue-paper patterns as a means of gaining ideas for the development of patterns for the newest fashions. The style possibilities of such patterns are many, as pattern manufacturers are quick to scent style changes and to issue new patterns by means of which new effects can be obtained.

Use tissue-paper patterns merely as style safeguards and study them sufficiently to make them yield to your desires. But use foundation patterns to attain exact proportions. Then, if you select materials and trimming with care and thought and with attention to style tendencies, smart and attractive garments will result.

4. Fitting Garments Cut From Foundation Patterns.—Frequently, the new appearance of a garment depends entirely on the fitting, as when a kimono waist is loose almost to bagginess in effect, or when it is fitted up snugly under the arms and pulled down with little fulness at the waist. Still another example of fitting as it affects fashions is the gored skirt that flares at the hem and is fitted closely over the hips—a skirt that is not in the same class as the gored skirt that hangs from the waist line and does not define the hip shaping.

The question of fitting, then, is a point that must be considered, even with drafted patterns, in order always to obtain the effects that the pattern is intended to bring out. Thus, if the shoulders of a waist pattern are found to be longer than the draft or foundation pattern calls for, it is advisable, before altering this line in the pattern, to ascertain whether this little added length is not one of those fashion changes, the elimination of which would rob the new garment of its smartness; likewise, if this change is the shortening of the shoulders, the reason may still be there. Thus, it soon becomes evident that an inch more or less at a certain point is often the vital feature of a new fashion.

5. Suiting Method to Individual.—You, as an individual, should find the best way for you—perhaps to design as you draft, to block out and flat design from your blocks, to make your own muslin models, to buy each season the outstanding design in commercial patterns or muslin models or copies of imports that are for sale by importers, and then to draft and design from these.

Any one of these means you should find fascinating, for designing is an artistic work and every phase is interesting. Consequently, every available means should be used to make your work inspirational and creditable.

_____

PROPER SELECTION OF DESIGNS

6. The success of a garment is primarily dependent on the proper selection of the design used for its development. For this reason, you will find it decidedly worth while not to choose designs promiscuously, but rather to consider the purpose for which the garment is intended, the material of which it is to be made, and the method of its development, the size that is best suited, also the suitability of the design to the individual, to the desired purpose, and to the material selected.

7. Purpose of Garment.—Before attempting to select a design or even to decide on the material of which to make the garment, consider the purpose for which it is intended; that is, whether you will need it for general utility wear or for service or for "dress-up" wear alone. Also, consider whether it will be necessary for you to wear the garment for several seasons. With these points in mind, you may then decide on the kind of material and the nature of the design suitable for your purpose.

8. Material Selection.—In determining the kind of material to choose, consider seasonal offerings in texture, design, and coloring in comparison with your individual requirements. If you wish a general-utility garment that must serve for several seasons, shun extremes or novelties in texture, design, or color, and choose a plain, staple fabric of a conservative color that, with repeated wear, will not prove distasteful to you nor appear decidedly out of date a second or third season.

As a rule, it is best not to obtain the material until the design is selected, for this prevents the purchase of too great or too small a quantity. In the case of a commercial pattern, the envelope gives information as to material requirements of different widths for various sizes. The amounts suggested are always ample, so there need be no concern that the stated requirements will not prove sufficient.

9. Suitability of Design.—Several points must receive attention in regard to the suitability of a design. First of all, consider whether it is becoming to your particular type. Then consider the purpose for which it is intended, being mindful of the fact that a style having good lines that are in keeping with style tendencies and yet not exaggerated in the least is the most desirable selection for a garment that must serve for several seasons, while a style extreme as to line and detail is permissible for a garment that need be worn for only a few occasions.

Usually, one design is illustrated two or three times in a fashion book or a quarterly, and it is well to observe the various adaptations of each pattern so as to understand better its possibilities in development.

10. The kind of material, too, helps to determine the design to choose. Select a design that will bring out the material to the best advantage. For instance, if you have chosen a soft, clinging fabric, select a design that has soft, long lines rather than one in bouffant effect, and unless the material is of very firm weave, avoid circular effects. If the material of your choice has a large figure or plaid or a broad stripe, select for its development a design that is as simple and has as few seam lines as possible, rather than one that would break the pattern of the material frequently and give a patchy effect.

11. Selecting Designs Within Your Ability. The selection of a style involving details that are much more complicated or require a much greater degree of skill than your experience in dressmaking would enable you to carry out satisfactorily, would undoubtedly cause regret and disappointment. Keep within your ability, letting your judgment rather than your desire be the dominating motive in the selection of a design. It is far better for you to turn out a garment simple in line but well made than one of complex design showing traces of amateur ability. Not that you need be hesitant about attempting new construction details, however; simply take logical rather than distant steps in advancement so that the foundation you have acquired will give you sufficient assurance and ability to make a success of the new details.

12. Before the design of a foundation pattern or draft is changed in any way, it is advisable to take care of any alterations that may be required in it to make it fit the individual figure properly. Many of the changes that are necessary for various types are considered in connection with plain-waist, sleeve, and skirt and close-fitting waist and sleeve drafts in Chapters II, III, IV and V. These drafts, if carefully individualized, will serve as foundations for most of the designing you care to do. The majority of the alterations suggested for the plain drafts may be applied to the changing of practically any foundation pattern you may select, but as a few of the alterations require special treatment they are considered at this time.

13. Altering Kimono-Waist Patterns.—A kimono waist is not intended to fit with so much snugness as a plain waist and for this reason does not require nearly so much precision in the altering. Unless you are entirely satisfied that the pattern is correct for you, cut a muslin model, adding any length you may have found necessary in the sleeve, front, or back portions, and make a very wide seam allowance at the under arm, provided you think the armhole should be made deeper. Then, in the fitting, make any adjustments that seem necessary.

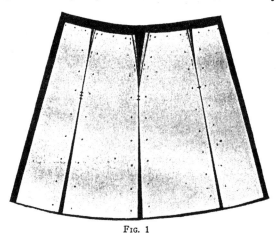

FIG. 1

14. Altering Gored-Skirt Patterns.—If alterations are required in a gored-skirt pattern, it is generally necessary to make a change on each gore rather than attempt to increase or decrease the size at only one point. For instance, if the waist measurement of a pattern must be increased, divide the amount to be added among all the seam lines except those of the center-front and center-back gores, which, in almost every case, should be left without change. It is not necessary to add the same amount on each seam line, however. Rather, consider the figure and observe where unusual straightness requires a less decidedly curved line in the pattern; then make the alteration accordingly.

15. In most cases, the greater change should be made at the center-side seam, as in Fig. 1, because a change at this point will be less noticeable than a decided change made at the side front or side back.

To avoid making entirely new pattern sections, you may slip strips of paper underneath the gore edges, pin these strips in position, and then shape them properly, as indicated by the illustration. When only a slight alteration is required, it may generally be made complete on the center-side seam line or on the front and back edges of a center-side gore.

In similar manner, follow this suggestion, also, in regard to decreasing the size of the waist measurement, drawing the new curves in from the original seam lines and making the alteration more pronounced where deep curves of the figure require more decidedly curved pattern lines.

Alterations in length above the hip line require much the same consideration. Thus, if an alteration is required for a prominent abdomen, for prominent hips, or for unusual size across the hips at the back, graduate the alteration according to the shaping of the figure, taking care to keep the length of the corresponding seam lines the same.

16. In case the width of the lower edge of a gored-skirt pattern requires changing in order to make it suitable for the width of the material or to produce some particular style characteristic, the amount of alterations should be divided among the various gores.

To reduce the width of a pattern, first subtract from the actual width of the pattern half the width that is desired in the skirt so as to estimate the amount the width of the pattern must be reduced. Then divide the amount to be taken out into as many parts as there are gores, and fold each gore back half the estimated amount on each side, folding from the lower edge and keeping a true line to the hip line, but never extending the reduction above the hip line.

If a skirt pattern must be enlarged at its lower edge, ascertain the amount that must be added to it to meet the requirements, and divide this amount by the number of gores so as to determine how much must be added to each gore. Then add half the required amount to each side of each gore, adding from the lower edge in a diagonal line to the hip line, but never above it.

17. It is not advisable to make any greater alteration in width than can be effected by bringing the lines of the gores in or extending them out about 1½ inches. Usually, however, the alteration does not require even as much change in width as this. An even greater alteration requires different shaping of the waist line and, for this reason, it is advisable to obtain another pattern of more satisfactory width to use as a foundation.

18. Altering Circular-Skirt Patterns.—In Fig. 2 is shown the manner in which the waist measurement of a circular-skirt pattern may be decreased without changing the hip measurement. To make the change, first slash the pattern from the hip line to the lower edge and then separate it enough to make possible the folding in of the pattern at the waist line, as shown at *a*, so as to take out the necessary fulness without cupping up the hip line or reducing its size. In an alteration of this kind, make the slashes at the back of the pattern so that they will not throw any additional fulness in front. Such fulness should be avoided in a circular skirt, unless a complete circle is used as a pattern; then extra fulness in the front is permissible. In the average circular skirt, however, unnecessary fulness falling to the front from the sides is a fault that should be overcome in fitting.

If the waist line of such a pattern must be increased, slash it from the waist line down to the hip line, and then fold the lower part of the pattern directly below each slash so as to separate the waist line the required amount. In making such changes, remember that the pattern must be kept flat and not be permitted to cup up in any place.

For small waists, fulness will, of course, be added to the lower edge of the pattern when the waist line is reduced, and when the waist is made larger the lower edge will become narrower. The only way to avoid changing the skirt width in either instance is to provide waist-line fulness.

When a circular-skirt pattern requires more length above the hip line in order to increase the front, back, or side-dart length, add this length at the point where it is needed, as suggested for a plain foundation skirt, and gradually blend this alteration into the original waist-line curve, thus forming a new curve at the waist line.

19. Precautions in Preparation for Designing. After a pattern has been individualized, or changed according to individual measurements, whether this be of a true foundation type or of some particular design that you wish to change in several details, it is well to remove all seam allowances as a precaution to insure greater freedom and satisfaction in the designing. Otherwise, such allowances might prove confusing and make it difficult to outline details and new seam lines in correct position and to produce the proper balance in the finished garment. Also, the marking of foundation lines and the indicating of normal seam lines will be a convenience in the designing as a guide for outlining the desired new features. When only a slight change is to be made in a pattern of special design,

the removing of seam allowances and the indicating of foundation and normal seam lines are not essential, however, for you may very easily mark the position for the new feature you desire with the pattern held in position over the figure.

As a rule, a narrow peplum, or skirt, portion is not objectionable in a guide or plain-waist pattern used for designing, as, with the waist line marked, the

Fig. 2

peplum portion should not be confusing. In fact, it may prove a convenience in some cases, for designing features that extend below the waist line may be marked on it and, besides, the extra length serves as a precaution.

Many of the waist patterns illustrated as foundations for the designing taken up in the following instruction have a peplum portion, but in each instance the waist line is indicated so that no confusion will result.

FLAT DESIGNING

INTERPRETING STYLE LINES

20. As mysterious as it may seem to some persons, the changing of patterns to produce garments that conform to Fashion's demands calls for nothing more than the application of a correct understanding of style lines. And this matter of style lines is simply a matter of being able to discern foundation lines, for once they are perceived the style lines stand out boldly and indicate immediately what must be done to a pattern to make it conform to the lines required.

Thus, to illustrate what is meant, assume that a fashion picture is before you. It may be a photograph or a picture from a daily paper, from the fashion section of a Sunday paper, or from a style magazine. Analyze this picture very critically, being as careful as a chemist would be in analyzing a compound. Notice particularly what foundation might be used in developing the garment, whether it is a plain or a kimono waist, a plain or a circular skirt, a one-piece or a two-piece sleeve. Then determine just where the foundation pattern would be used, remembering that approximately 75 per cent. of the garments made carry some foundation-pattern lines, that the garments are built over skeleton foundations cut by the aid of foundation patterns, and that their exteriors are shaped somewhat from foundation patterns.

It may be that the neck, the shoulders, the armholes, the under arms, or possibly only a foundation skirt is used and the waist itself is draped; in any event, though, some foundation lines must be used either in the lining or in the outer portion to insure its staying in position on the body.

After determining what foundation pattern or patterns are used, the next step is to determine what changes must be made. If the garment has more fulness than the foundation pattern gives, it must be ascertained how much this fulness is and just where the pattern must be slashed and separated to allow for the fulness, for this must be made to come at the exact place for the right effect.

21. Sometimes, in the elongated fashion figures, that are developed with the brush or pen, a stripe or frill or pocket or waist line is placed to suit the picture, but often this feature is technically impossible in copying the design in materials. When you study fashion pictures, therefore, try to visualize the effect you can obtain in the material, omitting anything in the design that does not have a definite reason for its being there.

22. In this section, only the changes or designing features that may be outlined on the flat pattern or draft are considered, this work being termed **flat designing.**

The designing features that are illustrated were selected not so much for their style value as to include the changes most often made in patterns and the foundation principles on which flat designing is based. By studying the style illustrations in comparison with their respective pattern diagrams, which show exactly the changes that must be made to produce the various effects, and then applying these suggestions in your practical work, you will find that you have gained a very thorough understanding of flat designing and that you will be able to proceed with assurance and pleasure in copying almost any design that does not require modeling on the figure.

23. In any designing that you do, keep in mind the normal position of the various lines of the foundation patterns, for it is on the correct position of these lines in the completed garment that its success depends. Thus, while it is possible to cut the pattern pieces into sections to allow for tucks, for fulness, for yokes, and so on, and to twist and arrange the pattern pieces to procure the effect desired, this fact must always be remembered: *Each line of a foundation pattern must always come at the place it is intended to come.* No matter into how many pieces a guide, or an individualized, waist pattern, for instance, may be cut, if all the pieces are carefully put back together again, so that they will assume the outline of the original foundation pattern, a perfect fit will be assured.

If you are in doubt as to the position any designing details should assume on the pattern, hold the pattern up to the figure and determine and indicate the point where you consider they will appear best.

24. Pay particular attention to the drawing of any curves you may wish to apply, striving to make these curves just as smooth in effect and as attractive as possible. A little practice or repeated attempts in drawing the same curve will give you assurance and skill in outlining any effect you desire. In joining two curves, if any angle forms, blend the lines gracefully, holding as closely as possible to the original curves. An angle in a seam line would prove awkward and ill-fitting, for the seam could not possibly follow the curves of the figure.

25. Trying Out Flat-Designed Patterns in Muslin.—Flat designing, besides providing a simple means of forming patterns for designs that it is desired to copy, is also an aid to the development of a sense of proportion and the relation of pattern lines to those of the individual figure. But until you have gained considerable experience in this work and feel confident that the new seam lines and details you have outlined on the foundation pattern are entirely suitable for the individual type, you will do well to try out the pattern in muslin, seaming this and observing it on the figure.

Muslin models are the very essence of economy and a safeguard where individual becomingness is essential, for they give assurance before the garment fabric is cut that the lines of the pattern are in the correct and most becoming position for the individual. The purchase of muslin for this work may seem to you to balance the cost of a special pattern you might purchase for the design, but when you realize that muslin modeling will enable you to make changes for individual becomingness and that you can keep recutting the muslin for smaller pattern sections or can piece it for larger ones, you will fully appreciate its economy. Besides, the development of a muslin model is generally advisable, even when few if any changes have been made in the pattern used for the cutting.

In case you find it advisable to make any changes in the muslin model, mark these accurately on the flat pattern and then use this in cutting out the dress fabric.

WAIST AND COLLAR DESIGNING

OUTLINING YOKES AND VESTS

26. Mannish-Yoke Effect and Vest.—A waist in which yoke effects at each shoulder, similar in appearance to those in a man's shirt, are formed by extensions made on the back portion of the waist is shown in Fig. 3. This design also has fulness gathered into the yoke effects and a vest with square neck line.

 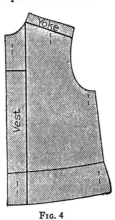

FIG. 3   FIG. 4

As the style appears to have a normal armhole line, a plain-waist pattern is immediately suggested as the correct foundation for the designing. Be guided by Fig. 4 in outlining the various features on the pattern.

Determine, first, how deep you wish the shoulder yoke, measure down this distance from the shoulder line along the neck and armhole edges, and connect these two points with a straight line, as indicated by the heavy line on the diagram.

The sides of the vest portion appear to extend on a straight line from the yoke portion. Therefore, mark the vest, as shown, by drawing a straight line from the inner end of the yoke line of the pattern to the lower edge of the waist, keeping this parallel with the center-front. Then determine how deep you wish the neck line, measure down this distance at the center front, and draw a straight line across to the vest line.

With the designing features outlined, pin the waist pattern to a piece of paper large enough to accommodate its full size, placing the center front along a straight edge of the paper, and then trace on the heavy lines and cut around the pattern. Then, with the foundation pattern removed, cut on the lines traced

to the paper underneath to form separate vest, side-front, and yoke sections.

27. To provide fulness to be gathered into the yoke, first slash the side-front section from the center of the edge that is to be joined to the yoke portion, on a line parallel with the center front, to the lower

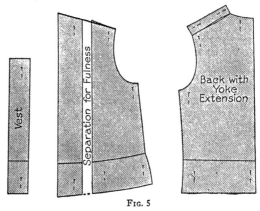

FIG. 5

edge. Then pin the sections to another piece of paper or directly to the material as in Fig. 5, separating the slashed edges from 1 to 3 or 4 inches, depending on the amount of fulness you desire, and taking care not to change the slant of the edge that is to be joined to the yoke portion. This will require that the corresponding corners of the separated portions be kept on exactly the same level, as shown. Then, to avoid the angle that would be formed in the edge, connect the upper and lower ends with a straight line, as indicated by the heavy line on the diagram. Blend the lower edge with a curve in the manner illustrated.

In order to cut the back in one with the shoulder-yoke portion, lay the two pattern pieces so that their shoulder lines meet, as shown. The shoulder edges may part a trifle at the center, but this small amount will not prove undesirable and, for this reason, no seam or dart will be needed at this point.

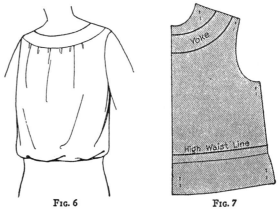

FIG. 6   FIG. 7

28. Round Yoke and Raised Waist Line.—Fig. 6 shows a round yoke into which considerable fulness is gathered and a waist line that is above the normal position. This design appears also to have a regulation armhole line and, therefore, requires a plain-waist pattern as a foundation.

131

Outline the round yoke on the pattern, as in Fig. 7, which shows only the front-pattern section, first determining how deep you desire the neck line at the center front and shoulder and then connecting the points indicating this depth with a smoothly curved line. Also, mark the neck line on the back portion in practically the same manner as the front.

A point to observe in the marking of neck lines is that the back be made somewhat higher than the front so as to maintain better balance in the design. The difference in the height of the front and back neck lines may be made just a trifle or a considerable amount, but, except in the case of an extremely low neck, or decolleté, the back should almost invariably be higher than the front.

With the low neck outlined, draw a curved line parallel with this for the lower edge of the yoke portion, as shown, making the yoke of the depth you desire it.

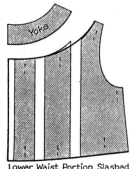

Lower Waist Portion Slashed and Separated for Fulness
FIG. 8

After determining how high you desire the waist line, mark the raised waist line this distance above the normal waist line, keeping these lines parallel, as shown. Then pin the pattern to a larger piece of paper, trace on the designing lines, cut around the shoulder, armhole, and underarm lines of the pattern and, after removing the pattern, cut along the lines traced to the paper underneath so as to form the separate pattern sections.

29. The separate front-yoke pattern and the lower-waist portion slashed and separated to provide fulness are shown in Fig. 8. When fulness is to be added along a curved edge, it is advisable to make provision for this at several points so that a correct curve may be maintained. Regulate the number of slashes by the amount of fulness you wish to add and, in pinning the pieces to another sheet of paper or to the material for cutting, place the center front ½ inch or a trifle more back from the edge or fold, and separate the other pieces from 1 to 2 inches, keeping the corresponding corners in line, as suggested for the waist pattern previously considered. Then redraw the curves at the upper and the lower edges, as shown.

Add fulness to the back portion in this same manner, provided you desire it.

30. Yoke Cut in One With Waist.—A waist in which the yoke effects are cut in one with the front and back kimono-sleeve sections is shown in Fig. 9.

A kimono-waist pattern having a shoulder seam extended through the center of the sleeve is the correct foundation for this design, as with a slight change it can be made entirely suitable.

FIG. 9

Be guided by Fig. 10 in designing the pattern, first pinning the front pattern portion to a piece of paper of ample size. Outline the round neck as low as you desire it; then mark the yoke of the depth you wish. In the case illustrated, it is marked so that its lower line is a trifle above the point on the pattern that corresponds with the tip of the shoulder. Let the yoke line extend as far toward the front as you wish, considering the length of line that will prove most becoming.

To form a seam line for the yoke effect, slash the pattern on the marked yoke line. Then, if you wish to remove any fulness through the lower portion of the waist, fold a vertical dart, as illustrated in Fig. 11, folding under as much as you desire at the lower edge and tapering the dart to nothing at the yoke line. This will cause the sleeve and the yoke portion to part slightly, as the illustration shows, and will, in many instances, improve the fit of the sleeve at the under arm. However, it is not necessary that this dart be taken if the entire amount of waist-line fulness in the foundation pattern is desired.

31. In order to provide fulness in the upper edge of the sleeve portion to be gathered into the yoke, extend the line, as shown, from 1½ to 2½ inches beyond

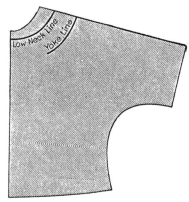

FIG. 10

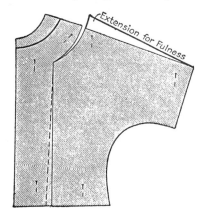

FIG. 11

the edge of the pattern, letting it follow the same general curve as the line drawn for the yoke, but taking care that the distance from the end of this curve to the lower edge of the sleeve is the same as the length of the original outside-seam line of the sleeve portion. Then, to form the new outside-seam line, draw a straight line to connect the end of the curve with the lower end of the sleeve, as shown.

To form the designed pattern, first trace the new neck line; then cut on the lower edge, the under-arm, and the sleeve lines, then along the new outside sleeve line and around the yoke portion, and, after removing the foundation pattern, cut the designed pattern on the traced neck line.

Treat the back portion of the pattern in practically the same manner, making the yoke portion of the same depth as the one in the front, and regulate the length of the yoke line by its becomingness to the individual type. If you prefer, you may extend the yoke entirely across the back.

OUTLINING SIDE-CLOSING AND SURPLICE EFFECTS
AND FLAT COLLARS

32. Side-Closing Waist.—As a foundation for the side-closing waist shown in Fig. 12, use a plain-waist pattern and be guided by Fig. 13 in forming the side-

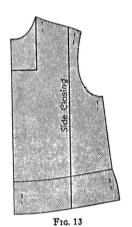

FIG. 12   FIG. 13

closing pattern. First of all, draw the neck line, making it as deep as you desire at the center-front.

Determine the point on the shoulder from which you wish the side closing to extend and draw a straight line from this point to the lower edge, keeping it parallel with the center front, if little or no fulness is desired across the waist line at the center front, or slanting it somewhat toward the under arm if the lower edge of the pattern has considerable fulness.

For a very prominent bust, this closing line might be more desirable if curved a trifle over the bust portion.

After outlining the neck line and the side closing, pin the foundation pattern to a folded sheet of paper large enough to form a double pattern, placing the center front along the fold of the paper. Then trace the new neck line and side closing and cut around the outline of the foundation. Next, remove the foundation, and with the paper still folded, cut out the new neck line on the traced line; then open out the new pattern and cut it at the left side on the traced line

indicating the side closing. This will give two pattern sections, as shown in Fig. 14.

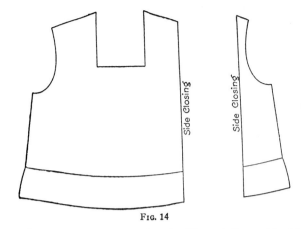

FIG. 14

33. Surplice Waist With Flat Collar.—Besides the outlining of the surplice effect and flat collar, the design illustrated in Fig. 15 requires, also, the dropping of the waist line, for the waist appears to extend considerably below the normal waist line.

Use a plain-waist pattern as a foundation and proceed as shown in Fig. 16 to duplicate the design.

First, pin the front-pattern section to a piece of paper about 6 inches wider than the pattern and several inches longer, placing the pattern section so that the lower edge is within a few inches of the lower edge of the paper and the center-front line is about 6 inches from one of the side edges of the paper.

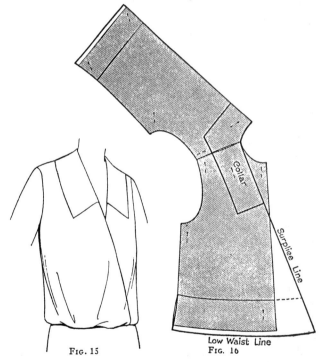

FIG. 15   Low Waist Line
FIG. 16

To make the extension below the normal waist line, first determine how deep you desire it, and then draw a curved line this distance below the waist line of the foundation pattern, making it exactly parallel with this waist line.

133

Also, determine how deep you wish the V-neck line and place a mark on the center-front of the pattern to indicate this depth. Then, to outline the surplice, draw a line from the end of the shoulder line at the neck through the point indicating the V-neck depth to the marked waist line, making the surplice line straight or curving it in a graceful manner, whichever effect you prefer.

The depth of the neck line regulates the extension of the surplice at the waist line, provided a straight or very gradually curved line is desired. If you wish the surplice to overlap considerably, you may plan a fairly high neck line, but if you prefer a short overlap, it will be necessary for you to mark the neck line extremely low and plan to have a little vestee as a filler in the front.

34. The easiest and most satisfactory method of forming a flat-collar pattern is to outline it directly

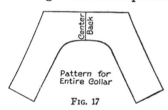

Fig. 17

on the waist pattern, using as the neck line of the collar pattern any new neck line that has been marked on the waist pattern in order to insure accurate results.

In order to outline the collar in one piece, first lay the back portion of the pattern, as shown in the illustration, so that its shoulder line meets that of the front, and the neck ends are exactly even. Then outline the collar, making it of the depth you desire at the center front, shoulder, and center back and shaping it according to the design you are copying.

This method of outlining applies to the formation of practically any type of flat-collar pattern.

35. With the designing finished, prepare to form a complete collar pattern by folding a piece of paper large enough to accommodate the collar size, lengthwise through the center, and slipping this under the outlined collar pattern without changing the position of the front and back waist-pattern sections. Pin this piece of paper in position so that its folded edge is exactly under the center-back line of the collar pattern and the remainder of the paper extends under the marked collar outline. Then trace the neck line and outer edge of the collar, and after removing the pins that hold the paper in place,

cut on the traced lines in order to form the complete collar pattern, which will appear as in Fig. 17 when the paper is unfolded.

To form the front surplice pattern, first trace the V-neck line, then cut around the shoulder, armhole, and under-arm lines of the foundation and along the lines marked for the low waist line and the surplice, and, after removing the foundation, cut along the traced neck line, thus completing the pattern.

OUTLINING DROP-SHOULDER, RAGLAN, AND DEEP-ARMHOLE LINES

Fig. 18

36. Drop-shoulder and raglan lines, because of the broad armhole essential to these styles and the absence of the normal armhole line, suggest a kimono-waist pattern rather than a plain-waist pattern as a foundation for designing. More doubt as to a correct foundation pattern seems to exist when a style having a deep armhole that assumes a natural position at the shoulder seam is to be considered, for this suggests a possibility of deepening the armhole line of a plain-waist pattern or of outlining the deep armhole on a kimono-waist pattern.

The latter method is preferable, as this insures a sleeve that will fit the armhole of the waist perfectly, while, with the use of a plain-waist pattern, the separate sleeve pattern would require very careful changing to make it suitable for the deepened armhole of the waist-pattern portion, a task involving much more work.

Observing the changes made in a kimono-waist pattern to produce the various effects illustrated here will help you in determining how to proceed in making various other changes in kimono-waist patterns, which are usually the most desirable foundations for designs that have considerable armhole depth regardless of the position of the armhole line.

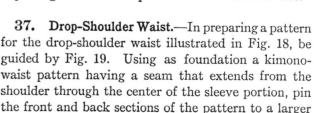

Fig. 19

37. Drop-Shoulder Waist.—In preparing a pattern for the drop-shoulder waist illustrated in Fig. 18, be guided by Fig. 19. Using as foundation a kimono-waist pattern having a seam that extends from the shoulder through the center of the sleeve portion, pin the front and back sections of the pattern to a larger piece of paper so that the center front is along a straight edge of the paper and the shoulder lines of the pattern meet, as shown.

To determine how deep you wish the drop-shoulder effect, place a tape around the upper arm in the position you desire the drop-shoulder line and measure from the neck line at the shoulder over the top of the arm down to this point. Then, as a guide for drawing the drop-shoulder line, measure this same distance down from the neck line on the shoulder seam and, as indicated by the heavy line, draw a gradually curved line from the center of the deep curve at the front under arm to the corresponding curve at the back, extending the line through the point marked for the drop-shoulder depth.

If the foundation pattern has short sleeves, make an extension beyond the lower edge of the sleeve portion for three-quarter sleeves, as shown, or for full-length sleeves, if you prefer, flaring the seam lines a trifle if you wish a broader effect at the lower edge.

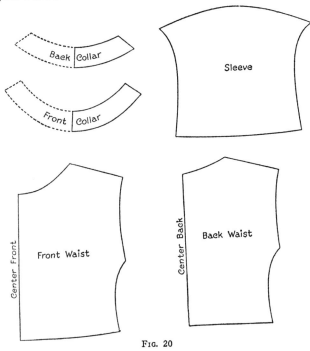

FIG. 20

To outline the collar, which consists of two pieces meeting at the neck line on the shoulder seams, first determine how deep you wish the neck line at the center front, shoulder, and center back, and mark the neck line, being guided by these depths; then outline the lower edge and the ends of the collar portions, making them as deep as you desire.

38. To form the various pattern sections, as shown in Fig. 20, first trace along the new neck line and drop-shoulder line and along the natural shoulder line from the neck line to the drop-shoulder line. Then cut around the foundation-pattern lines that have not been changed and along the newly marked sleeve lines, and after removing the foundation pattern, cut along

the traced drop-shoulder, or armhole line, the natural shoulder line, and the new neck line, thus forming separate front, back, and sleeve sections, as shown.

For the collar-pattern pieces, slip a piece of paper underneath the marked collar portion on the front and back foundation-pattern pieces, trace the collar outlined on these sections and also the center-front and center-back edges, and, after removing the foundation-pattern pieces, cut along the lines traced to the paper underneath to produce the collar pieces shown.

FIG. 21

39. Raglan-Sleeve Waist.—To develop a pattern for the raglan-sleeve waist illustrated in Fig. 21, follow the designing lines shown in Fig. 22.

With the front and back sections of a kimono-waist pattern pinned to another sheet of paper, as suggested for the drop-shoulder waist, first of all outline the new neck line, making it round, as illustrated, if you wish, and of the depth you desire.

If you wish to deepen the width of the armhole portion, as in the style illustrated, draw a new curve as indicated on the diagram, extending this as far below

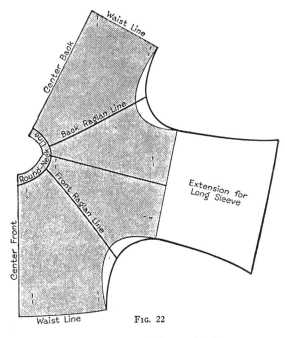

FIG. 22

the original curve as you desire and taking very great care to make the curve smooth and gradual in order to blend the sleeve and under-arm lines in a satisfactory manner.

In order to determine points from which to draw the raglan lines, measure on the figure from the natural shoulder line along a neck line shaped as you desire it to a point in front of the shoulder line where you wish the raglan seam to terminate.

Apply this measurement to the pattern along the new neck line, indicating a point in front of the

is, measure from the neck at the side to the tip of the shoulder, or the natural armhole line, and then apply this measurement to the pattern, measuring along the shoulder line from the natural neck line.

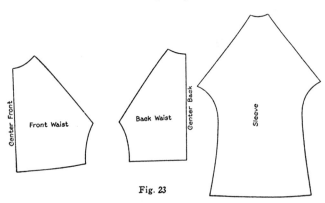

Fig. 23

shoulder line, and then in the same manner measuring the required distance back of the shoulder line and marking a point from which to extend the back raglan line. From the points in both the front and the back, draw very slightly curved lines, as shown, to the center of the front and back curves that blend the sleeve and under-arm lines. Aim to make these curves as attractive as possible, curving them up just a trifle from the front and back portions so as to make them curve in slightly on the sleeve portion. If you wish a long sleeve, also make an extension for this, as shown.

40. To form the various pattern sections, trace the raglan lines and the new neck line, then cut around the foundation pattern, following the new curve at the under arm, if one was drawn, and the outline for the sleeve extension.

Fig. 24

After removing the foundation pattern, cut on the traced lines in order to make separate front, back, and sleeve sections, as shown in Fig. 23.

41. Deep-Arm-hole Waist.—To develop a pattern for the deep-armhole waist shown in Fig. 24, follow the method of outlining illustrated in Fig. 25, first pinning the front and back sections of a foundation kimono-waist pattern to another sheet of paper as directed for the drop-shoulder blouse.

As a guide for drawing the armhole, measure the length of the natural shoulder line on the figure, that

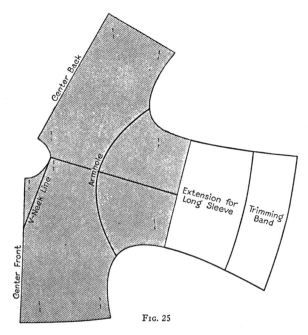

FIG. 25

With the point for the height of the armhole marked, draw an attractively shaped curve to form the armhole, extending it from the center of the deep curve at the under arm, as shown, through the point marked on the shoulder to the opposite under-arm curve. Aim to make the upper part of this curve similar to the upper portion of the armhole curves of the plain-waist pattern so that they will follow the correct line on the figure.

To make the sleeve of the desired length, extend the sleeve lines, and, after drawing the curve for the lower edge, outline the trimming band, first measuring up an even distance from the bottom to locate guide points through which to extend the curve.

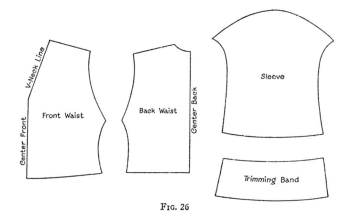

FIG. 26

42. Form the various pattern sections by first tracing the neck, armhole, and natural shoulder lines. Then, cut around the foundation-pattern lines that are to be retained and along the outline of the long sleeve and, after removing the foundation pattern, cut on the traced neck, shoulder, and armhole lines and on the line marked for the sleeve-trimming band. This will provide separate front, back, sleeve, and trimming-band sections, as shown in Fig. 26.

OUTLINING OVERBLOUSE AND BASQUE EFFECTS

43. Forming Overblouse Patterns.—A blouse that extends below the waist line over a separate skirt portion requires a waist pattern having its under-arm, center-front, and center-back lines extended to provide the required length below the waist line. Before extending these lines, consider the effect at the lower edge of the overblouse design you wish to copy. If it hangs with considerable fulness or flare, it will undoubtedly require slashing and separating the waist pattern to provide extra fulness at the bottom. Provide this fulness as you pin the waist pattern to a piece of paper of sufficient size to form the length of overblouse you desire, slashing the foundation where you consider the fulness should be inserted and separating the pieces as much as you consider necessary. Then extend the lines to make the blouse of the length you desire and outline the lower edge, shaping it to correspond with the style you are copying.

FIG. 27

44. Panel-Effect Overblouse.—In Fig. 27 is shown a type of overblouse that is rather close-fitting at the bottom, a feature requiring that the waist pattern have some of its fulness removed at the lower edge. In order to remove this fulness, fold a dart through the lengthwise center of the pattern, as shown in Fig. 28, taking sufficient in the dart to make the under-arm line comparatively straight and letting the dart terminate between the shoulder and bust line.

Next, proceed to draw the oval neck line and to outline the panel effect, making this of a width that you consider will be becoming across the shoulders and gradually curving it out toward the under arm, making the line as deep as you wish at this point.

In drawing the line for the lower edge, if you wish fulness gathered in at the under arm, as illustrated, make allowance for this, drawing a practically straight line from the desired distance below the waist line at the center front to the side rather than following the same general curve as the waist line.

Leave the shaping of the under arm until you try out the muslin model; then you may draw the over-

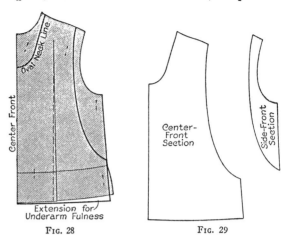

FIG. 28   FIG. 29

panel portion in as closely to the figure as you desire and adjust the fulness in any manner you wish.

45. To form the front-pattern sections, as shown in Fig. 29, first trace the new neck line, the panel out-line, and the lower edge, provided this is not drawn below the pattern; then cut along the shoulder, arm-hole, and under-arm lines and, after removing the foundation pattern, cut along the traced lower edge, and the neck and panel lines.

You may design the back portion of the pattern with a panel similar to that of the front, or plan to use a plain back gathered in at a normal or low waist line under sash ends or a belt portion joined to the front-panel extensions.

46. Semifitted Basque.—A semifitted basque which may serve as an over-blouse, because of its low waist line, or as a part of a dress, is shown in Fig. 30. This, also, has fulness gathered in at the under arm, a feature that is essential even in a comparatively straight, un-darted, basque style for a person having a rather prominent bust. If the bust is not prominent, gathers at the under arm may be used as a point of design, but they are not necessary to produce a correct fit unless very close shaping is desired.

The collar shown on this model is of the bertha type. Because it lies flat

FIG. 30

at the neck line, it may be outlined directly on the basque pattern.

47. Proceed to develop the basque and collar patterns as shown in Fig. 31. First of all, fold a dart in the front of the foundation-waist pattern to reduce the waist-line fulness as suggested for the overblouse previously considered. Fold a similar dart in the back section of the pattern, also, if you consider that this is broader at the waist line than you would care to have it in the basque. Then, pin the front and back sections of the foundation pattern to a large piece of paper, placing them, as shown, so that the center front is along a straight edge of the paper and the back shoulder line meets that of the front. This arrangement will permit the bertha-collar pattern to be outlined in one piece.

Extension for Underarm Fulness

FIG. 31

With the pattern pieces in place, draw the line for the lower edge, starting it as far below the normal waist line at the center front as you wish the finished basque to extend, with ½ to 1 inch additional allowance for ease in the length, and giving more length below the waist line at the side, as shown, in order to provide for fulness if this is necessary or desired at the under arm.

As no fulness is essential in the back under-arm seam, you may measure the line for the lower edge of the back an even distance below the normal waist line.

To outline the bertha collar, first outline the neck of the depth and shape you desire. Then, measure down on the figure from the normal neck line at the center front, the center back, and over the shoulder as deep as you wish the bertha collar at these points and, after designating these corresponding measurements on the pattern, connect the points at the center front, center side, and center back with a smooth, gracefully curved line. The lower edge of the collar illustrated extends on a comparatively straight line around the figure, but this effect requires a curved lower edge and greater width at the side than at the center front and center back, as indicated on the pattern diagram, because of the length that is taken up by the shoulders.

Form the bertha-collar pattern, as shown in Fig. 32, by slipping a piece of paper underneath the portion outlined, then tracing the collar, and afterwards cutting the paper underneath the traced lines.

138

FIG. 32

Form the waist pattern by first tracing any other lines that may be needed to the paper pinned underneath; then cut around all the lines that are to be retained, remove the foundation pattern, and cut on the traced lines.

48. Fitted Basque.—When a closely fitted effect is desired in a basque, extra seam lines are generally needed to maintain the correct grain in all parts of the garment. This type of basque with seam lines provided at each side front and side back is shown in Fig. 33, the very low neck line, in this instance, suggesting a style for evening wear. With a higher neck line, the fitted basque is likewise used for day time frocks in seasons when such effects are in vogue.

The method of developing a comparatively close-fitting basque pattern with a plain-waist pattern as a foundation is shown in Fig. 34. However, a tight-fitting lining pattern makes a very desirable foundation, also, in case its seam lines are arranged in practically the same manner as they are desired in the

FIG. 33

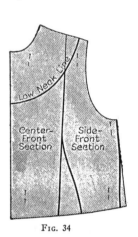

FIG. 34

basque. In using a tight-fitting lining pattern, simply provide as much "ease" as you consider necessary in the various seam lines, giving more width especially at the bust and waist lines, for a basque is seldom molded to the figure so closely as a tight-fitting lining.

In developing the pattern with a plain waist as a foundation, first of all cut off the portion below the waist line so that this will not prove confusing when you are removing some of the width at the waist line. Determine how broad you wish the center-front section at the waist line and locate a point half this measurement in from the center-front waist line. As a rule a trifle more than one-third of the length of the front bust line of the pattern is the most satisfactory width for the center-front section at the waist line.

Locate another point at about the center of the shoulder line and then connect this with the point marked at the waist line by drawing a straight line, as indicated on the diagram.

49. In order to determine how much fulness to remove from the waist line of the front portion of the pattern, hold this up to the figure, fold a dart in it at the side front to make it as close-fitting as you desire, and then measure the amount taken up in the dart.

This estimated amount must be removed from the waist line of the side-front section. Take out from $\frac{1}{2}$ to 1 inch of this amount on the under-arm seam, gradually curving the new seam line, as shown, so that it will follow the natural under-arm line of the figure.

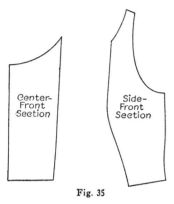

Fig. 35

Take out the remainder of the amount at the side front, measuring along the waist line from the side-seam line already drawn for the center-front section and locating a piont to indicate the termination of the side-seam line for the side-front section. Then draw this seam line, connecting it with the straight seam line drawn through the bust line and shaping it, as shown, to correspond with the natural curve of the figure. In making the garment, be careful to work in the slight fulness at the bust line so that the line is smooth.

After outlining the neck as low as you desire it, trace on the designing lines, which are indicated by the heavy lines on the diagram. Then, to form the two front-pattern sections, cut first around the waist line, then around the shoulder and armhole lines, and, after removing the pattern, cut on the traced neck, side-seam, and under-arm lines, cutting away the width between the two side-seam lines below the bust line. This will form center-front and side-front pattern sections, as shown in Fig. 35.

If you wish to provide side-seam lines in the back portion of the pattern, also, outline them in much the same manner as those in the front. First, draw a line from the center of the back shoulder line to the waist line, extending this through approximately the center of the back bust line, that is, midway between the upper end of the under-arm and the center-back lines. Then remove as much width as you desire at the waist line, taking out most at the center side and curving the separate seam line up to meet the seam line drawn first at the bust line. Take out some of the width at the under arm, also, as suggested for the front portion of the pattern and, unless the center-back section is to be cut without a seam, take out just a trifle at this point.

Then, too, when you are fitting the muslin model, make any alterations that you consider essential in the front and back portions of the basque, being especially careful to see that the side-seam lines are in the correct position on the figure and attractively shaped.

DEVELOPING ONE-PIECE DRESS PATTERNS

50. Essential Features.—The development of a one-piece dress pattern, like that of overblouse patterns, requires that the under-arm, center-front, and center-back lines be extended to form a skirt portion of sufficient length. In addition, the pattern requires, in most instances, special treatment to make the skirt portion hang properly or to make possible a comparatively straight grain at the lower edge.

If you wish to form a pattern for a dress having an especially narrow-skirt effect and a waist that fits rather closely over the bust, make a lengthwise fold in the center of the front portion of the waist pattern, taking out sufficient to make the pattern as narrow as you desire at the waist line and tapering this fold to nothing toward the shoulder line. Then, in extending the under arm, let it follow a practically vertical line so as not to introduce any extra fulness in the skirt portion. It is not advisable to remove any width from the back section of the waist pattern, as the full width is needed to make the skirt portion sufficiently large across the hips.

In making a straight-hanging, one-piece dress pattern, always consider the width through the hip portion, and provide at least several inches more than the hip measurement of the figure.

51. Making Provision for Darts.—In order to retain all the width through the bust portion of a pattern and to prevent the dress from falling to the front, it is usually necessary, especially if the bust is prominent, to make provision in the pattern for a dart. If you wish to provide a shoulder dart, that is, a dart extending from the shoulder line to the bust line or a point above it, slash the pattern on the line marked for the dart and separate the slashed edges at the shoulder line an amount sufficient to drop the under-arm section as much as you consider necessary. This will naturally cause a fold in the lower edge of the pattern and reduce the width at the waist line.

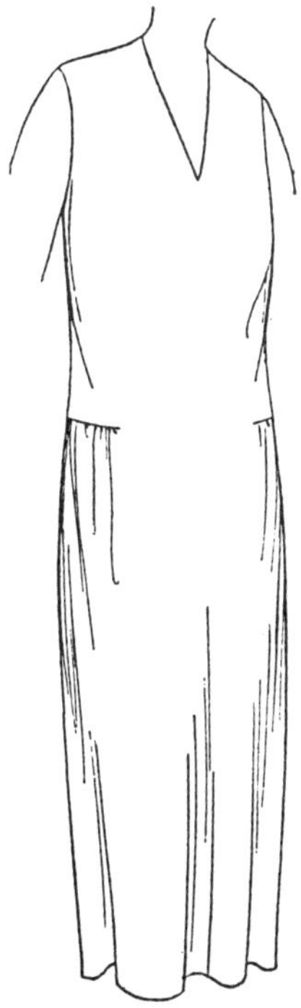

52. One-Piece Dress With Under-Arm Dart.—Fig. 36 illustrates a simple type of one-piece dress having a dart at the under arm, which permits the front to hang straight from the bust line and also provides a means of adding considerable width to the skirt portion, if this is desired.

Fig. 36

Proceed, as shown in Fig. 37, to develop a pattern for this dress. First of all, pin the front portion of the waist pattern you desire to use as a foundation to a piece of paper of sufficient size to form the full-length dress pattern, placing the center front along one lengthwise edge of the paper with the shoulder line close to one end. Then mark the neck line of the shape you desire and extend the under-arm line, as shown, in practically the same direction as it follows in the foundation pattern, making this the required skirt length.

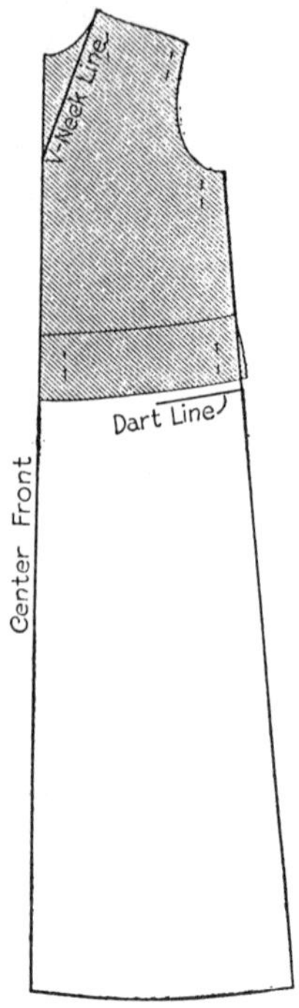

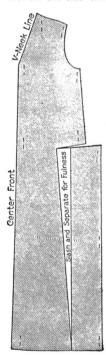

FIG. 37

In order to draw the correct line at the lower edge, first measure down from the center-front waist line the required skirt length and also from several points along the waist line and connect these points with a smooth curved line, as shown, extending the line to the end of the under-arm, or side-seam, line.

After outlining the full-length dress pattern in this manner, trace the new neck line and then cut around the shoulder, the armhole, and the under-arm line of the waist pattern and along the lines marked for the skirt portion. Then remove the waist pattern and cut the dress pattern underneath on the traced neck line.

53. You may make provision for the dart, as shown in Fig. 38, when laying the pattern on muslin for cutting a model. First, mark the dart line in the position in which it will prove most desirable, either at a point where it will be covered by a belt or waist-line finish or lower on the figure as a point of design. Regulate the length of the dart by the curve at the lower edge of the dress pattern; the more decided the curve at the lower edge, the greater the length required in the dart to make possible a more nearly straight grain in the skirt bottom. After outlining the dart, slash on the marked line and, if you wish fulness gathered into the dart, slash the pattern, also, from the end of the dart lengthwise almost to the lower edge of the pattern. Then separate the lengthwise slashed edges at the inside end of the dart, as shown. This will cause the dart edges to separate and lower the side-seam line, and besides

FIG. 38

will make greater length in the lower dart edge, thus serving to make a well-balanced pattern.

If you wish to provide a little more width in the lower edge of the skirt, you may outline an extension beyond the side-seam line of the portion of the skirt below the dart, making this of uniform width its entire length.

If you prefer to make the dart without any fulness and to reduce the width at the lower edge, make a lengthwise fold in the pattern, tapering this from nothing at the inside end of the dart to 1 to 2 inches in width at the bottom.

In cutting the muslin model, follow the outside lines of the pattern, slashing in merely to form the dart and leaving the width between the parted edges below to be gathered into the dart.

Develop the back portion of the pattern in a similar manner, with or without the dart, as you prefer.

FIG. 39

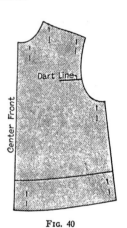

FIG. 40

54. One-Piece Dress With Armhole Dart.—A horizontal dart placed in the front armhole of a blouse or a dress, as shown in Fig. 39, permits a more nearly straight grain at the waist line and also more fulness across the bust. The method of forming an armhole dart in a plain-waist pattern and then extending the lines of the waist pattern to form a skirt portion is shown in Figs. 40 and 41. Mark the armhole dart at the point you desire it, as in Fig. 40; for the average figure, a dart placed about 4 inches below the shoulder line and made about $2\frac{1}{2}$ inches long is usually satisfactory.

In order to straighten the lower edge of the pattern and provide fulness in the lower edge of the dart, slash on the line marked for the dart and also from the inside end of the dart on a line parallel with the center front to the lower edge, as shown in Fig. 41. Then, in pinning the pattern to the large piece of paper in preparation for forming the dress pattern, separate the lengthwise slashed edges at the top $\frac{3}{4}$ to $1\frac{1}{4}$ inches, as shown, and overlap them at the bottom to take out as much width as you desire. See that the lower edge of the side section does not extend below the other pattern piece, for this would give an undesirable slant to the dart line.

55. With the pattern pieces securely pinned in position, draw the lower dart edge, extending it on a straight line from the inside end of the dart to the armhole end of the lower dart edge of the waist pattern. Then draw the under-arm line, giving as much width as you desire at the lower edge of the skirt, and afterwards draw the line for the lower edge.

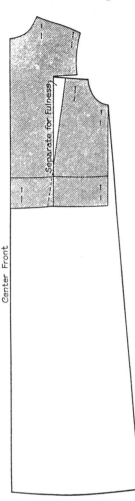

FIG. 41

Make the back portion of the pattern without an armhole dart as this is not needed in this portion and might prove unbecoming and undesirable.

56. One-Piece Kimono Dress.—If a one-piece dress having kimono sleeves is desired, the lines of the kimono-waist pattern may be extended to form a skirt portion in practically the same manner as with the use of a plain-waist pattern. As a rule, a kimono-waist pattern having a seam that extends along the shoulder and the center of the sleeve is the most desirable foundation, as it makes possible a more nearly straight line at the lower edge.

When a one-piece kimono dress, as shown in Fig. 42, has full-length front and back panels, however, a pattern made so that the center front and center back may be placed along a fold of the material is advisable as a foundation. The method of forming the pattern is shown in Fig. 43. In order to outline the new pattern, first pin the kimono-waist pattern to a piece of paper of sufficient length to accommodate the front- and back-skirt portions. Then mark the neck line of any desired shape and draw lines for the front and back panels, making them of a width that you con-

FIG. 42

sider will be becoming. Then, as a means of preventing the dress from falling to the front, draw a new front line for the side-front section of the pattern, slanting this from the bust line to the lower edge so as to remove 3 to 6 inches from the bottom, the amount depending on the prominence of the bust and the shaping that is required to make the dress hang straight from the bust line. This line is indicated on the pattern illustration.

If you wish a very broad effect at the armhole, draw new under-arm curves, as shown, and also extend the sleeve portion to make it of the desired length. Then, extend the under-arm lines so as to produce as much fulness as you desire at the lower edge, and draw the line at the bottom.

With the pattern outlined, trace the markings made on the kimono-waist pattern and remove this; then cut around the outer edges of the dress pattern and also on the marked panel lines to form the separate pattern sections and use these as a guide in cutting out a muslin model.

57. A dress of this type, if made for a person having a prominent bust, almost invariably requires a waist-line dart, at least in the front, or a side-skirt portion cut separate from the waist. Make provision for the dart in the manner suggested for the one-piece dress with under-arm dart.

58. In fitting the muslin model, strive for smartness and the style effect you desire, rather than precision of detail, but make sure that the dress hangs, or "sets," properly and that its lines are becoming. If you find it difficult to make the model hang properly, substitute separate, side-skirt sections for the front- and back-skirt portions that are cut in one with the waist. These side-skirt sections

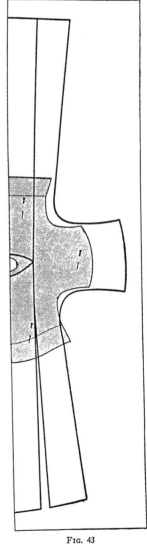

FIG. 43

will make additional skirt width possible, a feature often found very desirable, as they may be either plaited or gathered.

CHANGING OUTLINES OF COLLAR PATTERNS

59. A collar pattern that is satisfactory as to both the length and the shaping of the neck line may serve as a foundation for the development of any other styles

that differ only in outline. This holds true whether the pattern is for the flat or the rolled type of collar, but if the shaping of the neck line requires changing or a more or less decided roll is desired, the use of an entirely new pattern is advisable.

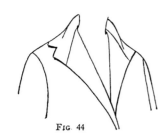

Fig. 44

60. In Fig. 44 are shown two styles of roll collars, each having apparently the same amount of roll and joined to the neck line in practically the same manner, but with a difference in the shaping of the outside edge. The manner in which the pattern for the first d e s i g n may be altered to make it suitable for the other style is shown in Fig. 45. In forming the new pattern, change simply the outline, as indi-

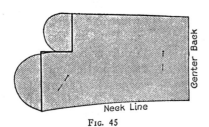

Fig. 45

cated by the heavy line on the diagram, making it conform to the shaping of the desired style.

SLEEVE DESIGNING

ESSENTIAL FEATURES

61. The changing of sleeve patterns to produce sleeves of different shapes seems like a difficult problem to those who are unfamiliar with the true measurements that control sleeves; namely, the inside sleeve measurement and the armhole measurement. But when these measurements are fully appreciated, sleeve-pattern changes prove to be just as simple as other pattern changes.

In order to show how sleeve patterns may be changed, there are here considered a number of

different types of sleeves that should suggest the method of developing patterns for practically any style of sleeve. In connection with sleeve patterns, it will be well to bear in mind that if the inside sleeve length is correct in the original pattern, a cuff as wide or as narrow as is desired may be used with any style of sleeve, it being necessary simply to subtract the width, or depth, of the cuff from the sleeve, so that when the cuff is joined to the sleeve the inside length will correspond exactly to the inside sleeve measurement.

PROVIDING FULNESS

62. Puff Sleeve.—In Fig. 46, is shown a *puff sleeve,* by which is meant a sleeve having considerable

Fig. 46

fulness restrained in a band to produce a puffed effect. Usually the fulness is at the armhole as well as at the lower edge of the sleeve and, therefore, the inside-seam line is kept practically straight.

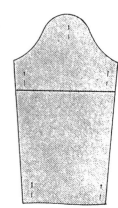

Fig. 47

As a foundation for the development of such a sleeve pattern, use a plain-sleeve pattern, first marking on this the length you desire the sleeve, as shown in Fig. 47. Then trace the upper portion of the sleeve and cut on the traced lines. Slash this pattern lengthwise in several places, and pin it to another piece of paper, separating the pattern pieces, as shown in Fig. 48, to give the amount of fulness you desire. Then outline the upper and lower edges, blending the curves so as to remove the angles and form a well-balanced pattern line.

This method of forming a puff-sleeve pattern applies to the making of a three-quarter or full-length sleeve as well as to a short one.

Fig. 48   Fig. 49

63. Leg-o'Mutton Sleeve.—The leg-o'm u t t o n sleeve, shown in Fig. 49, is so named because of its similarity in silhouette to a leg of mutton. This type of sleeve is old in fashion's history, but occasionally it is heralded as something very new on fashion's calendar.

As a foundation for a pattern for the leg-o'mutton sleeve, use a two-piece, close-fitting sleeve pattern. Pin the two parts of the pattern to a piece of paper, placing them together in the manner shown in Fig. 50; that is, overlap them so that the sleeve bottom, as at a, will be $\frac{1}{2}$ inch longer than the wrist measure and

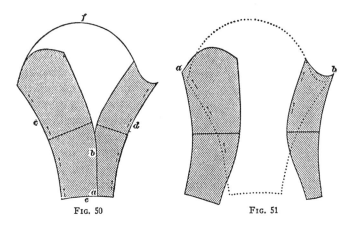

FIG. 50　　　　　FIG. 51

the sleeve at a point a little above midway of the lower arm, as at b, will be the correct size. Next, outline the outside lines of the pattern, as at c, d, and e, and connect the upper edges of the pattern pieces with a graceful curve, almost a half circle, as at f, the purpose of which is to provide for the desired amount of fulness at the top of the sleeve. When the outline is made, it should appear as shown by the dotted lines in Fig. 51.

With this done, it is necessary to shape the armhole line so that the sleeve pattern will be properly shaped to fit the armhole of the waist comfortably and correctly. To do this, swing the foundation-sleeve pattern pieces around in the manner shown, lifting the under-arm points a trifle, as at a and b. Then outline the armhole lines and extend the inside sleeve lines up to them, after which remove the foundation-sleeve pattern pieces and cut out the leg-o'mutton sleeve pattern.

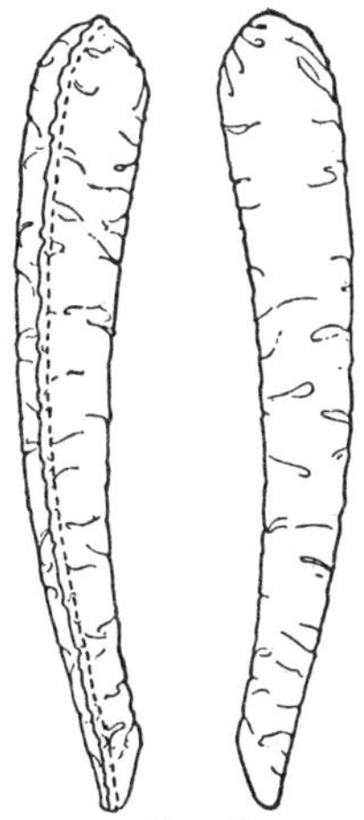

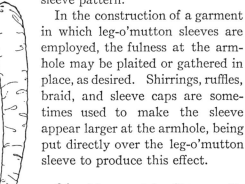

FIG. 52

In the construction of a garment in which leg-o'mutton sleeves are employed, the fulness at the armhole may be plaited or gathered in place, as desired. Shirrings, ruffles, braid, and sleeve caps are sometimes used to make the sleeve appear larger at the armhole, being put directly over the leg-o'mutton sleeve to produce this effect.

64. Mousquetaire Sleeve.—To make a pattern for the mousquetaire sleeve, by which is meant a shirred, close-fitting sleeve like that shown in Fig. 52, proceed in the manner shown in Fig. 53, using a two-piece, close-fitting sleeve pattern. Slash the pattern crosswise and then separate it, as

shown, to allow for the length desired. As a rule, it is necessary to add about 5 inches to the length of the sleeve. In order to distribute this extra length, it is advisable to slash the pattern sections crosswise in several places, as shown, and separate the pieces thus obtained an amount sufficient to provide the additional length that

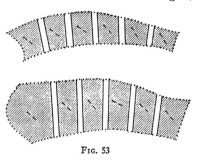

FIG. 53

is needed, keeping the spaces of uniform width. When the pattern is slashed, separated, and pinned to a piece of paper, trace the outside edges, remove the pieces, and cut out the required mousquetaire-sleeve pattern pieces. This pattern should be used in cutting the outer portion of the sleeve, and the plain-foundation pattern fitted close to the arm should be used for the foundation lining. Then, in the construction of a garment in which mousquetaire sleeves are to be used, the full portion should be shirred in place on the lining, which will give the effect shown in Fig. 52.

65. Bishop Sleeve.—The bishop sleeve shown in Fig. 54 derives its name from the sleeve used in a bishop's robe. As it is loose at the hand and has little or no fulness at the armhole, it requires that the inside-seam lines be flared to provide the desired width at the lower edge. The fulness at the hand may be held in with a cuff or with shirring, or the edges may be left loose and trimmed with ruffles, with braid, or in some other manner that is in accord with fashion.

FIG. 54

To develop a pattern for a bishop sleeve, proceed as shown in Fig. 55. Pin a close-fitting, two-piece sleeve pattern to a sheet of paper, placing the sections so that the elbow lines of the two pattern pieces are even and the back seam edges meet near the elbow, as shown. Because of the curved lines, the sleeve lines will not come together exactly at the elbow. Then proceed to connect the upper and lower edges, as indicated. To do this, draw a slightly curved line from the top of the sleeve, as at a, to the upper left corner of the underneath sleeve piece, as at b, thus forming a true, graceful curve for the armhole of the sleeve and also providing the required fulness. Then connect

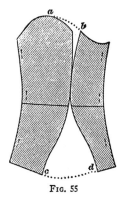

FIG. 55

the lower points *c* and *d* with a slightly curved line, as shown, so as to provide the fulness for the lower part of the bishop sleeve. With this done, trace all the way around the outside line of the pattern, as well as on lines *ab* and *cd*. Then remove the two-piece, sleeve-pattern pieces and cut out the bishop-sleeve pattern.

66. One-Piece Sleeve With Dart.—In a closely fitted, one-piece sleeve, a dart extending from the wrist to the elbow at the back of the sleeve is usually essential for comfort and to provide sufficient freedom to raise the arm. You may form a pattern for such a sleeve by using a close-fitting, two-piece sleeve pattern as a foundation, arranging the pattern pieces as shown in Fig. 55 for the bishop sleeve and cutting away the space between the two sections on the lower portion of the pattern, thus forming the dart edges. Do not cut between the sections in the upper part of the pattern, however. Rather, leave the upper portion in one piece the same as for a bishop sleeve.

If you prefer, you may cut a bishop sleeve in muslin and pin the dart in position when the sleeve is on the arm. This will make it possible to fit the sleeve as closely as you wish and also will insure a dart line placed as you desire it.

67. Bell Sleeve.—By a bell sleeve is meant a sleeve that is snug at the top and full and flaring at its lower edge; it therefore has a contour not unlike that of a bell, as shown in Fig. 56.

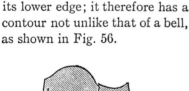
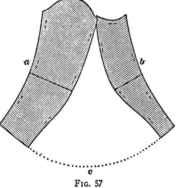

FIG. 56   FIG. 57

To produce a pattern for a bell sleeve, which is frequently in fashion, especially when full skirts are in vogue, place the pattern pieces of the two-piece sleeve on a sheet of paper, as in Fig. 57, separating the bottom of the two pieces enough to give the required width at the lower edge, which must suit the lines of the garment in which the sleeves are used, as well as the material itself. With these pieces pinned securely in place, outline the other lines *a* and *b* and connect the lower points of the sleeve with a graceful curve, as shown at *c*. With this done, bring the elbow lines of the pattern pieces together, as at *a*,

Fig. 58, and outline the upper edge as shown, shaping this edge so that the armhole line of the sleeve will fit the armhole of the waist properly. If the sleeve is to

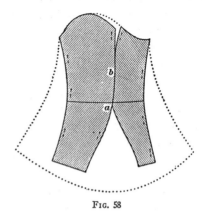

FIG. 58

fit absolutely plain without fulness, it will be necessary to overlap the edges of the pattern at *b* enough to reduce the top of the sleeve until it measures only 1 to $2\frac{1}{4}$ inches more than the armhole measurement. The amount to be allowed over the actual measurement will depend on the material and whether the fulness can be adjusted or shrunk out. With the upper edges connected, outline the remainder of the upper edge and then remove the pattern pieces and cut out the pattern for the bell sleeve.

68. In Fig. 59 are shown examples of how a bell sleeve cut with the aid of a pattern thus developed may be arranged for finishing. In (*a*) the dotted line *a* represents a seam, the material below which may be cut to permit the center of the sleeve to hang in a point. Such a sleeve is very effective for a dress made of soft material. The cuff in such a case might be simply a straight strip $2\frac{1}{2}$ inches wide in the center and as long as the hand measure. If you prefer to have the point of the sleeve extend up to the elbow, cut below the dotted line *b*, thus reducing the lower part of the sleeve to fit the wrist and the lower arm.

In Fig. 59 (*b*) is shown how the fulness may be arranged so as to be held in underneath a cuff.

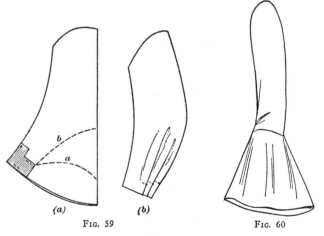

(*a*)   (*b*)

FIG. 59   FIG. 60

69. Sleeve With Circular Frill.—A sleeve cut in two pieces with a plain-fitting upper portion and a flared lower portion is shown in Fig. 60. To design a pattern for such a sleeve, first mark on a plain-foundation sleeve pattern the width you desire the frill, or flared portion, as shown in Fig. 61. Trace the lower section thus outlined, cut on the traced lines, and then slash this portion of the pattern lengthwise

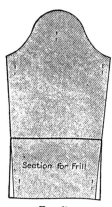

Fig. 61

in a number of places from the lower edge almost to the upper edge, and pin it to another piece of paper, as shown in Fig. 62, separating the slashed edges at the bottom an amount sufficient to produce the flare you desire. Regulate the number of slashes by the amount of flare you wish in the frill, making the slashes comparatively close for a decidedly rippled effect or slashing in only three or four places to produce a moderate flare. Also, make the spaces of even width so as to distribute the flare evenly.

Outline the lower edge by drawing a smoothly curved line, as shown, in order to prevent a jagged effect that might result if lines were drawn merely to connect the different sections. Then, in cutting out the pattern, form a smooth curve at the upper edge of the frill.

For cutting the upper part of the sleeve, use the portion of the foundation pattern above the marked line.

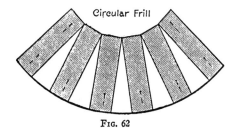

Circular Frill

Fig. 62

In case you wish to apply a circular trimming piece over a plain sleeve, simply outline this on the pattern at just the point you desire it, then slash and separate the traced pattern as illustrated.

SKIRT DESIGNING

ESSENTIAL FEATURES

70. Skirt-pattern designing is, as a rule, somewhat simpler than waist designing, principally because of the less intricate shaping of the foundation skirt pattern. The principal point to observe in the designing of a skirt pattern is that the hip line be kept in correct position in order to maintain the balance of the skirt. Another point to note is the length of the pattern. Either mark on the pattern the line for the hem turn or cut off any surplus length or hem allowance so that you may not be confused in trying to keep the designing features in good proportion with the

length. Otherwise, you may extend the designing feature too low on the pattern and produce an undesirable effect.

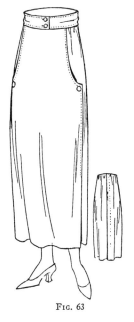

Fig. 63

CHANGING WAIST LINE AND PROVIDING FULNESS

71. Skirt With Pocket Effects and Gathered, Raised Waist Line.—In Fig. 63 is illustrated a skirt having a plain-fitted front shaped for pockets at the upper edge and a gathered back in two pieces, which are extended, at the upper edge, around under the shaped fronts. The waist line is raised but appears to be normal at the front because of the wide belt.

As a foundation for this design, use a plain two- or three-piece skirt pattern. Pin the sections, as shown in Fig. 64, to a large sheet of paper so that the center front is along a straight edge of the paper and the side-seam lines meet from the lower edge to the hip line or just below it.

Mark the extension above the front and back waist line, as shown, by drawing a curve parallel with the waist line, regulating the amount of the "lift" by the distance you wish the raised waist line above the normal waist line of the figure.

Before outlining the pocket effect, determine how deep you wish this at the sides and how broad the front gore should be at the waist line. Then, from a point at the waist line one-half the desired front-gore width from the center front, draw a smoothly curved line, as shown, to the point determined on the side-seam line as the correct depth for the

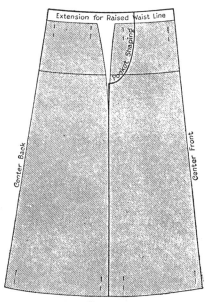

Fig. 64

pocket effect or a point directly above the meeting of the side-seam lines. Be careful to make this a smooth curve, using one of the curves of the Picken square.

To form the separate front- and back-pattern portions, first trace along the heavy designing line from the waist line, following the curve to the side seam and then straight along the side-seam line to the lower edge. Then cut around the raised waist line, center back, and lower edge; afterwards, remove the pattern pieces and cut the paper underneath on the traced side line. As the space between the curved side-seam lines above the hip line is included in the traced pattern, waist-line fulness is provided at the side, this being required when the seam line is omitted.

72. To provide fulness in the upper portion of the back-pattern section thus formed, slash it in two or three places from the waist line almost to the lower

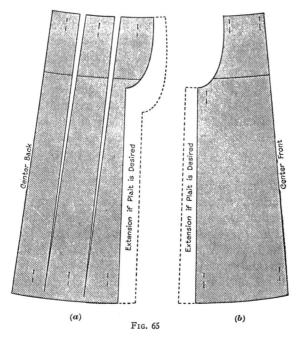

(a)   FIG. 65   (b)

edge and separate the pieces at the top, as shown in Fig. 65 (a), an amount sufficient to give the fulness you desire. This method of adding fulness does not change the width at the lower edge of the skirt.

If you wish to cut the skirt with a plait allowance and a pouch portion for the pocket, be guided by the dotted outline, making the pouch portion as deep as you desire and the plait allowance from $1\frac{1}{2}$ to $2\frac{1}{2}$ inches at the bottom, tapering this somewhat toward the top. This allowance is intended merely for the underlapping portion of the plait, the seam to be made at the inside edge.

The front section of the pattern developed in this manner, as shown in view (b), requires no alteration to make it suitable for the design that is illustrated. For plait allowance, be guided by the dotted outline, making the allowance the same at the lower edge as that of the back gore and narrowing the plait sufficiently toward the top so that it will not cause unnecessary bulk at the pocket edge.

146

73. Providing Fulness at Waist Line and Lower Edge.—Sometimes more width is desired through the hip portion of a skirt than at its lower edge, in order to give a "peg-top" effect. To make provision for this, separate the pattern pieces sufficiently at the top to make the skirt as much broader through the hip portion as you desire. In case you wish to make the skirt narrower than the foundation pattern at the lower edge, overlap the slashed edges at the bottom as you separate them at the top, taking out as much width as you desire in this manner.

If you wish to broaden the skirt at the lower edge as well as supply waist-line fulness, separate the pattern pieces their entire length.

In any event, keep in mind the fact that the number of slashes should be regulated by the amount of fulness that is to be added. The addition of a small amount of fulness requires but two slashes in a gore, but more slashes are needed if considerable fulness is to be supplied.

DIVIDING SKIRT PATTERNS INTO SECTIONS AND DECREASING WIDTH

74. Panel-and-Yoke Skirt.—Several designing details are involved in the style shown in Fig. 66, which has front and back panel sections accentuated by plaits and a shaped, one-piece yoke at each side joined to lower-side sections in which the center-side seam is omitted. The lines of the skirt, as you will note, are very straight.

Be guided by Fig. 67 in forming a pattern for this design, using a plain two-piece skirt pattern as a foundation and pinning the pieces to a large sheet of paper with the center front along a straight edge and the side-seam lines meeting, at least from the hip line to the lower edge. The pattern illustrated has straight side-seam lines, which give a little fulness at the waist line.

First of all, determine what panel width will prove most becoming and place a mark on the front waist line of the pattern one-half this width from the center-front line. As a rule, a panel should be a trifle broader at the bottom than at the waist line, even when the appearance of uniform width is desired, for if the panel is cut of the same width its entire length it will appear to be broader at the top than at the bottom when it is on the figure unless it is gathered slightly at the waist line.

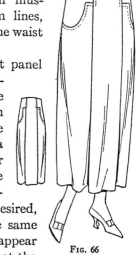

FIG. 66

In a comparatively straight-line skirt, an increase of from 1 to 2 inches is advisable in the panel width at the bottom. To make provision for this width, place a mark at the lower edge a distance from the center front equal to the width marked at the top plus from

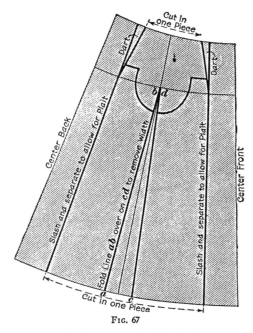

FIG. 67

½ to 1 inch, this being one-half the increase that is desired in the full panel width. Then, to form a panel line, draw a straight line from this point to the mark on the waist line, as shown by the heavy line on the diagram.

Mark the back panel in practically the same manner, making it just a trifle broader than the front panel if the figure is proportionately broad across the back hip line.

Outline the yoke by first drawing the straight extensions from the front and back panels. Then determine how deep you wish to make the yoke at the side and draw a gracefully curved line from the side to the termination of the straight lines drawn out from the panels, being guided by the general shaping of the yoke, as shown in Fig. 66, and also by the heavy line indicating the yoke marking in Fig. 67. Drawing a light dotted line as a foundation for the curve will aid you in forming an attractive final designing line.

75. If the side-seam lines of the pattern are separated from the hip line to the waist line, as would be the case if the pattern were fitted in at the waist line, disregard this space, planning to cut the yoke without a center-side seam, and shape the yoke along the side-front and side-back edges, as indicated by the dart lines on the diagram, removing the same amount as the side-seam lines are separated.

If the side-seam lines are straight their entire length, as in the pattern illustrated, and, therefore, do not separate at the top, make the waist measurement of the pattern correspond with that of the individual. To do this, first measure the waist line of the pattern and subtract from this one-half the individual waist

measurement in order to determine how much must be removed at the waist line for a close-fitting effect. Then divide this amount and take it from the side-front and side-back edges of the yoke, as indicated by the provision for darts shown in the diagram.

If there is a little more width than you desire at the lower edge, you may remove this at the side-seam line below the hip line, as indicated by lines *ab* and *cd* on the diagram, taking an equal amount from the front- and back-pattern portions. It is not advisable to take out more than 3 or 4 inches in this manner, as a more decided alteration might affect the balance of the pattern.

76. To form the various pattern sections, trace on the heavy lines; then remove the foundation-pattern pieces and cut the paper underneath on the traced lines with the exception of the lines traced from *ab* and *cd* on the diagram, provided these were drawn to reduce the width at the lower edge. Instead of cutting on these traced side lines, simply fold one over on the other in order to keep the lower-side section in one piece so that it may be cut without a seam line.

In cutting the material for this skirt design, make allowance for a plait along each panel edge, and, if you wish pockets on the sides, make allowance for a pouch portion on the lower edge of the yoke sections.

OUTLINING TUNICS OR OVERSKIRT PORTIONS

77. If you wish to form a tunic pattern or any overskirt portion that is joined to the foundation merely at the waist line, outline this on the foundation pattern in just the position you desire to have it assume. In some cases, a plain-skirt pattern will serve as the correct foundation, and, other times, a circular-skirt pattern would prove more desirable, this depending on whether the overskirt portion has considerable flare.

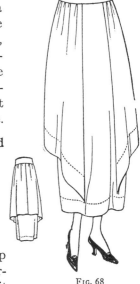

FIG. 68

78. Skirt With Shaped Gathered Overskirt.—In Fig. 68 is shown an overskirt with the edges parted at the center front to form a panel effect and with the lower edge curved from the lower front corners up toward the back. The overskirt has fulness but, as it hangs in comparatively straight lines, it suggests the use of a plain-skirt pattern rather than a circular one as a foundation for designing.

147

To form the overskirt pattern, first lay the front and back gores of a plain-skirt pattern so that their side-seam lines meet, at least from the hip line to the lower edge. Then outline the overskirt, as indicated by the heavy line in Fig. 69, making the panel line of a width you consider becoming, shaping the lower edge in the manner illustrated, and making the overskirt portion as long as you desire at the front and the back.

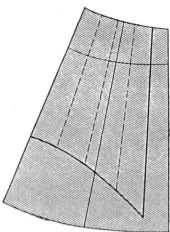

Slash on Dotted Lines and separate Pieces to provide Fulness

Fig. 69

After tracing the outlined overskirt to another piece of paper, slash it as indicated by the dotted lines and separate the pieces an equal amount their entire length to provide the amount of fulness you desire.

OUTLINING FLOUNCES AND TRIMMING BANDS AND PROVIDING FLARE

79. Shaped Circular Flounce.—A pattern for a skirt having a shaped circular flounce, as in Fig. 70, may be prepared in the manner shown in Figs. 71 and 72.

As a foundation, use a plain-skirt pattern if you wish the upper portion of the skirt to hang in comparatively straight lines, or use a circular-skirt pattern, as shown, if you desire to have the upper portion flared also.

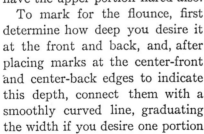

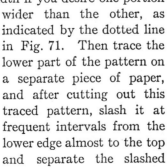

Fig. 70

To mark for the flounce, first determine how deep you desire it at the front and back, and, after placing marks at the center-front and center-back edges to indicate this depth, connect them with a smoothly curved line, graduating the width if you desire one portion wider than the other, as indicated by the dotted line in Fig. 71. Then trace the lower part of the pattern on a separate piece of paper, and after cutting out this traced pattern, slash it at frequent intervals from the lower edge almost to the top and separate the slashed edges to give the desired fulness. Then, with the slashed pattern carefully pinned to another piece of paper, as shown in Fig. 72, cut out the required

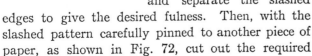

pattern. In making such a pattern, take extreme care to curve the upper line of the flounce evenly and gracefully, so that it will fit the foundation skirt accurately.

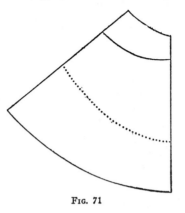

Fig. 71

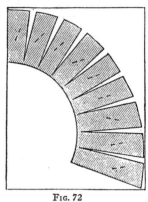

Fig. 72

80. Outlining Trimming Bands.—Patterns for fitted or circular trimming bands may be outlined on a skirt pattern in practically the same manner as a flounce. Simply decide what foundation-skirt pattern should be used, determine by measuring on the figure the exact position for the trimming bands, and then outline the bands on the skirt pattern in a corresponding position.

If the bands are to be fitted plain, use the traced pattern without change for cutting them, but if a rippled or circular effect is desired, treat the traced pattern as suggested for the circular flounce.

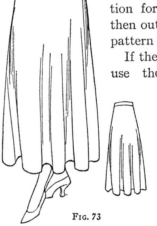

Fig. 73

81. Increasing Flare of a Skirt Pattern.—The principle of slashing and separating, which applies to the forming of circular-flounce and trimming-band patterns, may be likewise applied to increasing the flare the full length of a skirt pattern. For instance, the skirt shown in Fig. 73 has a great deal of flare, more than would be supplied by an average circular-skirt pattern. To make provision for this flare, slash the pattern and separate the pieces as shown in Fig. 74, making the separa-

Fig. 74

148

tions wider in the back than in the front in order to throw more fulness in the back.

You may treat a plain-skirt pattern having practically straight lines in this manner, also, but increase the number of slashes if you wish to produce the extreme flare that is characteristic of the skirt illustrated in Fig. 73.

In making allowances for flare in skirt patterns, avoid fulness at the center front, because a skirt that has fulness falling out directly at the center appears very ungainly unless it is in the form of a drape that is in harmony with the remainder of the design. You may provide fulness 1 or 1½ inches from the center front but not directly in the center.

REVIEW QUESTIONS

(1) If there is any doubt as to the points where designing details should be placed on a pattern, how may the correct position be determined?

(2) What are the advantages of trying out flat-designed patterns in muslin?

(3) What point is it well to observe in the marking of neck lines?

(4) If fulness is desired along a curved edge of a pattern, why should it be added at several points rather than in one place?

(5) What is the purpose of darts in a one-piece dress?

(6) Select one of the designs shown below and by means of a small diagram, show how you would develop a pattern for it. Make the diagram similar to those shown in this chapter, aiming for accuracy and neatness.

LACIS publishes and distributes books specifically related to the textile arts, focusing on the subject of lace and lace making, costume, embroidery, needlepoint and hand sewing.

Other LACIS books of interest:

MILLINERY FOR EVERY WOMAN, Georgina Kerr Kaye
"STANDARD" WORK ON CUTTING (MEN'S GARMENTS): 1886
LADIES' TAILOR-MADE GARMENTS 1908, S.S. Gordon
FASHION OUTLINES (1932), Margaret C. Ralston
GARMENT PATTERNS FOR THE EDWARDIAN LADY, Mrs. F. E. Thompson
SMOCKING AND GATHERING FOR FABRIC MANIPULATION, Nellie
       Weymount Link
THE ART OF HAIR WORK, HAIR BRAIDING AND JEWELRY OF SENTIMENT,
       Mark Campbell
THE ART OF TATTING, Katherine Hoare
TATTING WITH VISUAL PATTERNS, Mary Konior
TATTING; Designs From Victorian Lace, ed by Jules & Kaethe Kliot
THE COMPLETE BOOK OF TATTING, Rebecca Jones
NEW DIMENSIONS IN TATTING, To de Haan-van Beek
BEAD EMBROIDERY, Joan Edwards
EMBROIDERY WITH BEADS, Angela Thompson
BEAD EMBROIDERY, Valerie Campbell-Harding and Pamela Watts
THE BEADING BOOK, Julia Jones
THE BARGELLO BOOK, Frances Salter
FLORENTINE EMBROIDERY,   Barbara Muller
THE ART OF SHETLAND LACE, Sarah Don
KNITTED LACE, Marie Niedner & Gussi von Reden
THE CARE AND PRESERVATION OF TEXTILES, Karen Finch & Greta   Putnam
THE ART & CRAFT OF RIBBON WORK, ed by Jules & Kaethe Kliot

For a complete list of LACIS titles write to:

LACIS
3163 Adeline Street
Berkeley, CA 94703